WEAPONS OF MASS PERSUASION
Marketing the War against Iraq

With nearly 60 per cent of Americans initially against a pre-emptive war without sanction from the United Nations – and even higher anti-war numbers in most other nations – the 2003 war against Iraq quickly became an enormous public relations challenge for the George W. Bush administration. The subject of *Weapons of Mass Persuasion* is a war in which American patriotism became so mired in commercial jingoism that the demarcations between entertainment and political conduct disappeared.

In this engaging and disturbing book, Paul Rutherford shows how the marketing campaign for the war against Iraq was constructed and carried out. He argues not only that the campaign epitomized the presentation of real-time war as pop culture, but that it constitutes a significant chapter in the history of modern democracy. Situating the war against Iraq within an existing tradition of war as narrative, spectacle, and, more broadly, commodity, Rutherford offers a brief overview of the history of civic advertising and propaganda, then examines in detail the different dimensions of the war as it became a branded conflict, processed and cleansed to appeal to the well-established tastes of veteran consumers of popular culture.

Weapons of Mass Persuasion includes incisive analyses of speeches, editorial cartoons, media political commentary, and news reports of such sound-bite events as the bombing of Baghdad, the toppling of Saddam Hussein's statue, and the rescue of captured soldier Private Jessica Lynch, as well as extensive polling data from around the world and interviews with the actual consumers of TV war. The work chronicles the making and selling of a Hollywood-style war against Iraq: a fast-paced and heroic struggle between good and evil resulting in a triumphant, sanitized, and commodified outcome.

PAUL RUTHERFORD is a professor in the Department of History at the University of Toronto.

Weapons of Mass Persuasion

Marketing the War against Iraq

PAUL RUTHERFORD

UNIVERSITY OF TORONTO PRESS
Toronto Buffalo London

48.00

© University of Toronto Press Incorporated 2004
Toronto Buffalo London
Printed in Canada

ISBN 0-8020-8995-X (cloth)
ISBN 0-8020-8651-9 (paper)

∞

Printed on acid-free paper

National Library of Canada Cataloguing in Publication

Rutherford, Paul, 1944–
Weapons of mass persuasion : marketing the war against
Iraq / Paul Rutherford.

Includes bibliographical references and index.
ISBN 0-8020-8995-X (bound).   ISBN 0-8020-8651-9 (pbk.)

1. Iraq War, 2003.   2. War in mass media.   3. Iraq War, 2003 –
Public opinion.   I. Title.

DS79.76.R87 2004   956.7044'3   C2004-900098-5

University of Toronto Press acknowledges the financial assistance
to its publishing program of the Canada Council for the Arts and
the Ontario Arts Council.

University of Toronto Press acknowledges the financial support for
its publishing activities of the Government of Canada through the
Book Publishing Industry Development Program (BPIDP).

for Rio

Contents

List of Figures ix
Acknowledgments xi

Introduction 3

ONE
Marketing's Moment 8

TWO
The War Debate 22

THREE
Managing War 50

FOUR
Real-Time War 79

FIVE
Consuming War 111

SIX
Perceptions of War 144

SEVEN
The Phallic Dimension 164

EIGHT
The Propaganda State   183

Postscript: Summer/Fall 2003   194

APPENDIX
Consumer Voices / Citizens' Panel   199

Sources   201
Index   209

List of Figures

2.1 The UN as joke, 16 March 2003
(www.mideasttruth.com/cartoonsiraq) 23

2.2 Weapons of mass destruction, 24 August 2002
(www.edivu.com) 37

2.3 The lust for oil, 11 March 2003 (www.insidevc/vcs) 40

2.4 What anti-war really means, *De Telegraaf*,
Amsterdam, Netherlands, 27 February 2003
(www.mideasttruth.com/cartoonsiraq) 44

3.1 Mr Rumsfeld's war, 30 March 2003
(*Sunday New York Times*) 51

3.2 Smart weapons, *The Australian*, Melbourne,
25 January 2003 (cagle.slate.msn.com) 56

3.3 The first casualty, *Melbourne Express*
(cagle.slate.msn.com) 63

3.4 The embedded journalist, 2 April 2003
(cagle.slate.msn.com) 75

4.1 The overwhelming coverage, 3 April 2003
(cagle.slate.msn.com) 80

4.2 War as ad, *Chattanooga Times–Free Press*, 27 March 2003
(www.edivu.com) 92

4.3 Media patriotism, 3 April 2003 (cagle.slate.msn.com)   98

4.4 The two wars (cagle.slate.msn.com)   101

4.5 The evil eye, *Reforma*, Mexico City
(cagle.slate.msn.com)   109

5.1 Making meaning? 26 March 2003
(cagle.slate.msn.com)   112

5.2 The pundits, *National Post*, Toronto
(cagle.slate.msn.com)   128

5.3 Looting, *Vancouver Sun* (cagle.slate.msn.com)   134

6.1 The exhausted viewer, 28 March 2003
(cagle.slate.msn.com)   145

6.2 The misguided public, 28 March 2003
(cagle.slate.msn.com)   154

6.3 Democracy is coming, 23 March 2003
(www.globecartoon.com)   157

6.4 After Iraq ..., 15 April 2003
(www.globecartoon.com)   162

7.1 Real-time war, *El Universal*, Mexico City
(caglecartoons.com)   165

7.2 Macho games, 4 January 2003 (www.edivu.com)   169

7.3 Bush as cowboy, *Baslter Zeitung*, 5 January 2003
(caglecartoons.com)   173

7.4 The big media, 2 April 2003 (cagle.slate.msn.com)   175

7.5 The new master, 10 April 2003
(cagle.slate.msn.com)   180

Acknowledgments

An author always incurs debts writing a manuscript. I would not have written *Weapons of Mass Persuasion* but for the initiative of three people at the University of Toronto Press: Bill Harnum (Senior Vice-President, Scholarly Publishing), Melissa Pitts (Sales and Marketing Manager), and Virgil Duff (Executive Editor, Social Sciences). Back in April 2003, over dim sum at a midtown restaurant in Toronto, they suggested I write a book that would explore the marketing of the Iraq War. I owe a special thanks to Virgil, once again my editor, who shepherded the book through the birth process, always time-consuming and sometimes difficult, and to his assistant Stephen Kotowych, especially for his success in arranging the permissions to use the editorial cartoons. I would also like to acknowledge the contribution of John St James, who brought a keen eye to the copy-editing of the manuscript.

My second debt is to the twenty people I interviewed for this project. Some of these individuals I knew before, some I did not. No matter: they all agreed to submit to my probes and freely expressed their opinions on the crisis and the invasion. The reader will soon discover just how significant these interviews were to the final shape of the book.

I must also thank the anonymous referees whom the Press selected to evaluate *Weapons of Mass Persuasion* in its initial manuscript form. These individuals gave the book a speedy and thorough read and produced valuable reports. I did not follow all their advice. But many of the suggestions were worked into the final revision of the book.

My greatest debt is to Margarita Orszag, however. In effect she lost her partner for much of the summer of 2003, since my time and energies were consumed by the tasks of research and writing. She had to suffer both the ups and downs of what proved a most intense project. Once again she has my deepest gratitude for her understanding of the needs of the moment.

Paul Rutherford
December 2003

WEAPONS OF MASS PERSUASION

Introduction

War by Disney: that is how Glenna, an artist I interviewed, described the Iraq War she had witnessed on television and read about in Toronto newspapers. 'You could almost say this was a war invented and produced by Disney studios. It was monumental, it was full of slogans and images, it was like a production. And it happened, and [they] got it over so fast, they got away with it too.' The House of Mickey had nothing to do with the actual war. But the way the war was presented, at least in North America, seemed very similar to the style of shows the Disney studios, and other major production houses, had offered audiences in recent years. It bore the signature of some of the most successful products of a made-in-America popular culture that had captivated the world in past decades.

This book discusses the peculiar nature of the war so neatly summarized by Glenna. For the record, I was opposed to the attack on Iraq because that action lacked the sanction of the United Nations – had Washington secured the support of the UN, thus won legitimacy, I would have supported the war, and in particular the removal of Saddam Hussein. But I am not writing about the justice or otherwise of what happened in the spring of 2003. Nor do I intend to chronicle the diplomatic manoeuvres in the year preceding the invasion, the military operations of the coalition forces during the roughly three weeks of conflict, or the aftermath of disorder and confusion and resistance – at least not directly. Rather I will explore the experience of war, chiefly in North America, and to some extent in the world at large. I will treat the war as narrative and spectacle, as a form of 'infotainment' and, more broadly, as a commodity, something that was consumed by millions of people via the media. The intervention became a branded war, a co-production of the Pentagon and of newsrooms, processed and cleansed so that it could appeal to the well-established tastes of people who were veteran consumers of popular culture. This triumph of marketing is one reason to count the war against Iraq significant: it marked a new stage of the ongoing story of democracy, particularly in America.

Much of what follows details the efforts of two groups of producers, which for the sake of convenience I will call the Pentagon and the newsrooms, meaning chiefly the American television networks, to sell the war to a variety of domestic and foreign audiences. The crisis and then the invasion captured the attention of media and people throughout the world. The Internet made it possible to sample an extraordinary wealth of information about the marketing exercise. So my evidence derived not so much from my own experience of using the media as from a wide assortment of materials – television clips, radio interviews and documentaries, newspaper reports, magazine stories – all readily available via the Internet. I could inspect the leaflets the Americans had dropped over Iraq as part of their 'PsyOps' campaign in the months before the conflict: these were available at the website of Central Command. I could see the live report offered by the Canadian Broadcasting Corporation (CBC) of the bombing of Baghdad on 21 March, the day when commentators argued the Americans had initiated the infamous 'Shock and Awe' campaign. I could read the English version of reports posted by Al-Jazeera, itself one of the success stories of the war. I could view the British Broadcasting Corporation's (BBC) version of what happened in Baghdad on 9 April, that day of triumph and chaos when the Iraqi regime collapsed.

My focus on the marketing exercise, however, has necessitated two special features of the book. Whatever its prominence these days, marketing has remained a kind of communication that is both criticized and widely disdained. It works but often not perfectly. I have made extensive use of editorial cartoons drawn from publications around the world, though mostly from North America, to offer another way of seeing what this war meant. The crisis and the war provoked all kinds of talented people, of different persuasions, to produce a wealth of images mocking the pretensions and the behaviours of the antagonists. Humour, especially satire, has a marvellous way of highlighting conventions and contradictions. Its ability to exaggerate the import of ideas, words, and actions, to caricature figures and faces, renders public affairs grotesque, and does so in very interesting ways. The serious business of politics is invaded by the spirit of carnival. And so, samples of these cartoons are scattered throughout the text, to enliven, to enlighten, to criticize. (Nearly all of these cartoons I secured online in the summer of 2003. I have cited the artists and permission data with the actual cartoons, and the sources and the dates, where available, of this material in the 'List of Figures.')

Likewise I have incorporated the views of a select group of 'consumer voices' in what I will call a 'citizens' panel.' (The two monikers express the double nature of these volunteers, as an audience and as a public.) The analysis of any marketing exercise requires attention not only to what the producers were doing but to the responses of consumers as well. Did they buy into the rhetoric and the images? In May, right after President Bush declared that the war was won, I interviewed twenty people in the region of Toronto about their experience of the crisis and, most especially, the conflict itself. As one reader correctly pointed out, this panel was 'more Starbucks than Tim Hortons': it was not representative of the whole public. I chose women and men who belonged to the articulate public, people inside and outside the university community, who paid a lot of attention to public affairs – members of what is sometimes called 'the political class.' My purpose was to capture a wide variety of views, at one moment in time, before the course of future events had fogged memories. Most of the participants were interviewed individually, though I also held three joint sessions to probe how people discussed the war. I sought a rough balance among the competing views. Some subjects were peace activists, a few were sympathizers or supporters of the coalition, and still others were just alienated consumers. Some participants were retired; others were students. I managed to talk to 'newly minted' and 'native' Canadians, to citizens who were on the right and the left, to people who were Christian, Jewish, and Muslim. The interviews, lasting about an hour and a half, were designed to explore the meanings people derived from the experience of watching the invasion from afar. Their opinions are identified in the text by a first name and, if necessary, a last initial, to ensure their anonymity as well as to mark their special status as voices of consumers and citizens. (The participants and their affiliations are outlined in a brief appendix.) What I discovered forms much of the chapter entitled 'Consuming War.' But their views are also scattered throughout the book. The opening comment by Glenna was one of those views.

Of course this citizens' panel can only be counted as an expression of the type of opinions present in one city in one country. There is an old saying in the real estate business: 'location, location, location.' A similar maxim prevails in communications, even in this era of global marketing. The way a public responds to any message depends on its past experiences, its collective memory, in a word on its locale. So I have supplemented the findings of my interviews with a wide variety of data drawn from polls, letters, and newspaper stories that report views among the populace, particularly in North America but also globally, and notably in the Arabic world. Polls proved especially important. This is an era when the public mind is continually being scrutinized by all kinds of agencies. The significance of the Iraq crisis and the succeeding invasion meant these agencies went into a frenzy of surveying. While their findings do not make for the most inter-esting reading of the mind of citizens, polling results remain an invaluable way of understanding that elusive but signifi-cant property we call public opinion. The results are found chiefly in two companion chapters entitled 'The War Debate' and 'Perceptions of War.'

My argument explores the recent history of journalism, marketing, and entertainment because the convergence of these supposedly distinct discourses fashioned the character of the war commodity consumed by North Americans. Likely the emphasis on pop culture will seem the most peculiar thrust. Yet the practices and the character of entertainment were central to how people explained and interpreted what they saw: 'War becomes the ultimate reality TV,' announced a typical headline in Toronto's *National Post* (25 March). Mass culture has become so ubiquitous that it guides both the actions and understandings of producers and consumers in the realm of politics. I have favoured hit movies, and espe-cially the action/adventure genre, because they construct and popularize icons, stereotypes, archetypes, visual clichés, say-ings and slogans for such a wide audience that they offer us (and in this case 'us' takes in much of the world's population) the means to comprehend what happens in public life, in the corridors of power, and on the battlefield.

In summary: this book tracks how the weapons of mass persuasion were deployed, what their effect was, and why the experiment was significant.

ONE

Marketing's Moment

It is hard to exaggerate the significance of hype in the political as well as the commercial life of the United States. Nothing really big, no new product meant for the millions enters the marketplace unless heavily promoted to feed the demand, the desire to possess – often well before its release. The August 1995 launch of Microsoft Windows 95, a new version of the operating system for the mainstream PC market, was preceded by an extraordinary burst of publicity involving television commercials, print ads, in-store promotions, public relations, and publicity stunts. It was variously estimated that Microsoft itself had spent $200 million, and that the total budget for promotion by all the various retail, software, and computer firms reached $700 million. The Win95 campaign made news around the world: it was a global sensation. 'It's a defining moment,' claimed one high-tech advertiser – a gateway into a future of super-hype.

Somewhere in the not-too-distant past the philosophy and the technology of marketing had entered into its golden age, a time when its sway extended across the much of the globe, first in America and then increasingly across the affluent zone of countries. Read the literature and marketing seems positively democratic: a 'goal-oriented, integrated philosophy practiced by producers of goods and services that focuses on satisfying the needs of consumers over the needs of the producing company,' according to a *Dictionary of Marketing Terms.* Marketing does work in this fashion. The launch of New Coke in the mid-1980s was one such effort, because it was designed to meet a preference for a sweeter cola that had been discovered through taste tests. But marketing is often much more than this. It works to channel desires, a part of human nature it treats as raw material, by constructing the very needs that make a brand or a product appealing. Consider, for example, how marketing built the demand for the personal computer, both as a tool of play and as an instrument of productivity: acquiring the IBM PC or the Macintosh, both much publicized in the early 1980s, satisfied people's desires for power and pleasure. Marketing is a way to direct behaviour.

I

Marketing's moment was rooted in the emergence since the 1960s of a total communications environment, centred around television of course, but encompassing innumerable newspapers and magazines, radio stations galore, movies, books, records, video games, and the Internet, that flooded homes and offices with an amazing array of symbolic products. It has become increasingly difficult to resist sampling some of these wares. In fact, most people do more than just sample. The communications expert Todd Gitlin recently concluded that this 'torrent of images and sounds overwhelms our lives.' In the United States, he noted, the television set was on in the average household over seven hours a day, and the average American watched about four hours a day. The nightly TV audience in 2001 was around 102.5 million viewers, aged two or more, which amounted to roughly 40 per cent of the total American population. 'Most people, most of the time, experience media as signs of society's generosity,' Gitlin argued. 'The profusion of images offers fun, stimulus, feeling, or a sense of connection, however fugitive. We feel flattered to have the access.'

The United States has exported its media goods to much of

the world. In 1999 the export of entertainment and advertising amounted to about $30 billion. The US product domi-
nated the international market for television: kids' shows,
drama, TV movies, light entertainment, less so film and fac-
tual content. The top grossing movie of all time by 2003 in the
world outside North America was *Titanic*, generating $1.2
billion in sales, a movie in which Paramount and Twentieth-
Century Fox had a hand, the latter being part of the media
empire of Rupert Murdoch (once Australian, now American).
As *Time* (25 October 1999) put it, Murdoch has built 'a diverse
media empire that informs and entertains half the world.' If
so, then much of the rest of the world was serviced by one of
his rivals, Time Warner, which owned what is arguably the
most important news outlet in the world, CNN.

More significant, though, the United States had also exported its habits along with its goods. The world wanted
much the same kind of access to a plethora of entertainment
and news that the Americans already enjoyed. After decades
of slumping admissions, movie-going revived during the 1990s
in the affluent regions of Europe and Australasia, as they did
in North America. Rates of television usage in western Europe paralleled those in the United States, and in Japan and
Mexico these figures were even higher. Satellite TV rapidly
expanded in the better-off regions of the Middle East: the
percentage of households boasting this service in 1998 had
reached 28 per cent in Jordan and Qatar, 61 per cent in Saudi
Arabia, 75 per cent or over in the United Arab Emirates and
Kuwait – well ahead of the United States, where only 12 per
cent of households (or Canada at 4 per cent) were connected,
presumably because cable served the same purpose.

The appropriate metaphor for this phenomenon, as Gitlin
argued, might better be 'the global torrent' rather than 'the
global village.' More and more people can get the same, or the
same sort of messages, but some live in favelas while others
reside in gated communities. Equally important, what they
get is very American, either imported or imitated: so much of
what passes for mass art in the world is made-in-the-USA –

celebrities like Jennifer Lopez or Bruce Willis, the global imagery of Coca-Cola and Pepsi-Cola, or the news styles pioneered by CNN. American stuff saturates the global superculture.

From another perspective, however, the flood of images, sounds, and words has extended the market economy into more and more places (indeed, one might fairly say it is everywhere) and increasingly fashioned a public sphere that spans the globe, though it is hardly worldwide – the 'torrent' of news never reaches large areas of Africa. The point is that such a milieu has proved a fertile breeding ground for marketing in all its many guises. Where the media provide one of the environments in which we ordinarily live, where clutter afflicts all consumers and all citizens, the most important and the most scarce resource becomes the attention of the public. 'I've become like the teenagers: if I'm gonna watch TV, you've go to blow me out of my seat with some spectacle,' reflected Savino. 'They've made me jaded,' he said of the media.

The first task of publicity is to break through the clutter and grab the eyes and ears of the public, especially that jaded public. Effective marketing focuses attention on whatever the sponsor, be that IBM or President Bush, wants. No wonder that marketing emerged as a leading social science in the United States during the last third of the twentieth century, the very time when the extent and the speed of the 'torrent' expanded enormously. Ironically, the technology of marketing, notably publicity, actually increased the overall problem of clutter and distraction. Promotional noise has grown much louder: critics lamented the fact that the average consumer was bombarded by thousands of commercial messages a week, on television and radio, in newspapers and magazines, on the Internet or by phone, billboards, and direct mail. The ordinary American would look at roughly a million commercials by the time she reached thirty, with another million or so to go before she retired. Seeing does not mean believing, of course, but the very presence of so many ads has always bothered people, and the situation has actually gotten worse throughout the affluent world.

II

The single most obvious instrument of marketing, the loudest and the most garish, is advertising, and in many case advertising is also the most important technique of marketing to huge numbers of consumers. Worldwide ad spending in 2002, not a stellar year for the industry, was estimated in the Bob Coen Insider's Report (for the ad agency McCann-Erickson) at about $450 billion US. Television often grabbed the lion's share of this lush revenue. In America it took in only about one-quarter of the total, although at nearly $60 billion (year 2000 figures) that was far larger than in any other country. Elsewhere TV captured well over a third of the revenues, reaching 45 per cent in Japan and Italy and fully 60 per cent in Brazil.

National or international brand-name advertising had always played a special role in the marketplace. It added value to products, acting a bit like the factory where raw materials are transformed into goods, or in this case, into brands. Unlike classified or retail ads, this form of publicity dealt regularly in stereotype, cliché, and archetype, in hyperbole, and above all in symbols. Speaking in a familiar tongue, of course, was one way of reaching consumers. But an equally important objective was to attach a particular image or meaning to the brand. Television, and especially colour television, made this practice a good deal easier than it had been in the era when magazines had dominated the field of national advertising. During the 1960s the makers of television commercials worked to reinvent advertising as a form of popular culture. It was all a part of what came to be called the 'Creative Revolution,' initially centred on Madison Avenue in New York, where young men and some women attached to new and old agencies strove to fashion ads that in their own right offered people a dose of pleasure. Just consuming the ad would provide viewers with diversion, fantasy, and entertainment.

It was inevitable that sooner or later these innovations in consumer advertising would affect the style of propaganda.

Of course, the history of propaganda throughout the twentieth century had always been influenced by the practices of advertising: during the First World War George Creel, a former publicist and promoter, became the head of a Committee on Public Education that sought to sell the American war effort – he later wrote up his experiences in *How We Advertised America* (1920). Yet for a long time propaganda followed a different path, its style much more akin to the sermon than the story, hardly surprising given its purpose. Propaganda seeks to determine happenings in the public sphere. Whatever its particular shape, propaganda is an intentional and sponsored message that works to persuade the body politic, or some significant constituency within that community. It normally addresses or constructs the model citizen: it promotes right thinking, right feeling, and right doing, in each case a moral property. Propaganda amounts to a monologue: it is an assertion, not an argument that presumes some sort of dialogue among rival parties. Propaganda attempts to pre-empt debate. No wonder it works best when twinned with censorship, when conflicting opinions are banished from print or the airwaves, thus ensuring that the message is never challenged.

During the Second World War propaganda in America often employed a hectoring tone and used fear to compel silence ('Loose lips sink ships'), or sell war bonds (a swastika shadows a group of children), or inspire a renewed commitment (a sinister soldier, helmeted, looks out from the poster – 'He's watching you'). Even the more positive messages, like the famous image of Rosie the Riveter, the official heroine of wartime industry, and the slogan 'We Can Do It!', were imbued with a spirit of earnest enthusiasm. Much the same pattern was apparent in a display of war propaganda in France at the Musée de la publicité in Paris in 2003. The Vichy messages rang the alarms about Bolshevism and the Jewish plot or urged ideal husbands to work harder, and work in Germany, to support their happy families. Two Liberation posters of women epitomized the dichotomy: one woman was strong, idealized, reminiscent of the Statue of Liberty, while the other, a more surreal image, portrayed a woman hurt, her body damaged by the Nazi occupation. In each case the aim was to get the citizen to assume the correct moral position.

Still a different kind of propaganda did slowly begin to emerge in the United States in the postwar years, partly as a result of the activities of the Advertising Council, which took up the task of managing what came to be called public service announcements (PSAs). The Advertising Council was composed of representatives from the media and advertising industries, and it worked closely with corporate and government elites as well as the leaders of the country's social agencies, call them a moral elite, to assist worthy causes by arranging for an ad agency to produce a campaign at cost and for the media to donate free space or time to that campaign. Perhaps its most famous effort in these early years was Smokey the Bear, who tried to get people to prevent forest fires: Smokey, though always the moralist, became an icon in his own right, particularly popular with kids. Such endeavours, eventually labelled 'social marketing' in the early 1970s, were only one part of a general reformulation of propaganda. Leading firms mounted campaigns to position themselves as good corporate citizens or to foster capitalism or to inspire productivity. That trend mutated into issue campaigns during the 1970s when American business, notably the oil and power industries, fought back against government regulations or left-wing critics. In turn, employing a species known as 'green advertising,' the environmentalist movement sponsored its own initiatives to save the land or protect animals. Then there was the extraordinary rise of political advertising, which in time, perhaps as early as 1968, became the dominant form of election discourse in the United States. Each of these American forms was soon exported to other countries: in Canada, for example, the state became the largest single advertiser during the 1970s and 1980s, promoting everything from fitness to anti-racism to the war on drugs, until the assault on the federal deficit after 1993 forced a cutback.

Advertising remains the most visible way to advance an

agenda: the increasing welter of PSAs, government ads, charity appeals, corporate-image and issue advertising, health and social messages, political spots, counter-ads or culture jamming, cause-related publicity (like the Benetton campaigns) – the list goes on and on – together constituted advocacy advertising, the most common form of propaganda in the affluent zone of the world in the last third of the twentieth century. But there are other means. Social marketers have used posters, comic books, and tons of brochures to improve health or defeat vice. There is some virtue to the 'propaganda' or 'hegemony' model of the news media popularized by Edward Herman and Noam Chomsky, where media speak the agenda of the elite, although this theory dismisses the importance of that sphere of debate the press constructs and nourishes on a daily basis when politics is not disturbed by a crisis. Recent times have witness the massive growth of a bureaucratic propaganda, apparent in a host of reports by all sorts of government organizations and agencies, and sometimes in popular television shows where an anti-drug warning or pro-health message might be inserted by obliging producers on behalf of a state-sanctioned cause.

Above all, the world of affairs is full of consultants and professionals who deal in public relations, who strive to put the right 'spin' on events, to do damage control when disaster occurs, to put out the best message that serves the interests of their clients or employers. According to Chomsky and Herman, 'there are, by one count, 20,000 more public relations agents working to doctor the news today than there are journalists writing it' in the United States. This brand of marketing encompasses news conferences, press releases and video news releases, selective leaks, direct mail and personal lobbying, public speeches and lectures, letter-writing campaigns, media appearances, even presidential addresses. But it works best when the purpose is masked by the media, the message seemingly coming to the public through the ordinary news channels. Over ten years ago, Christopher Lasch estimated that a lot of the news in American newspapers (as much as 40 per cent, though such a figure can only be a guess) 'consists of items churned out by press agencies and public relations bureaus and then regurgitated intact by the "objective" organs of journalism.'

All this propaganda promotes a special kind of commodity known as a 'public good,' and often seeks to warn against a common risk, terms borrowed from the discipline of economics. A 'pure' public good, such as national security, has two basic attributes setting it apart from ordinary 'private goods.' First, the public good is 'non-deductible' or 'non-rival,' meaning that no matter how many citizens use it, that does not diminish its utility to other consumers. Second, the good is 'non-excludable,' meaning that it is almost impossible to stop anybody from enjoying the product. This attribute gives rise to the problem of 'free riders,' citizens who use a good without paying in some way, perhaps by avoiding their taxes or by not making a voluntary contribution. In any case the community, however defined, stands to gain or lose from the consumption of these jointly supplied commodities. A public good becomes a means to an esteemed end, whether that be a healthy Britain, crime-free streets, or world security. The benefits flow from the widespread use of a particular object (it could be a condom), the adoption of some policy (like banning weapons of mass destruction), or the election of an individual (candidates Bush or Gore in 2000), and nowadays each good is usually presented as a branded product. These social or political brands are subject to the same rigours of the famous 'four Ps' of marketing lore (product, pricing, promotion, and placement): they are pretested and positioned; they are packaged to suit disparate tastes; and they are targeted at specific market segments.

The number of ends, means, and sponsors has grown rapidly over the course of the past generation. And so, too, has the list of social risks, which now includes air and water pollution, AIDS, torture, homelessness, nuclear proliferation, and terrorism. They are the result of a wide assortment of sins, like selfishness or hedonism, persistent evils born of waste or intolerance, and occasional villains, perhaps corporate (say the tobacco industry) or religious (the Islamic jihadists). The causes of social and world progress, consequently, often involve unselling a particular idea or behaviour and dishonouring those who perpetuate or sponsor the social risk, a task that is sometimes called 'denormalization.' Both public goods and social risks have an important moral dimension, an ethical character that is largely absent from their private counterparts (unless, like the SUVs, they become the target of moral obloquy).

Daniel Robinson has coined the phrase 'marketing polity' to describe the new kind of democracy that slowly rose to prominence over the course of the twentieth century. Politicians have become entrepreneurs, perhaps better yet retailers, and voters have become consumers, shoppers, and purchasers in the political supermarkets of the land. The term marketing polity, however, means a lot more than just the application of market metaphors to the political game. Just as in the ordinary marketplace, huge sums of money are required to bring success in politics. *Time* (1 December 2003), for example, reported that the George W. Bush re-election campaign was 'in high gear, on track to raise $200 million' for the 2004 presidential contest. For the new political order rested upon an elaborate and expensive technology. Contenders for high office have built and maintained extensive databases of voters, a virtual community of the faithful made possible by the computer. Politicians and their handlers plus a wide assortment of interest groups must fund all kinds of consumer research – interviews, surveys, focus groups, and above all the incessant polling of citizens – in order not only to discover public opinion but to provide the means to shape that opinion. Their efforts have been supplemented by yet more polling on behalf of media organizations, designed both to supply news and predict the political future. The results of such market research have informed the successive waves of promotion by political actors – whether in the form of advertising (often the single most expensive item in political campaigns) or public and media relations, sometimes targeted at specific constituencies, sometimes aimed at the nation as a whole – that are intended to sell what I have called public goods or to denounce social risks. Here is the political context within which war as commodity was fashioned.

III

War might seem a particularly difficult product to sell. My 'consumer voices,' whatever their views, evinced a distaste for war that was more than just politically correct. In the formal democracies, at least, there has always been a streak of pacifism. One attribute, perhaps also an agent of the much-touted global society, is an increasing sense of empathy for people living in other regions of the world, manifested especially in moments of crisis: a famine, an earthquake, a plague, a civil war, especially when the lives of children are at stake – as, indeed, they almost always are. So the notion that war might be a public good strikes many people as obscene.

But there is a counter force, a popular culture of violence where the scenes of conflict are enjoyed as entertainment. I do not mean just the tradition of war movies. Indeed, some of the best of these are sympathetic neither to war in general nor to the experience of the war they depict: the justly famous *Apocalypse Now* (1979) showed the confusion and the collapse, in fact the sheer horror, of the American war effort in Vietnam. Rather, the celebration of violence has been especially pronounced in the much broader genre of action/adventure films, a Hollywood speciality that has flourished in the last thirty years, and flourished across the globe: the ranks of the top twenty movies worldwide, judged by box-office performance, are overloaded with mostly recent examples of this genre. Consider the popularity of the Star Wars saga, Indiana Jones and Rambo, or the various Terminators where the heroes fight amazing villains, often modelled upon stereotypes of the Nazis (think of the imperial storm troopers in *Star Wars*) or the Communists (Rambo took on both Asian and Russian types).

Star Wars (1977) and its children rehabilitated the notion of a good war, a war of liberation, in the realm of pop culture. Thomas De Zengotita, writing in *Harper's* (July 2003), thought the escapades in Afghanistan and Iraq had borrowed the justifications embedded in 'those action-vengeance flicks' of Steven Seagal and Vin Diesel where the hero had to right a brutal wrong (that was 9/11) with some awesome display of violence.

One of the most interesting series was actually an Anglo-American enterprise, not a Hollywood product: the saga of James Bond, especially the updated, modernized version played by Pierce Brosnan beginning in 1995. The appeal of 007 always extended broadly across the normal divides of age, class, locale, nationality, and even gender. The movies had a global reach: between a quarter and a half of the population of the world had seen at least one Bond movie, either at the cinema or on television, by the end of the twentieth century. Kids relished the Bond adventures. Television ratings in Britain and the United States, presumably from the late 1970s or 1980s, showed that Bond found a lot of favour with women. But Bond was most fancied by men, as was demonstrated by the Christmas rebroadcast of Bond films by TBS during the 1990s in the United States: according to the *Washington Post* (21 December 1998), these movies attracted not only more men than women, an unusual situation around holiday time, but a lot of upscale males as well. Men with money to spend were an irresistible attraction to advertisers, particularly to companies who sold luxury cars, expensive toys, all sorts of gadgets, fine liquor and wine, and quality men's products. Indeed, 007 had a proven track record as a salesman: the *London Times* (13 December 1997) claimed that BMW had managed to generate 10,000 advance orders, worth about $300 million, for its new sports car as a result of its presence in *GoldenEye* (1995). The Bond movies were, in themselves, a promotional commodity, able to convey messages to buy to an audience of eager consumers.

All of this points to the particular charisma of the Bond

franchise, and to the subversive pleasures it promised male viewers. In the world of 007, life was organized by the rule of the phallus, meaning that masculine principle of challenge, command, and conquest in which sex and violence were inextricably linked – 'hot babes and cool weaponry,' to borrow the words of the novelist Jay McInerney. The movies largely obeyed the well-established conventions of melodrama. Bond as hero was poised, efficient, and effective, the quintessential tough man. The villains were unremittingly evil. The megalomania was particularly acute in the case of Elliot Carver, the media mogul (à la Rupert Murdoch?) in *Tomorrow Never Dies* (1997) who sought to provoke chaos to produce the news sensations that would enrich his media properties and satisfy his lust for power. The world, or at least some large part of the world, was menaced, in *Tomorrow Never Dies* by a naval and possibly nuclear confrontation between China and the United Kingdom. All sorts of different story elements were present. There was adventure galore, and in exotic places – the action in *Die Another Day* (2002) was initially set in North Korea. There were innumerable combat scenes, gun fights and hand-to-hand struggles. There were moments of romance, even more of lust, notably in *The World Is Not Enough* (1999), when Bond played protector and lover to 'a sultry oil heiress' (as the blurb puts it) who turned out to be bad. There was science fiction: 007 has to battle against an old compatriot in *GoldenEye* who commanded a space weapon that could shock a city with an electromagnetic pulse. There was human interest: Bond must worry about the fate of 'M,' his superior but also a woman, held prisoner in a variation of the captivity tale (*The World Is Not Enough*). There was humour, notably of a sexual kind: Bond pointed his big gun at an unseen woman (*GoldenEye*). His comment: 'No more foreplay.' And he cocked the pistol.

The movies did not provide what the culture critic Tom Wolfe once called 'pornoviolence,' where characters satisfied their bestial urges in some cruel and graphic fashion. Bond has always been sadism lite. The villains had usually enlisted some brutes to threaten something very cruel. The trailer of *Tomorrow Never Dies* ends with Elliot Carver declaring to his torturer, 'When you remove Mr. Bond's heart, there should just be enough time for him to watch it stop beating.' The gory details of mayhem and murder were not shown. Instead, 007 was surrounded by the signs of hi-tech, a computer, a digital map, huge video screens, a space vehicle. He operated a wide assortment of fabulous machines: his fast and elegant cars of course, but also a supersonic jet or a futuristic speed boat or a weaponized hovercraft. He might leave some bodies in his wake. But the most common results of conflict were gorgeous explosions, enormous eruptions of white and orange cloud signifying the demolition of some machine or citadel. Brosnan as Bond invariably and successfully mounted the equivalent of a 'decapitation strike' against whatever lord of misrule was the villain of the piece – take out the leader and you've won your battle. He waged a clean war, full of jeopardy and jolts but not blood. No wonder his version was so easy to market: a clean war is a much easier sell than its dirty rival.

The Bond pictures were a foretaste of the coverage of the invasion of Iraq. True, there were no 'Bond girls' in Iraq. Well, not quite: the British forces did call the assault on Basra 'Operation James,' complete with targets labelled 'Pussy' and 'Galore.' Nor was Bush a replica of Bond, though the President was presented as a phallic hero. But Saddam Hussein certainly fitted the stereotype of the cruel villain. Officials and journalists would recount stories of the brutality of his regime. There were fears of mass destruction, of Iraq visiting death throughout the Middle East, especially on Israel. Plus there was plenty of neat weaponry, explosions, and derring-do in the invasion itself. Indeed, the Bond phenomenon was an indicator of what would work on the audience, how war could be positioned so that it was made palatable, even enjoyable, to a large body of spectators. Again pop culture, a sometime laboratory of politics, had pointed the way to making war both a public and a private good, a moral product that might also serve as a source of entertainment.

TWO

The War Debate

That Colin Powell might be exasperated by the United Nations was hardly surprising (figure 2.1). The Secretary of State had been billed in the media as the most prominent moderate in the Bush administration, not because he opposed war but because he opposed unilateral action. Powell, along with Prime Minister Tony Blair of the United Kingdom, constantly sought to win the approval of the United Nations for a new war against Iraq to ensure its disarmament. Both men hoped to renew the coalition that had triumphed in Gulf War I. The trouble was that the UN had refused to accept their case, particularly the doubtful evidence of Iraqi evil that Powell outlined in a tendentious speech delivered early in 2003. Nor were a sufficient number of member states willing to submit to American pressure.

The cartoon expressed the deep disdain many Americans on the right felt toward the UN: no more than a bunch of clowns and fools who lacked the wit or will to run the world properly. Their clothes, their body language emphasized the worthlessness of the whole UN exercise. Here was an image of the UN as circus or carnival, a place full of illusions where nothing serious could be done. American hawks reserved a special hatred for France, whose representative in the cartoon was sticking his tongue out at Powell (perhaps a reference to Dominique de Villepin, the foreign minister, who had proved such a thorn in the side of Washington). The French govern-

Figure 2.1 The UN as joke (By permission of Gary Varvel and Creators Syndicate)

ment had stoutly resisted the American pressure, even threatening it might exercise its veto in the Security Council should the Americans try to push through a war resolution. This defiance had inspired a bizarre but much-reported campaign to 'de-Frenchify' America, including the renaming of 'french fries' as 'freedom fries.' Bill O'Reilly of Fox News, one of the most exuberant of the media hawks, simply told his audience, 'Don't buy French stuff': the French were now just 'weasels.'

The UN had been at the centre of a battle over what to do about Iraq, a battle carried on in the media and in the streets throughout much of the world. The UN served as a kind of global parliament and consequently enjoyed a considerable measure of moral authority: its sanction of any invasion would give legitimacy to the pro-war cause. The noisy debate, however, was often a sham, a gigantic exercise in public relations, hardly a triumph of democracy. Beginning in the fall of 2002, Washington and the British government mounted a major marketing effort to persuade their own citizens, the world's publics, and the world's governments of the justice of war. That in turn provoked one of the most extensive antiwar movements in recent memory, complete with huge marches and demonstrations, which peaked in February and March 2003. The result was not really dialogue, an exchange of views, but a series of clashing monologues. The competing barrage of sights and sounds amounted to a propaganda war, now waged on a global scale. The debate that occurred was mostly in the heads of the journalists and the citizens at the receiving end of all this propaganda.

I

The propaganda war was rooted in the tragedy of September 11, 2001. The event might have seemed to some observers like a horrible replay of disaster movies like *The Poseidon Adventure* (1972) and *The Towering Inferno* (1974), which had enjoyed such a vogue in the 1970s. But the destruction of the World Trade Center's twin towers in New York was a gruesome instance of 'the propaganda of the deed,' to borrow a useful term from the lexicon of Jacques Ellul, a noted theorist of propaganda. That was not just because the suicide bombers had devastated 'a symbol of American prosperity,' which President Bush admitted in his address to Congress on 20 September. In fact, the World Trade Center was perceived in much of the world as a symbol of American arrogance and power as well. No, the crucial element was the attention paid by the news media around the world to the devastation and its aftermath. It was the constant and global focus that drove home the message of America's humiliation and vulnerability, the inability of the world's superpower to protect its citizens against terror. Sad to say, al-Qaeda had managed to use the apparatus of their enemy, not only its planes but its media as well, to send a message of hate and anger and, yes, triumph to a global audience (though not all were fascinated: in Madrid at a bar and restaurant called Museo de Jamon I found the crowd that evening was much more interested in a soccer match). This was postmodern warfare at its best, or rather its worst, where a low-tech band of warriors scored a massive symbolic victory by appropriating the technology of their foe. The world had changed, as so many commentators noted in the following months.

There was a brief moment when it seemed as though the Bush administration might be humbled. It had so obviously failed to protect the country against a stunning blow. Any feelings of guilt, however, were swiftly overwhelmed by a wave of patriotism, clearly encouraged by a president who wanted to wash away the stain of dishonour. Indeed the government was rejuvenated: previously the Bush adminis-tration had lacked a sense of mission, suffering because its legitimacy was in doubt as a result of the way the Republicans had won the presidency – via a Supreme Court decision rather than the popular vote. There was little soul-searching, and none it seemed in Washington, about the culpability of Ameri-can foreign policy. The Americans were 'hurt' and angry, Orsolina noted: as an American friend told her, 'You don't attack Americans.'

Particularly crucial was the campaign to establish the mean-ing of the tragedy. In the immediate aftermath rumours spread rapidly through the Internet that the downing of the towers presaged a general catastrophe, and the rhymed prophecies of the famed sixteenth-century seer Nostradamus were, once more, deployed to justify such pessimism. Some initial efforts to find blame were clearly divisive – such as the abortive attempt by the Reverend Jerry Falwell to stigmatize gays and feminists and liberals as somehow responsible. The brief craze demonstrated that people always need explanations of the unusual and the extraordinary. Authority moved swiftly to provide these explanations, drawing upon the lessons of mar-keting. Alternately employing the rhetoric of crime and of war, officials and journalists identified al-Qaeda as 'terrorists,' the enemy as 'terrorism,' and so placed both Osama bin Laden and his jihadists outside the pale of civilized society as a global risk. One purpose of this semantic exercise was to deny the obvious, that the assault was rooted in the anger of radical Islam. Recognizing that would foil efforts to build a global coalition. It would also foster racist attacks against Muslims and Arabs in the multicultural West. Better to try to bring everyone onside, whatever their politics or religion or nationality, on behalf of a vague something called civilization – that way, there could be no free riders. The meaning of 9/11 was no longer debatable: it referenced not *The Ugly American* (1963), a movie about how the United States tarnished its own reputation, but *Independence Day* (1996), a very different movie where a defiant America, led by a determined president, struck back at a hideous enemy.

The result was the declaration of a war on terror by President Bush that swiftly won widespread public support inside and outside the United States. That brought the destruction of the Taliban government in Afghanistan, an ally of Osama bin Laden and al-Qaeda, a worldwide hunt for these and other 'terrorists,' and the installation of a new regimen of security in the United States. The production of fear, the regular security alerts, the speculation about gas attacks or biological warfare or water poisonings, the worries about new suicide bombings, the stories of jihadist plots foiled and terrorists imprisoned all served to feed a kind of paranoia and to condition a public to accept the idea of permanent warfare.

What became clear a bit later was that 9/11 had enabled the victory of a cabal of hawks in and around the administration. 'Within the Republican Party ...,' argued Dave, 'September 11 provided the room for a *coup d'état*, to take over the Republican party and marginalize everyone.' It was as if the children of Dr Strangelove had suddenly seized power. The names most often mentioned were Dick Cheney, the Vice-President; Donald Rumsfeld, the Secretary of Defense; Paul Wolfowitz, the Deputy Secretary of Defense; and Richard Perle, chairman of the Defense Policy Board that advised the Pentagon. They were associated with a wider body of intellectuals, like William Kristol (editor of a Washington political magazine called

The Weekly Standard), as well as right-wing think tanks like the Project for a New American Century (whose chair in 2003 was William Kristol). These were men with answers, confident, driven, at least that was their public persona, supporters of an ideology now labelled 'neo-conservatism.' The hawks imagined an assertive, tough America that would act alone, if necessary, to advance its own broadly defined interests, as well as the cause of democracy, throughout the world.

Bush was clearly captivated by this vision of an American superpower bestriding the world. Early in 2002 he denounced an 'axis of evil' (supposedly a term coined by David Frum, a Canadian neo-con, then a White House speechwriter) that was composed of Iraq, Iran, and North Korea, each of which had or were developing weapons of mass destruction and so posed a threat to the United States. Possibly by the spring, certainly by the summer, he had committed his administration to the idea of an invasion of Iraq as the next stage in the war against terror, even though there remained dissent in Republican ranks. In September 2002 he endorsed a war strategy declaring that the United States would take pre-emptive action to forestall a threat, a step that mightily distressed the once sympathetic publics among America's European allies. The worry was that a naive Bush might let loose a demon he could never control.

II

The propaganda war opened in the Islamic world. At first this had little to do with Iraq. Operation 'Enduring Freedom,' as Washington called its war on terror, had proved easy to sell to the West, also menaced by the threat of the jihadists. A Pew Research poll in the summer of 2002 found generally favourable attitudes toward the United States among its traditional allies and one new friend: in the 70 per cent range in Great Britain, Canada, and Italy; in the 60 per cent range in France, Germany, and Russia. The one region of the globe where people were not especially sympathetic to the United

States was in the Islamic countries. Pew discovered that only a minority of people there put any faith in the wisdom of Washington: Lebanon (35%), Turkey (30%), Jordan (25%), and Pakistan (a mere 10%).

The trouble was that neither the Arabic nor the Muslim 'street' had bought into the justification for 'Enduring Freedom.' Too many people, whether Islamic radicals or moderates, found themselves living under proxy regimes, dominated by rulers who were propped up by American money and might. According to some reports, the news of the 9/11 tragedy had actually caused jubilation in cities in the Middle East. Moreover, Islamic militants had scored an early propaganda triumph. A CBS News report (4 September 2002) recounted the popularity of a 'Big Lie' about the demolition of the World Trade Center, namely, that it was the work of Jews. Another version (not reported by CBS) blamed the CIA, acting either alone or with Israel. In any case, bin Laden was seen as innocent, though he remained something of a hero to many people. Muslims everywhere, so CBS claimed – and their findings were backed up by a Gallup poll – were taken with the story that 4000 Jewish employees at the Center had been warned to stay home the day of the assault. Reporters even tracked down the origins of this myth to comments in two papers in Jordan on 13 September that raised the issue of Israeli involvement in the disaster. The next day an Israeli ambassador mentioned to the press some 4000 telephone calls Israelis had made in search of their relatives in New York. On 17 September Al-Manar, a Beirut television station, put together the 'Big Lie' as a special report. It was immediately spread via the Internet and soon picked up and widely discussed in the press, on talk shows, and on TV and radio throughout the Middle East and beyond. A CBS reporter had discovered just how commonplace the myth of Jewish involvement was when he attended a wedding party in a small town in Pakistan: every one of the town's leading men, so he stated, accepted the 'Big Lie' as fact.

The lie worked because it readily fitted the prevailing views.

Anti-Americanism was pervasive: the reporter was told, 'People hate America. Yeah, that's true.' Blaming Arabs for 9/11 was just a new excuse the Americans were using to persecute Muslims and invade Islamic states. The other reason for the story's success was the hatred of Israel, whether based on anti-Semitism or fury over the way Palestine was being treated. The 'Big Lie' neatly exploited existing animosities and added that delicious morsel, how an arrogant America was actually trashed by its most fervent ally, Israel.

One of the people CBS News interviewed for this story was Charlotte Beers, the Undersecretary for Public Diplomacy and Public Affairs in the State Department. Beers was a retired advertising executive and brand specialist, in the 1990s the chair of Ogilvy and Mather and later of J. Walter Thompson. She had agreed to join the State Department to revitalize its publicity back in the spring of 2001, although her task was effectively defined by 9/11, and she took office in September. She found the intellectual terrain in the Middle East already controlled by the enemy. Osama bin Laden had quickly sought to establish the meaning of the war on terror. In a letter delivered to the Arab media, he warned against 'the new Jewish and Christian crusader campaign that is led by the Chief Crusader Bush under the banner of the cross.' That wording cleverly exploited a verbal misstep of Bush, who early on had identified the war against terrorism as a crusade, an allusion to a time many centuries ago when Christian warriors attacked Islam. History served here to justify bin Laden's effort to engage the Muslim public in his planned 'jihad' against an unholy America. Put this way, radical Islam was on the side of civilization, while the West, and especially the United States and Israel, were the barbaric aggressors. The 'terrorists' were transformed into 'martyrs.'

Beers had to find a way to counter the loathsome reputation of the United States in the Islamic world, to concentrate attention on America's positives. Part of the efforts of her staff involved organizing a series of interviews by Colin Powell and National Security Advisor Condoleezza Rice on Arab media, including Al-Jazeera, an Arabic TV channel based in Qatar that had won attention as the forum where bin Laden and his associates aired their propaganda to the Islamic world. Former American diplomats, able to speak Arabic, were recruited to give interviews and talks to combat the messages of bin Laden and his allies. Beers's department was also involved in the establishment in the spring of 2002 of Radio Sawa, offering rock and pop (Celine Dion was an early favourite) and some news aimed to please Arab youth. That latter effort had the advantage of using America's preeminence in the realm of pop culture to provide a vehicle for its propaganda. By the fall Sawa had already built up a fair audience, notably in Amman, Jordan.

But Beers had a much more breathtaking strategy. Her place was rife with adspeak. She set out to sell 'brand America' to a doubting population across the Islamic world, a goal in itself a testament to the extraordinary faith some Americans had in the power of publicity to transform opinions. Beers worked in association with Muslims and Arabs in America, as well as the Advertising Council. She hired McCann-Erickson to produce the 'Shared Values' campaign, a series of extended TV commercials for brand America meant for Islamic consumption. One of these efforts was composed of testimonials from a group of successful Muslims living and working in the United States: the owner of a bakery, the director of a health institute, a paramedic, a schoolteacher, a student learning broadcasting. They explained how America was really a tolerant society, a multicultural paradise of democracy, religious freedom, and opportunity where Arab and Muslim could thrive without fear of harassment or persecution. Indeed, according to one happy soul, America and Islam shared the same kind of family values. Beers was out to reposition America as a friend of Islam and Arabia, to counter the hatred marketed by bin Laden and his associates.

The 'Shared Values' campaign failed miserably. It was supposed to roll out during Ramadan, and it did air in some places (Indonesia was mentioned by the press). But Beers's department was unable to get Al-Jazeera, the most believable of the media, to carry the spots, reportedly because the Arab channel wanted too much money. Beers only had a budget of $15 million, a ludicrous amount given how daunting her task was. Such propaganda had to blanket the airwaves. Even then it would have been an impossible sell. Bob Garfield, the veteran ad critic of *Advertising Age* (25 November 2002), correctly deemed these sweet efforts naive: marketing meant supplying what an audience wanted, or at least appearing to do so, not 'putting the best face on that which you wish to sell.' A response from Muslims was that the propaganda amounted to a whitewash of US foreign policy, especially its support of Israel. There was no way that such a small dose of propaganda, no matter how slick, could push brand America in a region where anti-Americanism prevailed. Not even the prophet Mohammed could sell America in the present climate, quipped one Muslim expert. The campaign was halted early in 2003. Beers herself resigned from the position in March 2003. Washington had suffered its first defeat in the propaganda war, though it would redouble its efforts after the conquest of Iraq.

III

In the end the 'Shared Values' fiasco proved to be only an intriguing sideline. Selling the invasion of Iraq to America and the West was a much more substantial enterprise. Bush and company set out to exploit the fears and desires of Americans, the fears of more terror attacks and the desires for peace and security. Once more, Washington drew on a lesson of advertising: one key to persuasion was repetition – keep telling the public how evil, how dangerous Saddam Hussein was to ensure that some of the charges stuck. Oscar recalled how his daughter Karen, living in the United States, had been keenly aware of the whole crisis, and of the claims about why Iraq must be humbled, because of the constant barrage of propaganda.

There had been rumblings about Saddam Hussein and Iraq ever since 9/11, but the drum beats got much louder in the fall of 2002 when the White House rolled out its new product in the war on terror. Washington did not use the conventional marketing methods employed by, for example, Sony or Procter & Gamble: there was no state-sponsored ad campaign (although in early 2003 pro-war advocates, outside the administration, did launch some commercials to answer the peace agitation). Rather, Washington relied on lobbying, media appearances, and televised addresses. Bush spoke at the UN. Congress was soon persuaded to give its approval for war. Blair's government released a dossier on Saddam Hussein's atrocities. The White House used doubtful intelligence to claim the dictator was out to build a nuclear bomb. Administration heavies like Rumsfeld and Rice made themselves available to the press and television so they could tell, again and again, how Iraq was a threat to America and the world. The advocates of war kept up a constant invective against the sins of the Iraqi regime: it was during this period that Paul Wolfowitz became a household word in the United States, with his war ardour, his commitment to regime change, his belief in an American mission, which made him seem the most obvious successor of Dr Strangelove. And before long the press was harping away on the fact that the UN inspectors, newly returned to Iraq, had not turned up any weapons of mass destruction, leaving the impression that these really did exist somewhere other than in the imagination of the administration. Bruce W found the build-up to war 'almost agonizing.' Perhaps that was 'part of the show,' mused Glenna: 'getting people up to a pitch before ...' The propaganda blitz was a campaign as full of hype as any a business might launch to promote its new brand, of soap, or cola, or software. But what contributed to the success of this propaganda was that it used the news media, a more trusted source, and not the normal ad media, often discounted by consumers, to promote the Bush agenda.

Washington had a great advantage in America because the

war was already largely 'pre-sold.' That was the most obvious reading of a compilation of polls published later by the American Enterprise Institute, entitled *America after 9/11*. Surveys taken just after the tragedy showed that Americans were in a belligerent mood, ready to discipline any country which sponsored or harboured terrorism. The passage of time and the attack on the Taliban brought some abatement in the war fever. But not much: the war on terror remained very popular, able to command substantial majorities in the polls. People were ready for sacrifice, even for body bags: the much-feared aversion of the public to casualties, the death of 'our boys and girls,' the legacy of Vietnam, had receded. In particular, the time had come to deal with Saddam Hussein, whose very persistence so long after the victory of Gulf War I both irritated and frightened Americans. A few polls indicated a majority of Americans believed that Hussein did have a connection to al-Qaeda, that he had been involved in 9/11, and certainly did support terrorism. Two polls in the spring of 2002 even counted Hussein 'a greater danger to the United States' than bin Laden. There may have been some softening of support for war in the late summer, at least according to two polls in August (Gallup and ABC News), but even then a majority still favoured war, and the totals rose again after the administration launched its campaign.

What the majority of Americans wanted, though, was some approval: they wanted friends and a UN sanction, they did not want to go alone. Two polls in January 2003, for example, demonstrated massive support (at the 80 per cent range) for a war sanctioned by the UN and conducted by America and its allies, but not if the United States acted without UN sanction, and particularly not if it acted alone (support for a unilateral war fell dramatically to the 30 per cent range). The demand for war was there – all the administration had to do was satisfy that demand with the right product.

Not surprisingly, Washington's propaganda was tailored to suit the public mood. The task was to manage opinion, to nurture the sentiments that would ensure the success of the government's agenda. Witness the televised speech, broadcast live to the nation, and to the world at large, by President Bush on 17 March 2003, where he announced the commencement of the invasion of Iraq in the very near future should Saddam Hussein and his sons fail to leave the country immediately. This was one of those special moments in public life, a command performance, that the television age made possible. He was dressed in a sober, dark suit and stood at a podium that displayed his seal of office, with an American flag in the background. He used no aids, but spoke directly to the camera, which soon moved in to frame his upper body, a mode of direct address that established eye contact with the unseen audience. He never smiled or grimaced: indeed all his gestures, and there were a few hand movements, were carefully controlled. His tone was measured, reasoned – with none of the malapropisms for which he was notorious. Occasionally he enunciated carefully and emphatically every word in a clause or sentence. This was definitely a paternal moment. He reminded me of stars once common in the American medical dramas of the 1960s, men like Dr Zorba (*Ben Casey*) or Dr Gillespie (*Dr Kildare*), father figures who would always speak the 'truth,' usually a very moral truth, to their younger colleagues and to the watching audience. Perhaps, too, the fact that Bush was talking of war and sacrifice brought those paragons of tough medicine to mind. Such paternal moments may no longer be so frequent in the realm of pop culture, where flash and humour and speed reign. But they do connect to an archetype of the ideal father who, in a moment of crisis, delivers the law to his family.

This was not the time for novelty. The by now commonplace claims and clichés, so familiar because of the work of the propaganda mills, were carefully woven into a speech that lasted only a little more than thirteen minutes. Evidence was no longer necessary to justify this war. Rather, Bush had to reaffirm the master narrative of a righteous war that would capitalize on the existing views of the much-surveyed American populace. He began by asserting the necessity to disarm

Iraq, a pledge the regime had made in 1991 when Gulf War I ended, but which it had never honoured. He noted the failure of the UN inspectors, emphasizing the duplicity and deceit of the regime, a charge of immorality. He noted as well the failure of diplomacy, of the honourable efforts to bring about a just settlement and preserve the peace. His purpose was to establish just how hard he and others had worked to avoid the now necessary war.

What made war a necessity now was the persistence of Saddam Hussein. 'Today, no nation can possibly claim that Iraq has disarmed. And it will not disarm so long as Saddam Hussein holds power.' Here was the rationale for regime change, a project championed in particular by Wolfowitz and the hawks. The reputation of Saddam Hussein had been blackened back in 1990 and 1991, and the stain was renewed in recent months: Bush could assume his audience was well aware of the assorted atrocities, notably the gassing of the Kurds in northern Iraq in the 1980s. The successful demonization of Hussein was a crucial element of pro-war propaganda, the hinge of the whole exercise. A number of the 'consumer voices' expressed doubts about the reality of Hussein as Devil – he was no Hitler (Oscar), did he really gas the Kurds? (Glenna and Bruce W), 'a fairly typical Middle Eastern despot' (Michael), 'a common thug' (Richard). But none denied he was a dictator whose departure would make Iraq a better place.

No doubt aware of the internationalist sentiment of the American public, Bush carefully declared his commitment to 'the mission of the United Nations.' But he also explained that one rationale for the UN was 'to confront aggressive dictators actively and early, before they can attack the innocent and destroy the peace.' That body had already given its sanction for the use of force to disarm Iraq, and he carefully cited the three resolutions (numbers 678, 687, and 1441, the last passed in November 2002) justifying such action. Here was an effort to cloak the ultimatum in a garb of legality, the way a sheriff might evoke federal law to justify killing his foes in some old western movie. The trouble was not 'authority' but 'will.' Some members of the Security Council shared the American 'assessment' of Iraq but not the American 'resolve.' Fortunately, many other nations did share that 'resolve,' and here he made reference to a 'broad coalition,' elsewhere famously known as 'the coalition of the willing,' which was 'now gathering to enforce the just demands of the war.' This was Bush's surrogate UN. Put another way, the United States was acting in concert with like-minded countries, an important claim because it met the public's distress at the notion of going it alone.

Much of the talk over the past six months had revolved around the specific reasons for invading Iraq. Bush now laid out two clear justifications for war. The first was national and world security, the peril that Saddam Hussein's Iraq posed to every other country because of its weapons of mass destruction (see figure 2.2). 'Intelligence gathered by this and other governments leaves no doubt that the Iraq regime continues to possess and conceal some of the most lethal weapons ever devised.' Nor was there any question that the regime had 'a history of reckless aggression in the Middle East,' that it boasted 'a deep hatred of America,' and that it had 'harbored terrorists, including operatives of al-Qaeda.' Sooner or later Iraq would use or lend its weaponry to kill the innocent. America had to act to prevent 'the day of horror.' This was classic fear-mongering, a staple of the pro-war case because it so readily fitted into the wider frame of the war on terror. This was also the language of advocacy: Bush had underlined how Hussein was a public risk.

The second objective was to liberate Iraq from the tyranny of 'the lawless men' who now held power. The Americans and their allies would destroy 'the apparatus of terror': 'no more poison factories, no more executions of dissidents, no more torture chambers and rape rooms.' Instead, America would build a 'prosperous and free Iraq' that could 'set an example to all the Middle East of a vital and peaceful and self-governing nation,' a phrase that hinted at the goal of

Figure 2.2 Weapons of mass destruction (Mike Keefe, *The Denver Post*)

Many of the people I interviewed identified the charge that Iraq possessed weapons of mass destruction as the 'Big Lie' of the propaganda campaign mounted by Washington and the British government. Some had believed the charge had merit, whatever stand they eventually took on the war. Time and again television viewers were told that Saddam Hussein had biological, chemical, and possibly nuclear weapons that he was ready to launch against neighbours or give to terrorists. Time and again they were told this constituted a major threat to the security of the United States. The cartoon simply turned this fear-mongering on its head. The irony, as the peace movement pointed out, was that Washington had an enormous arsenal of these lethal weapons. According to Melissa, one of her students claimed it simply was not fair for Washington to ban other states from having the same kind of weaponry as the United States.

democratizing the whole region. Altogether Bush had cast America in the role of both avenging angel and world saviour. The messianic note in Bush's address harked back to a long-standing sense of mission rooted in the history of American thought, namely, the belief that the United States was a people's utopia with a responsibility to spread its values and its system, especially its democracy, to the less fortunate peoples of the world. This was yet another way in which to position war as a public good.

Running throughout Bush's speech was a sense of will, of resolve, words that he clearly liked. He was playing out a classic role in the mythology of the Old West, a role epitomized by Gary Cooper as the marshal in *High Noon* (1952) who stood his ground against the villains, even though abandoned by all the townsfolk. A more jaundiced reading, though, might activate the memory of the cyborg played by Arnold Schwarzenegger in *The Terminator* (1984), a killer who was indomitable, who would never listen to reason nor succumb to exhaustion, unstoppable until the end, that is, when he was literally crushed. Bush himself even evoked History, recalling the failure of appeasement to stop the dictators of the 1930s from ravaging Europe. Nothing similar would happen on his watch – shades here of Winston Churchill. 'We are a peaceful people, yet we are not a fragile people. And we will not be intimidated by thugs and killers.' Any who attacked the United States, or aided such fiends, would face 'fearful consequences.' These claims hinted at a third, unstated objective of the war: to alert other rogue nations to the fact that America would punish all offenders. The invasion of Iraq was, in that sense, an advertisement of a newly bellicose America.

IV

Opposing war was enormously popular in Europe, and only a bit less so in Canada. A Pew poll released on 18 March revealed a huge divide had opened between America and Europe. Six in ten Americans favoured an invasion of Iraq. In

Europe, however, the desire for peace, the horror of bombing, the fear of Armageddon, all had generated a mass movement against war and in support of the United Nations that filled the streets of cities with demonstrators (the London rally was supposedly the largest in its history) in the middle of February 2003. A variety of protest groups had formed their own 'coalition of the willing,' using the Internet to mobilize the traditional community of dissent against Washington – but not just that community, a fact which startled participants and journalists alike. 'You were getting millions of people out,' recalled Chris, who had been in Berlin during one of the marches, 'protesters for the first time who'd never protested anything, so not just these so-called professional protesters ... but actual people, actual in quotation marks, mums and dads, and middle-class people.' The planned war was variously condemned as unnecessary (let the inspections work), illegal (because it lacked the UN's sanction), dangerous (because it would provoke more terrorist actions), immoral (because it meant killing innocents). Invasion was the policy of warmongers like Bush, of imperialists like the neo-conservatives, of capitalists like Big Oil (see figure 2.3). Not only was the opposition strong in France (at 75%) and Germany (69%), the lands Rumsfeld had stigmatized as 'Old Europe' because they had blocked Washington at the UN. The publics of countries officially part of 'the coalition of the willing' were actually unwilling to join up: Italy and Spain (81%), Poland (73%), and even Britain (59%). Similarly, an EKOS poll in late February revealed that nearly three-quarters of Canadians opposed a war lacking the sanction of the UN: this time, anyway, Canadians were thinking like Europeans. Peace was always a much easier sell, because it was an intrinsically moral commodity, an expression of widely esteemed ideals about the human condition, at least to people who were not feeling threatened by some imminent peril.

In America, however, the antiwar movement remained much weaker, except in a few areas, notably Seattle, which did earn a reputation as a hotbed of peace sentiment. The peace advo-

Figure 2.3 The lust for oil (Steve Greenberg, *Ventura County Star*)

'It's all about oil, right?' That comment by a Canadian protester made to a CBC reporter (in a documentary entitled 'Protest') was an article of faith among peace advocates everywhere. All you had to do was decode Washington's rhetoric, as Greenberg did here. Sometimes, the claim reflected the age-old distrust of American business, Big Oil, which presumably wanted to use America's military might to generate super-profits. Were not Bush and Cheney past Texans whose political fortunes were linked to the oil industry? On other occasions critics evoked the charge of empire: oil was the essential fuel, the means of ensuring both American prosperity and American dominance. Iraq would be devastated to satisfy the base needs of the owners of SUVs and the sinister designs of American generals. But whether capitalism or imperialism motivated Washington was not the point. The charge itself, that Washington lusted after Iraqi oil, served to dishonour the whole pro-war case, at least in the minds of protesters.

cates had to unsell the populace, never an easy task as the war on drugs had proved long ago. Inevitably they employed the techniques of advocacy advertising to awaken the public. One difficulty was to find a way to counter Washington without appearing unpatriotic. Another part of the trouble was that the Democrats in Congress had largely accepted the administration's case, their silence a reflection of the general popularity of the war on terror. Instead, Hollywood and the like filled the void: a number of celebrities such as Martin Sheen, Susan Sarandon, Michael Moore, Sean Penn, and the Dixie Chicks, in different ways, gave voice to peace sentiments. Such stars of pop culture had the advantage of being able to command media attention, especially at a time when it seemed difficult to get the antiwar message out to the public. In January 2003 Comcast, a big cable enterprise, refused to air an antiwar spot on its CNN service in the Washington area, including some time during the coverage of Bush's State of the Union address. An appeal to the Federal Communications Commission, the government's watchdog, brought the response from its chairman that there was no need to act, whatever the cries of outrage from peace groups.

A similar problem bedevilled the career of one of the most interesting pieces of antiwar propaganda, an advocacy ad created by MoveOn.org in an effort to get Washington to 'let the inspections work' – in other words, to back the UN effort to disarm the Iraqi regime. MoveOn was billed in the press as one of the new-style protest groups because it existed primarily in cyberspace. Started by a Berkeley couple in 1998 to combat the impeachment effort against President Clinton, MoveOn had continued to work through the Internet to mobilize a middle-class public on behalf of a variety of liberal causes and candidates. This innovation in grass-roots activism proved itself when MoveOn managed to sponsor successful petitions as well as generate considerable funds, boasting a membership of around 650,000 people. Late in 2002 the organization decided to lend its support to the peace cause, allied with other protest groups in the environmentalist movement (such as Greenpeace), civil rights (the NAACP and the National Organization for Women), and the churches (the National Council of Churches) under the label 'Win Without War.' MoveOn purportedly raised $300,000, much more than was needed (as reported in the San Francisco *Sunday Chronicle*, 9 February 2003) to place antiwar ads in the *New York Times*. It organized 'Let the Inspections Work' petitions that were delivered to the home offices of senators and congressmen across the nation in late January. And just the week before, according to the *Los Angeles Times* (16 January 2003), MoveOn claimed it had secured some $450,000, mostly in the form of small donations, to mount a television campaign in Washington and other major cities.

The core of that campaign was a controversial ad that had been fashioned in association with Fenton Communications, a liberal public-relations firm noted for its involvement in progressive causes. The advocacy commercial was an update of *Daisy*, the most famous attack ad in the history of American politics. That spot had been aired during the 1964 presidential campaign by the Democrats: it began with an image of innocence, a little girl plucking a daisy, and ended with an image of horror, a nuclear explosion, all in order to awaken voters' fears that the Republican challenger, Barry Goldwater, might start a war. The ad was recalled as so effective (some people thought, incorrectly, that it had murdered the Goldwater campaign) that it was redone at least twice to suit different causes, in the 1996 and 2000 presidential campaigns.

The MoveOn variation stayed fairly close to the original, except that it was in colour and it only ran thirty seconds. Again the commercial started peacefully, presenting a series of pictures that were supposed to evoke ideas of harmony and childhood: a pretty blonde girl, dressed in blue, surrounded by bright flowers, in a quiet meadow somewhere, intently plucking the petals off a daisy, saying 'One, two, three, four, five ...' That idyllic scene was shattered by the voice of a male announcer who warned, 'War with Iraq, maybe it will end quickly. Maybe not. Maybe it will spread.' At which point the picture of the girl was replaced by scenes of conflict, the guns of a warship blasting away, a building or oil field ablaze, and a new countdown began, a missile count-down by an echoing male voice, 'nine ... eight ... seven ...' Back came the announcer: 'Maybe extremists will take over countries with nuclear weapons.' The warning was reinforced by an image of a foreign-looking mob trashing the American flag. Then the ad cut back to the little blonde girl, who looked up as the camera moved abruptly into a close-up of her face and froze. 'Maybe the unthinkable ...' The countdown reached zero. The screen filled with a billowing nuclear explosion, first the giant bubble and then the awesome mushroom cloud, always the hideous glow of red fury, accompanied by the sounds of destruction. 'That's why Americans are saying to President Bush ... Let the inspections work.' Those last words were superimposed on the screen, along with the address 'www.MoveOn.org,' as the image of nuclear terror receded.

Daisy redux had a number of purposes. First, it was designed to avoid any suggestion that the antiwar cause was sympathetic to Saddam Hussein – in short, peace was just as patriotic as war (see figure 2.4). Second, it sought to awaken the interest of the news media, which it certainly succeeded in doing: news organizations proved eager to get copies of the commercial, which was also covered in the international press. Third, it aimed at provoking the public to start thinking seriously about the consequences of war, just at a time when the peace movement was planning a series of marches. 'We wanted to run an ad that would highlight that very real possibility [of nuclear war] and help encourage a national discussion,' Eli Pariser, MoveOn's international campaign director, told the Associated Press. Yet this was a strange way to provoke a reasoned conversation. No less than Washington's declarations of imminent peril, the ad was also a form of scare propaganda, its mix of images, especially the nuclear explosion, meant to frighten. The Daisy remake suggested the war would radicalize the Middle East (was that a mosque in the background of the anti-American crowd?), thus broadening the

Figure 2.4 What anti-war really means (Fritz Alfred Behrendt,
Cartoonists & Writers Syndicate / cartoonweb.com)

The pro-war camp made much of the apparent moral confusion of
the peace movement. Here were a collection of people, some drawn
from the churches, who were in effect supporting a tyrant. Was
that not a form of appeasement? This European cartoon neatly
skewered these naive protesters. The way they held themselves
suggested they were somehow flaky. By contrast, there was a
gloating and triumphant Saddam Hussein, backed by his odious
henchmen, accepting the tokens of submission. In fact, in the
United States, the peace movement laboured under the charge that
its efforts worked against the liberation of Iraqis. Indeed Dave, a
peace activist, admitted that briefly he too had been swayed by 'the
idea that the job of a democratic nation is to spread democracy.'

war, although the only Islamic regime known to have nuclear weapons, Pakistan, lacked the means to launch its warheads against the United States. The claim, in short, was far-fetched, though still evocative, a way of exploiting the existing public fears of new horrors. One of the staples of antiwar rhetoric was that any invasion of Iraq would provoke the jihadists to launch new suicide assaults against the West, thus raising the spectre of another 9/11. *Daisy* redux just built on that fear to identify war as risking Armageddon.

Yet the potential of this *Daisy* was never fully realized. It had to get out to the public. The ad was shown on four national newscasts as well as on CNN's *Inside Politics* and *American Morning*, an excellent form of free publicity – except that in each case the journalists involved discussed, and sometimes doubted, the claims or the rationale for the remake. *Inside Politics*, in particular, drew a comparison between the 1964 and 2003 versions, noting how both had tried to play on the anxieties of Americans about war. On ABC's *This Week* Donald Rumsfeld, no less, saw portions of the ad and deemed it 'irresponsible' (like the original), indeed 'unhelpful' to the cause of peace. So the message of the ad was always mediated. Soon MoveOn discovered that it could not buy time on CNN, Fox, or NBC to air the ad, a spokesperson for that last network claiming such issues were better handled by its own news and public affairs staff. According to the Scripps Howard News Service (25 February 2003), four television stations actually pulled the ad off the air. Later efforts by MoveOn and other antiwar groups ran into this same kind of obstacle: whatever the rhetoric about a free press, they either lacked the monies to buy time or they were refused the privilege of buying time on the major broadcast and cable networks. The marches, the demonstrations, the personnel, sometimes the propaganda, these were covered as news in the media. But the peace movement could not easily employ the same media to reach the public directly. Such were the limits on debate in America.

Possibly the peace movement would have had more impact

if the agitation had begun earlier or the crisis lasted longer. Certainly the activists managed to mobilize a broad spectrum of people disturbed by the march to war. Polls did indicate that many Americans (fully 47 per cent in one mid-March survey) were not sure Washington had made an iron-clad case for waging war without the sanction of the UN or the support of America's traditional allies. But surveys also indicated that much of the American public was not listening very closely, and a goodly number of citizens simply did not want to listen: they had already concluded that war was inevitable. Nine out of ten respondents did not participate in a demonstration, nor did they know anyone who had. One poll, admittedly sponsored by the very patriotic Fox News, found that nearly two-thirds of Americans held an unfavourable view of the antiwar protesters. Another March poll, conducted by Pew Research, learned that 40 per cent had decided they had heard too much about the views of those people who opposed the war.

Yet after all the supposed debate there was still no happy consensus. Writing in the *New Yorker* (17 March 2003), Hendrik Hertzberg thought the polls he saw demonstrated that many Americans were increasingly troubled – 'The divisions are profound, and the most agonizing are not between people but within them' – because they could see justice in both the pro-war and the peace positions, because they found the prospect of war and of peace both risky, whatever their decision about how to deal with Iraq. Bush might admit he had no doubts – '"If anyone can be at peace," he said the other day, "I am at peace about this"' – but the American public did not go to war with an easy conscience.

V

The invasion of Iraq, even more the bombing of Baghdad, provoked the last great explosion of antiwar protest around the world. There were marches and demonstrations, especially around American consulates. A group in Halifax acted out a missile attack, another in Ottawa chained themselves to the gates and doorways of the British High Commission, protesters burned flags in Paris. In a number of cities there were riots when the angry crowds were confronted by the police – in Amman, Jordan, for example, the demonstrators were dispersed by tear gas. Bombing had a special horror because it visited death on so many innocents, so many children. A CBC TV report on 21 March captured this outrage and this empathy. 'I just see their faces and I just know they're experiencing the terror,' said a woman in Toronto, with a catch in her voice, 'you know, the bombs falling, and they don't know if they're going to make it through the day.' 'My heart's bleeding, I'm crying,' lamented another woman in Ottawa. 'It's just too much, it's just too much to do this in the twenty-first century, and the whole world is watching.' Protest leaders vowed to step up the pressure, to mount larger and larger demonstrations everywhere to force Bush and Blair to call off the dogs of war. To no avail: indeed the opposite happened. The antiwar protest as a mass movement dissipated after the first week of war, at least in the West.

No wonder, then, that most of my citizen's panel deemed the whole antiwar exercise a disappointment. Bruce and Glenna W, who had participated in peace marches, did believe the antiwar protests had an impact on the policy of the Canadian government, more particularly on Prime Minister Jean Chrétien, who consequently refused to participate in the Anglo-American assault on Iraq. And Reza, as a Muslim, was 'glad to see the antiwar movement' because of what it suggested about the inclusiveness of Canadian society. However: 'We are marching with millions of people around the world, an amazing phenomenon, and yet it means very little. The war is going ahead, the United Nations and its debates and votes and opinions are absolutely irrelevant, the course has already been set.' Likewise, Michael was amazed at 'how it collapsed as soon as the war had started and how ineffectual it seemed to be. Nobody seemed to pay any attention to it, certainly [not] in the US and in Canada, and in Europe it was but for the UK basically in support of the positions being taken by the politicians.' As a result, Bob concluded that the antiwar movement actually 'didn't happen,' not in any significant sense, which was a surprise to him since he had expected a much more lasting protest.

There was, indeed, something a bit strange, in a word festive, about aspects of the whole exercise. Reza pointed out how the peace movement soon became a bit of a 'fad,' at least in Canada, the thing to do 'if you're cool.' Richard, who supported the coalition, argued the protesters were just part of a long tradition of peace marchers evident over the course of the twentieth century: naive, ideological, and now so very anti-American. He could understand pacifism as a creed, even if he had little sympathy with its tenets. But the antiwar movement lacked intellectual substance. You could not reason with the protestors. There was no 'meeting of the minds,' no way to talk to people caught up in the emotion of the moment. 'They're idealists,' agreed Irene, 'if for the wrong reason. They still haven't got out of Woodstock in the '60s.' Likewise, Bob thought the Canadian participants were 'just thrilled' by the excitement of playing a part, something out of collective memory, 'the brave days of the '60s.'

All of which may seem a bit too harsh. There were good reasons why people should take to the streets to protest the war. But there was also a spirit of rejectionism, a grand refusal, akin to those performances that occasionally surface in the marketplace when consumers turn against a fashion or condemn a brand because it seems, however briefly, offensive. Think back, for example, to the great outburst against Coca-Cola in the mid-1980s when the company endeavoured to market a new flavour of its much-loved Coke in North America, and to retire old Coke. Or consider the way Madonna faced a boycott in the early 1990s when her explorations of the styles and images of pornography carried her too far into the realm of dirty sex for many consumers of her products. These outbursts express a resentment against an elite, the fashion designers say or an industry, that regulates the lives, more properly the consumption, of the affluent.

They were, in a way, a cry of independence. The protesters were engaged in a moral escapade which demonstrated their rejection both of the propaganda emanating from Washington as well as of the war commodity that Bush and the hawks were trying to sell the West.

Re-enacting the script of the sixties was a different sort of game where young and old, ordinary folk and celebrities alike could replay History. It seemed natural to market peace in a way that would resonate so widely. The anti-Vietnam protests, especially the marches, had been embedded in popular memory, especially by television's documentaries, as a triumph of people power when an engaged public had helped to bring Washington to its senses. The comparisons between then and now were on the minds of both observers and participants. A whole raft of celebrities followed in the footsteps of Jane Fonda, adding glamour but little substance to the peace movement. The media sought out aging peace activists like Pete Seeger, Joan Baez, or Tom Hayden to find out what they were doing to stop war. Old slogans were resurrected, albeit in a changed form: so 'make tea, not war' played in the United Kingdom. Some protesters noted how this was the first time they had been out on the streets since the great days of the anti-Vietnam movement, thus reliving a moment of youthful idealism.

The pleasure of participation, the re-enactment of the script of the 1960s, the ephemeral sense of common purpose, these were all a part of what constituted a brief rebellion by so many citizens in the realm of show and rhetoric that was now the public sphere. One item in a CBC feature on the protests captured this property. It highlighted an interview with two young men at a peace march in Toronto in February. They had brought along two huge puppets whose enormous faces looked like twisted, colourful versions of the statues on Easter Island. 'We have a surfeit of images of fear, right, so we want to bring some images of beauty, and peacefulness, and togetherness, kind of, into the world. It's really beautiful to see so many people come out.' No hippie could have said it better. Protest was its own reward in a world full of distress.

THREE

Managing War

'Let me begin by saying this will be a campaign unlike any other in history, a campaign characterized by shock, by surprise, by flexibility, by the employment of precise munitions on a scale never before seen, and by the application of overwhelming force.' That was how General Tommy Franks, the overall commander of coalition forces in what was now called Operation Iraqi Freedom, described the forthcoming invasion at his briefing on military operations on the 22nd of March. On the whole his prediction was right: the war took only three weeks, 20 March (Baghdad time) to 9 April, during which the Americans in particular stunned not only the Iraqis but the world as a whole with a display of unmatched military prowess. But, unlike his predecessor, Stormin' Norman Schwarzkopf, who commanded the coalition forces in the first Gulf War, Franks did not emerge as the star of this return match.

Not long after the invasion started, journalists came to call the whole affair Mr. Rumsfeld's War, as if he were the director and the producer of a movie (see figure 3.1). In the *New Yorker* (7 April), for instance, Seymour Hersh wrote at length about how this dynamic secretary of defence, a man who acted far more boldly than you might expect of a 70-year-old, broke the rules by insisting on 'micromanaging the war's operational details,' traditionally a task left up to the generals and their staff. '"He thought he knew better," one senior planner said.

Figure 3.1 Mr Rumsfeld's war (© 2003 *The Record*, Jimmy Margulies)

"He was the decision-maker at every turn."' Rumsfeld had designed, or rather redesigned, the war plans by dramatically reducing the troop strength that would be available for the actual invasion. He had forced a greater reliance on air power. He had argued the virtues of a fast war, as well as a cheap war, utilizing America's technological supremacy to overpower Iraqi resistance and minimize casualties. His would be a 'clean war,' not the old kind of 'dirty war,' full of rubble and blood and gore in which the body count kept mounting as the enemy was ground into submission. Indeed, some of his civilian advisers expected that the Iraqi army would likely collapse and that the Iraqi population would welcome coalition forces as liberators. So the Pentagon even 'planned' the actions of the enemy, an assumption that Jimmy Margulies mocked in his spoof: here the Iraqi soldiers were represented as incompetent extras who did not understand what they were expected to do. (In fact, as the *New York Times* [10 August] reported later, Washington did mount a major covert action to persuade Iraqi commanders not to fight.) The cartoon was published around the time when the coalition assault seemed to be stalled by Iraqi resistance and the weather. Yet within ten days the fall of Baghdad seemed proof of Rumsfeld's foresight.

Still, his public fame depended as much on his performances at the regular Pentagon briefings during the conflict, where he impressed the press and its audiences with his skill as a spokesman of war. Rumsfeld continually sold the military, the generals, the troops, the weaponry. 'He's brilliant,' claimed Reza, no supporter of the war itself. 'I'd love to have him as a propagandist as head of state because he, the manner in which he speaks, is so raw and down-to-earth and he addresses questions in such a direct, casual manner.' Better than Bush, Rumsfeld fitted the stereotype of the John Wayne character, an icon of traditional manliness. Rumsfeld seemed to relish the struggle with reporters over the messages embedded in the news. He usually exuded confidence. He could be scrappy. And he laid claim to a kind of moral authority, as a man of conviction and principle. More than any other single individual, he managed the war, in Iraq, in the United States, and so in the world. The articulate and blunt Rumsfeld emerged as the great media star of the Iraq War, at least on the American side. That also made him, in the words of the *New York Times* (20 April), 'the face of American strength – or, alternatively, of American arrogance' around the world.

I

The design of the war did not spring full-blown out of the head of Donald Rumsfeld, however. The origins of what Max Boot, a military scholar, has called 'the new American way of war' reach back to a host of studies and proposals made in the 1990s after the collapse of the Soviet Union and Gulf War I. One of these proposals came in a book written mostly by Harlan Ullman, entitled *Shock and Awe: Achieving Rapid Dominance* and published late in 1996. Ullman set out to explain how the United States ought to fight differently in the post–Cold War world. According to the *Washington Post* (22 March 2003), the book was an answer to a question then bothering the community of military analysts: 'How to maintain U.S. military strength in the post-Cold War era of declining military budgets?' Rather than employ overwhelming force, the orthodox strategy, America should wage a form of high-technology warfare in order to induce a state of 'shock and awe' that stunned the will of the adversary, who thus would collapse or surrender. In one aside Ullman claimed shock and awe was 'the non-nuclear equivalent of the impact that the atomic weapons dropped on Hiroshima and Nagasaki had on the Japanese.' But the whole purpose was to intimidate, not devastate, to stun the enemy, turning its soldiers and leaders into glassy-eyed survivors, ready to surrender. That success would limit both civilian and military casualties and contain the destruction of property, quite unlike the horror visited on Japan in the Second World War. Using adspeak, the book amounted to an outline of a brand strategy, constructing a commodity, the good war, that was produced and sold by only one supplier, the United States.

Not surprisingly, so evocative a phrase as 'shock and awe' captured the fancy of the media. In late January, noted *Post* reporter David Von Drehle, a CBS story had quoted an unnamed Pentagon source who used the term to describe what was planned for Iraq. Whether the doctrine actually did inform the planning exercise, and that was later denied by other officials, the appropriately sinister phrase gathered momentum over the next few months through the sheer fact of repetition in news stories, climaxing in the week before the invasion – when the *Post* found more than 600 references in the media. Ullman was a bit distressed by all the publicity. '"I'm a piñata for the antiwar forces," Ullman complained, as he prepared for his next interview.' Yet another reincarnation of Dr Strangelove had been found lurking in the halls of the Pentagon.

By this time the phrase was applied almost solely to the expected bombing of Baghdad, which actually took place on

21 March – and that was described as the beginning of the 'shock and awe' campaign. In the book itself, Ullman imagined a wide variety of assaults that might induce sufficient shock and awe, among them 'massive bombardment' (but using precision weapons), blitzkrieg (emphasizing speed and concentrated firepower), and decapitation strikes (the ruthless targeting of leaders), each of which would be employed during the course of the Iraq War. Indeed, Ullman had even imagined a renewal of the Gulf War, albeit twenty years hence, in which Iraq could be subdued in a matter of days, using a force of far less than the 500,000 troops required in 1991. 'Shutting the country down would entail both the physical destruction of appropriate infrastructure and the shutdown and control of the flow of all vital information and associated commerce so rapidly as to achieve a level of national shock akin to the effect that dropping nuclear weapons on Hiroshima and Nagasaki had on the Japanese,' wrote Ullman and James Wade, his co-author. 'Simultaneously, Iraq's armed forces would be paralyzed with the neutralization or destruction of its capabilities. Deception, disinformation, and misinformation would be applied massively.' The doctrine of shock and awe amounted to an application of the idea of theatricality to the practice of warfare, not in itself new though the techniques Ullman proposed were novel. America would put on a gigantic show to overawe the hapless Iraqis.

How would America produce such a show? Ullman pointed to an amazing mix of techniques available to the wise general bent on achieving 'rapid dominance': smart weapons, stealth machines, unmanned aircraft, surveillance and reconnaissance systems, intelligence gathering, special forces, 'brilliance' (another evocative term, meaning troops able to act autonomously and effectively), and psychological operations. The aim was an integrated and simultaneous application of all these techniques to bring about the swift collapse of the hapless enemy. One crucial component was the total control of information in all its many forms across the whole battle zone – the term 'information' and such derivatives as the information revolution, disinformation and misinformation, or information warfare cropped up constantly in *Shock and Awe*.

Central Command, the group organizing the invasion, proceeded to attempt exactly that during the three weeks of war in Iraq. Max Boot has outlined how the American military employed an extraordinary array of marvellous machines to dispel the infamous 'fog of war.' Unmanned aerial vehicles at different altitudes plus manned aircraft kept up a constant surveillance of the battlefields. That was supplemented by spotters on the ground who could use global positioning, satellite telephones, and wireless Internet devices to shape and forward their information. Headquarters was equipped with digital screens that provided colour-coded icons of troop deployments: the friendlies were in blue, of course. The addition of inexpensive Joint Direct Attack Munitions kits (JDAMs) transformed 'dumb' into 'smart' bombs, guided by satellite and able to operate in all weather conditions, which finally realized the Pentagon's claims about precision munitions (see figure 3.2). Intelligence officers sent e-mails and even made phone calls to Iraqi generals offering bribes and the like if they would fail to carry out their orders. Coalition forces targeted the command-and-control systems of the enemy so as to disrupt whatever plans the Iraqis had to slow the advance. American planes took out the transmission facilities of Iraqi TV, first its satellite service and later its domestic broadcasts, thus depriving the regime of its own weapons of mass persuasion.

One of the most intriguing weapons was 'PsyOps,' or the psychological operations campaign, really a propaganda blitz meant to sell Iraqis, and most particularly Iraqi soldiers, on the wisdom of disobedience and surrender. The campaign received considerable attention in the news media in North America during the first week of the war, though in fact it had been operating well before the commencement of military action. The purpose of starting early was to sap the morale of the Iraqi armed forces, to de-market the regime, and so pave the way for an easy coalition victory. The potential savings

Figure 3.2 Smart weapons (Peter Nicholson, Cartoonists & Writers Syndicate / cartoonweb.com)

A LATTER-DAY WILLAM TELL

Much was made before and during the conflict about the capabilities of America's missiles and smart bombs. These were crucial to the waging of a 'clean war,' because in theory the coalition could then target only the government and its loyal forces without devastating the cities or causing thousands of civilian casualties. Max Boot estimated that 70 per cent of the munitions were smart, compared to less than 10 per cent in the first Gulf War. But according to one research institute (reported in the *Guardian*, 29 October), there were up to 10,800 deaths among Iraqi combatants and 4300 among non-combatants, roughly double the ratio of civilian to military deaths than in 1991. The author of the report observed that the precision weapons had actually been used 'to pursue more ambitious objectives rather than achieve lower numbers of civilian dead.'

were such that the Americans went to considerable effort to design an effective campaign, no doubt in part because 'PsyOps' seemed to encourage the surrender of many Iraqi troops in Gulf War I. The air force dropped some twenty-five million leaflets over Iraq between 2 October 2002 and 23 March 2003. Nearly two million alone were dispersed on 19 March over twenty-nine different locations in southeastern Iraq in preparation for the coalition's advance. The leaflets were also made available, in Arabic and English, online at the website of Central Command. Usually each leaflet was more like a double-sided postcard, with one picture on the front, sometimes another on the back, plus a brief statement that explained and warned readers. The work of this mass mailing was supported by a series of radio and some television broadcasts from aircraft as well as ground transmitters to elaborate the claims and commands present in the leaflets. The radio broadcasts might run up to an hour, combining an assortment of music and the required message. Both varieties of propaganda, leaflet drops and broadcasts, were delivered by a branch of special operations called Commando Solo II, which regularly flew propaganda missions over Iraq   'We like to call ourselves "weapons of mass persuasion,"' claimed the detachment's commander.

Now selling surrender was never going to be an easy task, at least not in an age of nationalism, nor in a region where anti-Western sentiment was so rife, no matter how distasteful the regime. An additional problem was the Iraqis' fear of Saddam Hussein and his Baathist party, which had a fearsome reputation for exacting revenge. After the first Gulf War America had deserted Shi'ite rebels in the south of Iraq, this after encouraging their uprising, which then was savagely put down by the regime. Iraqis were even more likely to discount a new set of American promises. Consequently many of the leaflets told Iraqis what not to do: do not repair fibre-optics cables, do not fire weapons of mass destruction, do not shoot at coalition warplanes, do not burn oil wells, do not interfere with coalition forces. The likelihood was that uncer-

tain Iraqi troops would opt for this passive form of disobedience. Some leaflets, though, did advise a more active course:
the troops manning anti-aircraft emplacements were told to
abandon their weapons, soldiers in general were told to go
home or how to surrender, and families were told to help
downed coalition pilots. The families who did help were promised a reward for their 'hospitality.' Much more often than
rewards, however, Iraqis were promised imprisonment or
death should they disobey the instructions of the propaganda.
Again, a blunt warning was more likely to elicit compliance
than some vague promise.

The scare was backed up with images and words that conveyed the impression of coalition omnipotence. One stark
leaflet presented a map of Iraq viewed from the heavens,
where a satellite was able to spot a mobile missile launcher as
well as a toxic weapons site. The warning: 'We can see everything.' The American eye was all-seeing. This technology of
surveillance meant that anyone who fired a weapon of mass
destruction would be held responsible by the soon-to-be-
victorious coalition. It called to mind the looming Death Star
in *Star Wars: The Empire Strikes Back* (1980), an instrument of
terror that destroyed the beautiful rebel world of Alderaan.
Indeed, the whole scenario evoked what was and remains a
visual cliché in the history of advertising: a man (usually)
looking out and down from a privileged vantage point – a
hill, a horse, an office window, a plane – onto some landscape,
some objects that becomes his. The very gaze denotes command. No wonder this cliché has been called a particularly
masculine vision of domain. It had been used to sell Marlboro
cigarettes, Air Canada executive travel, ITT's System 12, etc.,
etc. Now it was recruited to help in Iraq.

At least two of the leaflets worked to assure Iraqis that they
were not the target of Anglo-American anger. One juxtaposed
a picture of Saddam Hussein ('He lives in luxury') and a
woman with child ('As your family struggles to survive'). The
back panel offered up a collage of images, saluting officers
versus smiling faces, to support the plea to reject the regime

and choose the home: 'Return to your home and family.' The whole concoction was reminiscent of comparison ads in North America: indeed mother and baby, the Madonna image, had always been commonplace in advertising for home products. In fact, the radio was deemed a more effective vehicle for dishonouring the regime, since it was possible to explain in some detail the assorted sins of Saddam Hussein. So the broadcasts told Iraqis how the man was consumed by a lust for power, like Stalin; how he threatened the world with weapons of mass destruction; how he and his family lavished funds on themselves but impoverished the army and the citizenry. Radio, in short, delivered the very kind of propaganda that circulated throughout the American media. This kind of rhetoric recalled the widespread practice of dishonouring employed in the notorious attack ads of election campaigns in the United States.

'PsyOps' amounted to a battlefield version of advertising. The messages were usually prepared by the 4th Psychological Action Group, headquartered at Fort Bragg, North Carolina, and composed of soldiers and civilian analysts able to draw upon different kinds of expertise. In military parlance these personnel were known as 'force multipliers,' meaning their activities enhanced the effects of other, more brutal modes of persuasion: bombs, missiles, tanks, bullets. The Iraqi campaign had not really sought to win the hearts and minds of Iraqi soldiers or civilians. It was not marketing 'brand America.' It was marketing safety. The range of warnings and the effort to dishonour Saddam Hussein were supposed to sap the commitment of the Iraqis to a regime that, so the Americans assumed, was not loved by its citizens; indeed, in some areas like the Shi'ite south it was actually loathed. So the campaign did not have to combat the kind of ideological commitment to a regime that 'PsyOps' had faced in Vietnam, where they were generally deemed of limited utility. Instead, they could play on notions of American superiority, fears of personal survival, the desire to return home. The price of compliance was kept low. The credibility of the campaign depended very much on the actual effectiveness of the coalition forces in delivering death to those who resisted. Thus, 'PsyOps' may have worked much better later in the military campaign, when the regime was obviously crumbling.

The final act came on 10 April. Bush and Blair inaugurated a new television service called Nahwa Al-Hurrieh or 'Towards Freedom,' which was broadcast using the specially equipped Commando Solo plane. The plan was to situate the service in Baghdad as soon as possible and to provide daily broadcasts of material created by the new military rulers and Iraqi exiles, who were expected to take charge, as well as British and American news, including Arab-captioned newscasts originating from the US networks. The prerecorded message was, inevitably, the liberation of Iraq. The two leaders told Iraqis the bad days of the regime were almost over, the coalition would respect Islam, the authorities would establish law and order, and the government would soon be theirs. 'You deserve better than tyranny, corruption, and torture chambers,' concluded Bush. 'You deserve to live as free people. And I assure every citizen of Iraq, your nation will soon be free.' 'Our forces are friends and liberators of the Iraqi people,' reiterated Blair, 'not your conquerors and they will not stay in Iraq a day longer than is necessary.' The signal might be a bit weak – not many Iraqis actually saw the speeches – but the real message was clear. The very style and content of the propaganda reiterated the fact that Iraq was now living under an Anglo-American co-dominion. Bush and Blair had just delivered the first ad for the new order.

II

A different kind of psychological warfare was played out in another arena of battle: the media. The Pentagon's desire for the total control of information extended well beyond Iraq into the living rooms and bedrooms in America and around the world. That was driven in part by a dubious assumption about 'the CNN effect,' the way television images could impact war decisions – for instance, the claim that 'television got us in and television got us out' of Somalia ten years before. More important, though, was the realization that victory was the single most important product the American military manufactured, and like any product it had to be sold to the citizens as taxpayers and consumers.

That meant the Pentagon had to find ways to script what constituted the news and how that news was reported. '"In wartime," Winston Churchill once said, "truth is so precious that she should always be attended by a bodyguard of lies."' Rumsfeld had cited these words just after 9/11 when asked whether the Pentagon might ever lie to the media. Early in 2002 rumours hit the press that the Pentagon was playing with the notion of 'black propaganda,' the planting of false stories in the press, not in the United States but elsewhere in the world. Indeed Maud Beelman, the director of the International Consortium of Investigative Journalists in Washington, told CBC Radio during the war that the Pentagon was grouping its public-affairs officers and its psychological operations into one 'discipline called information operations.' All of which added force to Michael Moore's call on the US military to withdraw from the media.

What played a more important role in the practice of news management than 'PsyOps,' however, was the 'philosophy' of marketing in the shape of public relations. Like all major corporations, the American military had come to realize how essential was a public-relations strategy that worked not just to keep the 'bosses out of the news,' as Philip Taylor put it, but to set 'the media agenda.' Victoria Clarke, the Assistant Secretary of Defense for Public Affairs at the Pentagon, hired in the spring 2001, came out of public-relations work, notably at Hill & Knowlton, a global operation notorious for its propaganda effort in Gulf War I (where it had orchestrated the atrocity story that Iraqi troops emptied Kuwaiti babies out of their incubators onto the floor to die). Even more important was Karen Hughes, a long-time Bush confidante and adviser stationed at the White House, who had served as his director of communications when the President was governor of Texas. She organized the new Office of Global Communications, launched in January 2003, to coordinate the public-relations strategy of the whole government, ensuring that it would speak as one voice on the issue of Iraq.

One of the first priorities was to control the language of war, really a continuation of the propaganda campaign launched to sell the policy of going to war (see figure 3.3). The struggle to get the right words out was in itself nothing new – two legacies of earlier wars were 'collateral damage' (civilian deaths) and 'friendly fire' (killing your own). But there was a novel twist this time: the effort amounted to a particular application of a hot new technique called 'viral marketing' that had been born out of the experience of selling on the Internet. The idea was to get any promotion to propagate itself by infecting other messages, much as a virus can spread rapidly through an unsuspecting population. Hotmail, for example, had enjoyed a runaway success in the late 1990s because it included a clickable tag line promoting the e-mail service on each and every message a user sent out, and that won the service some twelve million subscribers in about eighteen months. Similarly, the White House and the Pentagon could go some distance to ensuring the right spin on events if they could get reporters, and thus consumers, to utilize the appropriate terminology.

There were many examples of such efforts, not always effective. The Office of Global Communications mandated the use of the phrase 'war of liberation' by military and administration officials to describe the invasion of Iraq. The very term 'regime change' cast the Iraqi government in a negative light, or, as one editor at the Oxford English Dictionary said, made them 'more despotic.' Bush had consistently used the word 'thugs' to describe the Iraqi leadership and its troops (he used that term in the 17 March speech), which evoked the idea of crime and suggested the regime was illegitimate. The ballyhooed phrase 'shock and awe' was itself a tool to impress all, perhaps especially the Iraqi leadership, with the notion that a

Figure 3.3 The first casualty (Vince O'Farrell, Cartoonists & Writers Syndicate / cartoonweb.com)

The war provoked a small flurry of comment over just what died first in the rush of war. The classic formulation had the easy answer 'truth,' except that in these times many journalists and consumers were well aware that truth was not always a simple property. Yet another answer was credibility, an obvious problem for Mohammed Saeed Al-Sahaf, the Iraqi Information Minister, who soon became a global joke because his pronouncements about the war were so ludicrous. But the best answer was the one O'Farrell identifies: language. 'The first casualty of war is less often the truth itself than the way we tell it,' argued Geoffrey Nunberg, a Stanford linguist, in the *New York Times* (6 April 2003). Everybody's words coloured the facts.

coalition victory was inevitable. In addition, like the terms 'decapitation strike' or 'kinetic targeting,' 'shock and awe' was a euphemism for bombing. The reference to 'coalition forces,' like 'coalition of the willing,' masked the fact that this was chiefly an American war, assisted by a substantial British contingent. During the conflict administration spokespeople talked not of the paramilitary fedayeen who briefly caused the invading armies some problems but of 'death squads' who threatened the Iraqi people if they did not fight. The word 'fedayeen' had too much of a positive connotation. The Iraqis who kept on resisting became 'dead-enders,' people who could have no future in a post-Hussein era.

Observers were well aware of what was going on. According to Geoffrey Nunberg, writing in the *New York Times* (6 April), what was notable about this war was 'the obsessive attention we pay to the matter' of language. Britain's *Guardian* ran an occasional series of stories on the language of war where it decoded mostly military jargon for its readers. But what was most telling was the way the Pentagon's terminology did circulate through the media, not just because of the official briefings but because it was used by anchors, analysts, and reporters. That was most obvious in the case of 'shock and awe,' which became part of common parlance, recognized by just about everyone who consumed the war. But the contagion also spread to the very style of war reporting. 'Embedded reporters produce embedded language, the metallic clatter of modern military lingo,' claimed Nunberg: 'acronyms like TLAM's, RPG's and MRE's; catchphrases like "asymmetric warfare," "emerging targets" and "catastrophic success" ...' So it was that a commentary by NBC's Chip Reid, just outside Baghdad on 3 April, borrowed from the jargon of the Marines who were his hosts. The Pentagon had left its mark on the vocabulary of journalism.

III

Washington's second order of business was to keep on top of the news. The daily briefings were transformed into a pow-

erful weapon of persuasion. Washington built on the experience of the first Gulf War, when televised press conferences
had proved so effective in delivering messages directly to
the public, over the heads of reporters. The *New York Times*
(20 April) explained how even before the war key communications personnel from the White House, the Pentagon, the
State Department, and London arranged an early-morning
conference call to identify 'the theme of the day and who was
delivering it.' The Office of Global Communications sent out
a daily e-mail to embassies specifying the administration's
line. During the war this technique ensured not only consis-
tency but priority, being there first with the right slant. Starting at breakfast, cable TV viewers would receive a stream of
Washington's words and images. At the US Central Command forward headquarters in Doha, Qatar, the generals of
fered their summary of military operations on a special hi-tech
set designed by a show-business professional, a man who had
worked for Michael Douglas in Hollywood, at an estimated
cost of $250,000 US. Brigadier-General Vincent Brooks became
famous for showing his audience 'before' and 'after' photo-
graphs of bomb sites to emphasize how effective were the
precision munitions. At the White House, official spokesman
Ari Fleischer held three sessions a day with reporters to keep
the administration line at the front of the news. At the Pentagon there was, sometimes, the incomparable Donald Rumsfeld,
ready to speak his truth, field the questions of reporters, and
occasionally scold some critics. The onslaught of words and
images had an effect. 'You could see that most of the journalists and commentators were simply retailing what was being
given to them at briefings,' recalled Mike. 'So if you want to
get it from the horse's mouth, you'd better get it from the
briefing.'

Washington strove to get out two, sometimes contradictory,
messages. The first message was to maintain the fiction that
Iraq was a credible enemy, in part to ensure the war would
serve as an ad for American might. Time and again officials,
sometimes the President or Rumsfeld, would caution against
too much optimism. 'As we near the end of the regime, we

have to remember and underscore repeatedly, that the very toughest fighting could lie ahead,' Victoria Clarke said as late as 5 April. Washington never wanted to endorse the notion that the war would be a cakewalk, because that could only detract from the military achievement. One key in the early days of the war was to pose the threat of the assorted missiles and chemical weapons that Saddam Hussein might employ against the coalition forces. There was speculation about a line in the sand, purportedly around Baghdad, that once crossed would signal the time to unleash the chemical and biological assault. Another key was to hype the capabilities of the Republican Guard, typically labelled by the press 'elite' troops, the best trained and the best equipped. 'Too many reporters accepted the military's description of the Republican Guard as a formidable force, when in fact those units rolled up like a cheap carpet in the face of the US advance,' claimed Terence Smith, a commentator for PBS, in a retrospective on war coverage. A third ploy was to raise the spectre of a Baghdad hell, where Hussein would withdraw his forces into the cities and turn the capital into another Stalingrad. Rumsfeld himself told a congressional committee about the possibility of a siege to avoid the blood and gore of street fighting. 'News organizations accepted without much question the Pentagon's forecast that Baghdad would be fiercely defended,' added Smith. 'When it fell with only spotty resistance, the American performance seemed all the more impressive.' That was one reason Smith gave the media only a 'C–' for their resistance to gullibility.

But Washington was equally determined to preserve the integrity of the war plan, the idea that the war was going according to the script, which bespoke the brilliance of the Pentagon and the superiority of the armed forces. That became a problem in the first week of the war when it was clear the Iraqis were not welcoming their supposed liberators nor were Iraqi forces surrendering in any numbers to coalition forces. Things got especially messy when on 27 March Lieutenant-General William Wallace, one of the army commanders, declared in an interview, 'The enemy we're fighting is a bit different than the one we war-gamed against.' Somehow the qualifying words 'a bit' were dropped from the quotation circulated through the press. The revised comment set off a media frenzy in which reporters and commentators talked about a quagmire, a lengthy war, and the collapse of the war plan. The ghost of Vietnam returned, briefly, to haunt imaginations. A few retired or 'armchair' generals hired by the networks to reflect on the war suddenly became notorious because they argued Rumsfeld had not authorized sufficient troops and tanks to do the job properly.

It was time for damage control, a classic problem of re-marketing: how to deal swiftly with bad news. The White House and Pentagon took the offensive. First, critique the source: officials questioned the knowledge or the motives of the 'armchair generals' and the nervous nellies who delivered the news on television. Second, advise calm: Rumsfeld warned against premature judgments since events were moving very rapidly. The President's belief that this was all silly speculation soon found its way into the press. The setback eventually led the Pentagon to send out warnings to commanders to watch what they said to reporters.

Meanwhile Washington used the military briefings to divert criticism. The *Washington Post* (29 March) captured this ploy in an article entitled 'Military P.R. Force Wages a Battle to Stay on Message,' which claimed Central Command had proved not much interested in explaining why the coalition forces had faced resistance. 'Centcom officials are far more enthusiastic about using the podium day after day to spotlight reported abuses by President Saddam Hussein's government, a public relations strategy that officials said was worked out with the White House Office of Global Communications.' The line went out that Iraqi soldiers were victims of intimidation, forced to fight because the lives of their family members were threatened by the thugs of the regime. Similarly, Central Command never explained why ordinary Iraqis were not cheering. 'Brooks, instead, rolled a 45-second video on Thursday of US troops distributing humanitarian aid in southern Iraq. It showed an Iraqi boy waving to passing US troops as he motions to his mouth, indicating he wants food, another boy giving a thumbs up and a US soldier shaking hands with a local man.' As for the armchair generals, it was left to an unnamed official in a background briefing to pass along a sneer: 'Retired military officials, the day they retire, become out of date.' These were not necessarily lies. Call this misinformation, a mix of facts, none of which could be readily proved or disproved, that sought to obscure the views or behaviours the Pentagon found threatening to the integrity of the war script.

The most successful example of misinformation, however, grew out of the rescue of Private Jessica Lynch, a supply clerk who, along with other members of an army maintenance crew, had been taken captive by Iraqi forces on 23 March. Roughly ten days later, on the evening of 1 April, a special-forces team stormed an Iraqi hospital to free her from the clutches of the enemy. The operation was made to order for the propaganda machine. Private Lynch was young, nineteen years old, attractive, blonde, and a woman, an American victim saved by the heroics of her comrades, in short a natural for a retelling of that old yarn, the captivity narrative, that harked back to the legends of the Indian wars. The military made a video of the 'daring' nighttime assault, which was released to the media. At a briefing Brooks celebrated the rescue, proof of the skill and commitment of the special forces. 'It was a classic joint operation done by some of our nation's finest warriors who are dedicated to never leaving a comrade behind,' Brooks said. Much was made of her wounds, supposedly the results of a firefight. Unnamed officials in Washington turned Lynch into a female Rambo who fought furiously against her captors in spite of her injuries. There were rumours she had been mistreated or tortured in an Iraqi hospital that was really a military base. The American media and the American public ate up the story: it was at the top of the news on TV and in the press. Pictures of Lynch, including a pre-war photograph of her as a pretty, all-American teen, appeared in print. Journalists interviewed her folks, friends, and neighbours back home. Adding to the drama was the news that an Iraqi lawyer had given the army the information necessary to carry out the rescue. A bit later *Variety*, the entertainment weekly, reported that NBC already had in the works a TV movie detailing the story (which came out in the fall). 'This story is Mission: Impossible, but it's real,' said an NBC official, according to a BBC report (11 April). 'It's uplifting, heroic, compelling and dramatic. You see this sort of thing in spy movies and wonder if it's really true. Now we know it is true.'

It was not true. The military may not have set out to deceive the media, only to hype a good story which newspapers and networks then developed into an extravaganza of courage and skill. That became clear in May when notably the BBC (15 May) and other sources, including the *Toronto Star* (4 May), brought out new pieces of information. Certainly she had suffered. She may have been sodomized by her Iraqi captors, or so her later biography suggested. But Lynch had not played Rambo. Her rifle had jammed. Her extensive injuries were likely the result of the crash of her Humvee. She had been well treated by doctors and nurses. The special forces did not need to storm anything since the Iraqi military had deserted the site a day before. The doctors in the hospital felt they had been dropped into some bizarre Hollywood fantasy: soldiers rushing around, guns firing, like the action movies starring Sylvester Stallone or Jackie Chan.

The dramatic triumph, however, had come at exactly the right time, because the news served to buoy a populace worried by signs that Iraq was turning into a quagmire – polls later revealed a significant rise in public morale in the United States. No wonder: the Lynch story fitted so neatly into the existing web of perceptions fashioned by pop culture. All kinds of people took to calling the escapade 'Saving Private Lynch,' a direct reference to the hit film *Saving Private Ryan* (1998). Now the two stories were very different: the movie dealt with a Second World War incident in which a small platoon of Rangers find and protect the last of four brothers (the others having died), who was fighting in France after the Normandy landing. There was no exact match to the freeing of Lynch. But *Saving Private Ryan*, like another if darker rescue movie *Black Hawk Down* (2001), worked to humanize the American military as one big family where skilled professionals sacrificed their lives to look after their own people. These were studies in competence, commitment, and devotion that made of ordinary soldiers heroes who deserved the admiration of the citizens they served. 'Saving Private Lynch' could well appear to be a real-life version of an already existing mythology.

IV

The third technique of control was the practice of embedding journalists with military units so that they effectively became instruments of the marketing apparatus. This was the most novel technique, but also the riskiest, because it presumed that the sometimes unruly breed of journalists could be retrained, or rather tamed. These classic outsiders, who in the rhetoric of journalism owed no loyalty to the subjects they covered, would become insiders, the friends of the military.

The effort to manage war news had a long and difficult history rooted in the experience of the Vietnam War, when the relations between journalists and generals had reached their nadir. Journalists had been allowed a relatively free passage, at least outside the major battle areas, during the long conflict. Michael Arlen's classic book of essays *Living-Room War* detailed how in the early years television, in particular, usually did follow the government line. Journalists on the scene in Vietnam became increasingly cynical about the misinformation and deception of the generals, yet their reports were censored back in America. As time went on, however, and especially after the Tet Offensive early in 1968 demonstrated how hollow were the military's claims of inevitable victory, the editors at home also came to doubt the propaganda of General Westmoreland (the commanding officer in Vietnam) and the White House, in part because of the gathering anti-war storm in America. The most famous sign of change was the conversion of Walter Cronkite, the famed anchor of CBS News, the most trusted man in America. He made a special trip to Vietnam to investigate the situation after Tet and concluded that America could not win this war, a declaration that, in legend anyway, has been credited with leading President Lyndon Johnson to decide against running for office again. It became an axiom of faith in some military circles, and not only in the United States, that the American media had lost the war because their coverage of failure and disorder turned the American public against their armed forces.

That was a ridiculous claim – the war was lost by the White House and the military, not the media. But the myth persisted. It seemed the generals concluded that never again, never would the media be allowed so much freedom to cover any new war. The first test of this determination involved the British, not the Americans: during the Falklands/Malvinas War (1982), the commanders of the British armada censored all television coverage in order to create a 'boys own' adventure movie of the successful recovery of the islands from the grip of the Argentine dictatorship. The next year, when the Americans moved on the Caribbean island of Grenada, the media were kept out altogether until the action was finished. That sparked joint discussions between news executives and military officers over how to cover small wars, out of which came the notion of a pool of officially registered journalists who would be allowed access as long as its members followed certain guidelines. The test of that system in the case of Panama (1990) was no great success: at one point the pool was kept away from the fighting, and actually escorted to a room to watch CNN's coverage of the war! The pool did not work much better during the first Gulf War either, concluded Gary Woodward. The military were largely satisfied with their ability to manage the media, especially to avoid any harmful coverage. The working press, though, felt restricted, censored, unable to cover what was happening effectively, and some reporters broke away from the pool to join allied units when they moved into Kuwait at the end of the war. Things were even worse in Afghanistan in 2001, when journalists felt they had been frozen out of covering the battlefield.

The crucial difference in 2003 was that the Pentagon and the White House determined to co-opt – one wag said 'weaponize' – the news media, treating the journalists not as enemies or nuisances but as potential allies in a joint effort to promote the practice of war to the public. Supposedly the Pentagon had missed a grand opportunity in past conflicts, notably the first Gulf War, to tout the amazing feats of America's armed forces. The policy expressed that new maxim of corporate marketing: be proactive, set the media agenda. After the Afghanistan fiasco, according to the *Weekly Standard* (28 February), Victoria Clarke organized a host of meetings with military and news personnel out of which came a new policy of access, which she proceeded to sell to the top brass at the Pentagon and the White House. The details were left up to her assistant Bryan Whitman, a public-affairs veteran and an ex-commander of special forces in Somalia. The media were offered the chance to embed their reporters in designated military units, though only some of these were in the main invasion force. The individuals would undergo a mild version of basic training to prepare them for battlefield discipline. They also had to sign a contract to signify their willingness to self-censor so that information deemed vital to the ongoing military operations would not be released in their reports. Close-ups of dead or wounded soldiers, for example, were taboo, at least until the next of kin were notified. In return, the Pentagon and the military would do their best to make sure these embedded reporters could send their stories and their images back to their news outlets. Eventually over 600 correspondents, mostly American and British, accepted the terms of the agreement. The emphasis had switched from secrecy to publicity.

The approach would make the reporters, as Victoria Clarke

once put it, 'witnesses to history.' But the advantages to the Pentagon were far greater than this innocuous phrase suggested. Rumsfeld frankly admitted that it was 'self-serving' because it would enable the Pentagon to counter the kind of propaganda that the Iraqi regime and its allies might dispense to the world media. The Taliban and al-Qaeda had proved a bit too effective in getting their message out in Afghanistan. 'We have to face the reality that truth needs to be an issue in this conflict,' Bryan Whitman told PBS (18 February). 'Our potential adversary is a practiced liar. There's no doubt about it. He uses disinformation all the time. I can't think of a better way ... to counter such disinformation than to have objective reporters on the battlefield covering the news as it occurs.' Perhaps even more important, though, the embedded reporters were expected to sell the virtues of the American military: '[T]he American people really get an opportunity to see the dedication and the professionalism of their military and the care ... their military takes in executing these very lethal and dangerous operations if it comes to combat.' The goal was to return to the long-lost tradition of the Second World War reporter, what was called the Ernie Pyle tradition, when the war correspondent was also a patriot. Pyle had been a war correspondent who tracked the exploits of the armed forces in North Africa, Italy, and France before he died in the Pacific theatre. He was remembered because his reports had memorialized the ordinary fighting man, especially the lowly infantry. Their hardships, their courage, their heroism, these he eulogized in a vigorous prose that made war into a thoroughly American adventure. No wonder the news organizations were not allowed to replace any embedded journalist or to move that soul to another posting: the journalists were expected to bond with their units, and no newcomers could be expected to play out the role of an Ernie Pyle if they were new to the environment.

The Pentagon did not insist that all correspondents agree to this regimen. News outlets could also send along other journalists, independents, not linked to a unit, who were called 'unilaterals.' The CBC, for example, refused to agree to the terms of contract, fearful of becoming an arm of the Pentagon information machine, and so its veteran reporter Paul Workman had to make his own way to find the news. It was not easy, as he reported later to CBC News Online (7 April), explaining how he and his colleagues had to finagle themselves into Iraq, in the face of official hostility. 'An American officer in the public affairs division made his country's position utterly and maddeningly clear to my producer Ian Kalushner. "I don't give a damn about the unilateral journalists," he said. "We've fulfilled our obligation to the media and if you don't like it, you can go home." That was after telling us the CBC had been listed as a "state" broadcaster, much like the Russians and that we were little more than a mouthpiece for a government that doesn't support the war.'

In fact, the military had good reason to deny the independent reporters any assistance. Both Workman and John Donvan of ABC News (25 March), another unilateral, reported how ambivalent were the Iraqis who had just been liberated by the coalition forces in the south of Iraq. The people of Safwan, Donvan claimed, thought that the invasion was actually an American 'takeover.' They were angry because the Americans had shot at them, upset because they had not received any food or water or medicine. Even the children stole radios and a camera from the cars and banged on the windows demanding money and food. 'They weren't dancing in the streets.' Similarly, Donvan noted evidence of civilian casualties and discovered how disordered, how dangerous were areas the military had claimed were 'under control.' Clearly, some of the reports the independents sent home did clash with the Pentagon line.

The slant of the approved journalists proved much more amenable (see figure 3.4). Taking the risk of opening the war up to reporters proved a very wise move for the Pentagon. The practice did work to defeat Iraqi propaganda. 'It meant one thing for the Pentagon to deny an Iraqi spokesman's claim that coalition forces weren't in Baghdad,' said Whitman,

Figure 3.4 The embedded journalist (Graeme MacKay, *The Hamilton Spectator*)

The practice of embedding provoked a lot of comment and comedy, not the least because the very word 'embedding' could suggest all manner of vulgar epithets. But MacKay's cartoon raised the more significant issue of distance, the ways in which a journalist takes on the slant and the views of his or her subjects – a version of 'going native.' 'They depend on the military for everything, from food to a place to sleep,' reflected Chris Hedges, a veteran war correspondent, in *The Nation* (21 April). 'They look to the soldiers around them for protection. When they feel the fear of hostile fire, they identify and seek to protect those who protect them. They become part of the team. It is a natural reaction.' But in Iraq it was hardly 'natural.' What the Pentagon did was to exploit the team spirit so that the journalists could better serve the purposes of the war plan.

according to a paraphrase of his comments in the *Globe and Mail* (23 April), 'and quite another when Fox News Channel aired that spokesman on a split screen with reporter Greg Kelly riding a tank on a city street.' But the Iraqi propaganda was generally so inept, certainly by the time the American tanks reached Baghdad, that the much more important effect of embedding was to advance the cause of the American military. Many of the reporters became family; they lost that sense of distance necessary to 'objective' journalism because they developed instead a sense of camaraderie, an admiration, for the people in the unit – and they shared in the dangers and the triumphs of that unit. 'Even the most hard-bitten journalist is hard-pressed to criticize the efforts of young Americans fighting a war they were ordered to fight,' reflected Cynthia Bowles of CBS News (30 March), who served aboard the USS *Abraham Lincoln*. 'Living alongside young soldiers and sailors, breaking bread with them, and watching them every day put in their 12–18 hours without complaint, can't help but elicit my and many others' non-grudging respect.' Mike Cerre of ABC News (16 April) talked about how difficult it was to report when the unit took casualties; his colleague Dan Dahler spoke of 'the many acts of heroism we got to see over there.' In short, the approved journalists often did act as cheerleaders, their copy a kind of free publicity for both the military and the war. It was like having '500 Ernie Pyles,' stated one retired general in a conference report published by *Editor and Publisher* (11 April).

The Pentagon was very pleased with the results of the experiment. General Tommy Franks said he was a definite 'fan.' 'Transparency works,' Victoria Clarke told an audience later at the Brookings Institution (Fox News, 17 June). 'The good news gets out. The bad news gets dealt with quickly.' The good news, as she named the approved reports, had even served to balance all the captious objections raised by commentators at home. Rumsfeld found an additional benefit, the retraining of a body of journalists as patriots. 'The side benefit, it seems to me, is there's now a new generation of journalists who have had a chance to see first hand what kind of people volunteer to put their lives at risk,' reported the *Globe and Mail* (23 April). Equally pleased, however, were the media and many of the correspondents who served as embeds, because they finally had access to the battlefield, despite the fact that only a few (fifty to seventy according to one estimate) actually saw any significant combat. It had meant more exciting and more intimate coverage of the most dramatic of stories, a victorious war. Even erstwhile sceptics were impressed by the copy and the images that arrived back in the United States. Now the generals and the journalists were not only at peace but locked into a symbiotic relationship: the military delivered the show and the media promoted it to the public. No wonder both were thinking, in the immediate aftermath of their joint victory, about how to make the next war an even better experience.

V

When Baghdad fell on 9 April, the veteran CBC reporter Don Murray ended his account of that amazing day by explaining that the American military had swiftly moved in to invest the Palestine Hotel – 'this was symbolic' – where many journalists had their base of operations. 'It's as if the control of information and the watching over the journalists from the world over is one of the key components of this new government that the Americans are clearly on the point of setting up tonight.' How perceptive: the Americans were simply registering their triumph in the information war the Pentagon had waged even before the armed struggle began.

What Murray did not discuss, however, was whether the Pentagon's determination to watch over the media might have a more sinister side. According to the *Guardian* (16 April), the invasion had taken a toll on the ranks of journalists: it counted fourteen dead, some of these unilaterals who died under suspicious circumstances. Early on an ITN correspondent, a unilateral, died in the south of Iraq, possibly the victim of 'friendly fire.' A cameraman was killed when bombs hit the Baghdad home of Al-Jazeera (8 April), despite the fact the station had alerted the Pentagon to the site's location. The American forces had actually fired on the Palestine Hotel (8 April), killing two more cameramen and leaving four journalists wounded. Abu Dhabi TV was also struck. These were only accidents, according to coalition spokespeople, unfortunate events inevitable in war, and a warning to news media to keep their journalists out of harm's way. Other voices wondered whether the incidents might also be a warning to journalists who did not submit to the leash of the coalition forces. 'I have a feeling that independent journalists have become a target because the management of the information war has become a higher priority than ever,' claimed Martin Bell, a former war correspondent for the BBC (*Guardian*, 9 April). Did this spell the death of 'the independent witnessing of war'?

FOUR

Real-Time War

Pity the poor viewer (see figure 4.1). 'I watch as soon as I get home from work and I stay up until midnight watching,' a college professor from Iowa, a young man of thirty-three, told Reuters (2 April). Before, so he said, he had only watched an hour of television a night. 'It drives my wife crazy because I keep watching the same things over and over,' he told the reporter. 'It seems like every hour there's some little tidbit that's new, it might be three minutes worth of news every hour that are different than the stuff you've heard, but that's enough to keep me hooked.' There spoke an addict of what came to be known as 'the real-time war,' a war brought live and brought constantly into the living rooms and bedrooms of the whole world via television. You could now experience war as it was happening.

That real-time war was not just the concoction of the Pentagon and the White House, no matter how effective the script or how wise the policy of access. Indeed, in some ways Washington found the pace and the character of war coverage disturbing, so fast and so extensive that no officials could control the message the way they wanted to. The real-time war was constructed as well by the media, by the technology of instant communications, above all by the television networks. Radio, newspapers and magazines, the Internet, all played a role, but a supplementary one. There had been some

Figure 4.1 The overwhelming coverage (James Casciari, *Vero Beach Press Journal* / Scripps Howard News Service)

EMBEDDED.

talk that this might constitute the first Internet war, where huge numbers of people regularly surfed the web to find out what was happening. Not so; or rather, not enough people turned to their computers for answers. The core of coverage, as before, remained television, because it alone could deliver the experience, the images and the sounds, that made of war a live spectacle. The war the television networks co-produced, however, was more than just that, a spectacle meant to inform and to please millions of viewers. The war was also a commodity, indeed a promotional commodity, albeit not quite of the same kind as the Bond movies. What war coverage promoted were the networks as they struggled for fame and power in the marketplace of signs. The last grand affair, the first Gulf War, had made CNN the first successful all-news cable channel, indeed a master force in the realm of television news. The real-time war was also a media war, another time of opportunity, when rivals might show their prowess and expand their reach.

I

TV news has long been a target of academic criticism, ever since it became the most common source of knowledge about the nation and the world, something that occurred four decades ago in the case of North America. (Pew Research learned in 2002 that the triumph of TV news was now global – its survey took in 44 countries.) In the mid-1980s, the American professor of communications Neil Postman published a popular polemic against television called *Amusing Ourselves to Death*. It exploited the continuing suspicion that television was corrupting American culture, a suspicion that persisted in reaction to the dominion TV had already won in the living rooms and bedrooms of the nation. Drawing on the work of Marshall McLuhan, among others, Postman argued that the medium of television had an intrinsic and unfortunate bias. The 'peek-a-boo' world of disconnected images constructed by TV could only serve as a form of showbiz which worked to divert its viewers. He was not much concerned with all the junk entertainment the networks showered on the public. He was exercised by the serious stuff. 'I should go so far as to say that embedded in the surrealistic frame of a television news show is a theory of anticommunication, featuring a type of discourse that abandons logic, reason, sequence and rules of contradiction.' Postman believed television posed the most serious threat when it tackled matters of public import, because it could produce only 'entertainment packages' that must debase the quality of public discourse and thus public life.

In the mid-1990s, the famed French sociologist Pierre Bourdieu published his own diatribe against TV news, entitled simply *On Television*. That too became popular, indeed notorious in France where, amazing as it sounds, the grumpy book was a bestseller and the target of much controversy because journalists took the polemic as an assault on their profession. Bourdieu shifted the argument about what made TV news bad news away from the intrinsic nature of the medium to the structures that operated on journalism, most especially the impact of ratings and the general phenomenon of marketing. He made much of the way television dramatized events, seeking what was sensational, and constantly moralized about their significance, always to avoid boredom and to keep things amusing. Bourdieu seemed particularly ticked off by the taste for human-interest stories. That type of journalism was 'at once dehistoricized and dehistoricizing, fragmented and fragmenting,' depicting the world in terms of 'a series of apparently absurd stories that all end up looking the same.' In the process, TV news appropriated, reduced, or trashed other better varieties of knowledge, science or law and, it seemed, sociology. Like Postman, Bourdieu saw television as a threat to democracy.

The coverage of the Iraq War would bear out some of these strictures, such as the notion that TV served up a lot of infotainment. Even more, it justified Bourdieu's phobia about the ill effects of marketing. But Iraq did counter the claim that TV news was unable to offer little more than a debased or irrational package of disconnected information. This time, as we shall see, the news media did weave a series of sometimes compelling stories about the invasion, the weaponry, the coalition soldiers, and the downfall of a regime. That aside, realtime war was a new chapter in the ongoing story of TV news. Neither Postman (understandably) nor Bourdieu (and here the absence was more puzzling) took any account of the way twenty-four-hour cable news networks had transformed the possibilities of TV news. Newsrooms could now really generate an all-encompassing vision of 'reality,' impossible to do when they only had a half-hour news slot. A succession of big stories during the 1990s, like the earlier Gulf War, the flight of O.J. Simpson, or the death of Princess Diana, had shown the way to cover, and hype, this kind of news.

The news media had been gearing up for the war many months before the bombs started falling on Baghdad. They arranged for transmission facilities, collected and shipped equipment, sent off embeds for training, and began dispatching journalists and camera technicians to places around the Gulf. After the fact, the *Guardian* team of reporters estimated that around 3000 journalists, double the number in 1991, were stationed in the region, 'the largest media war force ever assembled.' (Not quite: there were 4000 accredited journalists for the Kosovo conflict.) At one point Baghdad had about 350 journalists, although some would leave or be forced out by the government once the war began. *Newsweek* sent about 30 people into the region, the CBC had 40 employees, the BBC 200 journalists and technicians, and CNN fully 250 staff members. Only two American networks, ABC and NBC, had correspondents in Baghdad for most of the war. Just a few of the journalists, at home or abroad, could be called veteran war correspondents or military experts.

What was novel about the war (well, almost, because Afghanistan had given a foretaste of the new rivalry) was the presence of a series of indigenous Arabic and Islamic satellite services that were bound to offer a different perspective on events than the big Western networks. Aside from Iraq's international service, which American warplanes would soon take off the air, there was Al-Manar, a Lebanese station, Abu Dhabi TV, out of the United Arab Emirates, and the newcomer Al-Arabiya, based in Dubai and heavily bankrolled by Saudi investors among others, which had started in March. The latter had been launched as an alternative, supposedly more moderate, to the single most important channel, Al-Jazeera, founded in 1996 and based in Doha, Qatar. Al-Jazeera had won fame and viewers (it claimed 35 million) across the region because it looked American, like CNN in short, but acted Arabic, adopting a critical stance towards the Western powers. Not without cause, American hawks were inclined to view Al-Jazeera with deep suspicion, as a vehicle of anti-Israeli and anti-American propaganda. The network was ready to provide an Arab eye on the war: it had five correspondents in Iraq and two stationed with the coalition forces. Al-Arabiya claimed twenty-five correspondents in the region. The point was that this time, unlike the situation during the first Gulf War, the war would not be viewed just through an Anglo-American lens.

The media could deploy their own array of marvellous machines, akin to those weapons of war the coalition boasted. The journalist and the photographer had at their disposal satellite phones, digital cameras, videophones, and lightweight portable computers. Indeed, pretty well everything was lightweight: the satellite phones in the first Gulf War that could amount to over 50 pounds were now less than a pound. There were the 'tank cam' videos that attached to a moving vehicle could convey the impression of being right there. Yet another signature of the war were the grainy, greenish images produced by the night-vision cameras. ('One of the things that really jolted me I think, after a while,' said Bruce R, 'a great deal seemed to happen at night, cooler I suppose, and this constant image of green, that greenness on the screen ...') If everything worked right, and sometimes it did not, the journalist could connect easily from anywhere via satellite to deliver that live feed which made for real-time war. The feed was then massaged back home, labels added, perhaps a musical introduction, a bit of graphics. If the pictures came from somewhere else, and Western networks often used material from Al-Jazeera, then the channel might mute the sound and add a voice-over. The talking head in the desert might be juxtaposed with the anchor in the studio. The program host could interrogate the correspondent. Then there were all the digital animations, the maps and the moving arrows and the simulations, which sometimes gave the coverage the appearance of a video game. Real-time war had a distinctly high-tech 'look and feel.'

The scale of the whole enterprise generated its own brand of hubris. The news media were continually fascinated by their own doings and people and ways. There was constant marvelling at the cutting-edge technology that was on display. The program hosts, noted Rick Salutin, a columnist for the *Globe and Mail* (11 April), 'seemed to think we'd feel comfier if we identified with them and *their* issues – long hours, early rising, strange pronunciations and geography, adapting to time zones – so when they changed over, there was lots of *You take care now* chitchat.' Some of the embedded journalists, cast as knight errants, were clearly on a grand adventure. CNN's Walter Rodgers, reported Antonia Zerbisias in the *Toronto Star* (25 March), really got carried away: he explained 'how he has been moving inside "a huge wave of steel,"' and how he knew, 'if it ran into Iraqi troops, "We'll simply kill them, we'll find the enemy and grab him by the nose."' It all had the flavour of an Indiana Jones story, where a professional (recall Jones was an archaeologist) was thrust by circumstances into a world of excitement and peril.

Not just Donald Rumsfeld (though his views received a lot of attention), but all sorts of officials felt called upon to make comments about the media's performance. So the fall of Baghdad allowed Dick Cheney, the Vice-President, to make a sneering comment about the foolishness of 'retired military officers embedded in TV studios.' At another level newspapers carried lots of stories about how the television networks were delivering the news, about the difference between Western and Arab media, whether people were watching and what they were watching, how they felt about the torrent of war coverage. The CBC radio station in Ottawa first got listeners to sound off about the wall-to-wall coverage on CBC Radio and Television in the early days of the war, and then questioned a network official who had to defend this as a necessary 'service to Canadians.' Probing the nature of the real-time war had become a matter of consuming interest across the media.

II

The conceit of the real-time war was its capacity to create an illusion of being there, right when something was happening, all in order to transmit the virtual experience of war to viewers. An early story in the *New York Daily News* (21 March) marvelled at the 'shocking scenes': CNN's Nic Robertson, stationed in Baghdad, reporting live on a midday wave of strikes, was so panicked by a huge flash and explosion that he ordered everyone away from the windows – here peril was brought right into the American home. It was not long before media critics tried to capture the unique properties of the product television was now serving up. 'Today's television broadcasts unfold not like narratives, edited for sense, context and continuity,' asserted Julie Salamon in the *New York Times* (6 April), sounding a bit like Postman, 'but like animated Cubist paintings with sound and multiple images appearing simultaneously.' Richard Goldstein in *The Village Voice* (26 March–1 April) argued that this was really a new genre of hyperreality, drawing his inspiration from the work of that guru of postmodern thought, the French theorist Jean Baudrillard:

> What's truly new, and memorable, about this sequel is its aura of intimacy. Embedding journalists with the troops has produced its desired effect, creating a feeling of thereness that many an action-movie director would envy. But the insignia of this event is its distinctive low-res look. It resembles early generations of video games but with a far more resonant edge. The visual plane is flattened, the voices of reporters crackle, the image breaks up into pixelated squares. It's the cubism of postmodern combat. And like cubism, low-res forces the viewer to fill in the semiotic blanks. Gaze at these images long enough and you enter a semi-rational state. Your mind may find it offensive but your senses say sit back and enjoy *The Shock and Awe Show*.

Goldstein concluded by stigmatizing live war as a more sinister version of 'Reality TV,' presumably like the hit *Survivor* series, boasting 'the same voyeuristic kick, the same aura of faintly forbidden intrusion,' that offered viewers a 'safe and secret' stimulation.

Whether the result was Cubist art, an action movie, or reality TV, all of these claims had merit, even if the analogies were contradictory. The fact is that real-time war was not always the same product. Sometimes the broadcasts were full of spectacular images. Consider one of the most intense moments in the whole conflict, when American bombers and cruise missiles launched their assault on Baghdad, the opening of the supposed 'shock and awe campaign,' on Friday, 21 March. Television around the world carried these pictures live, often using the facilities of Al-Jazeera and Abu Dahbi TV. The CBC's coverage that night featured Peter Mansbridge, the anchor, in the studio, a person he referred to as an 'admiral,' and a third expert connected by phone. They carried on a fragmented discussion, Mansbridge as the official witness who talked about what they were seeing, the two others as military observers who watched through the lens of their expertise. They were looking at a live feed (we knew that because the word 'LIVE' was stamped on the screen) from an Arab television service, marked occasionally by the sounds of Arab voices. The cameras had two modes, night scope and regular vision, and over the course of about seven minutes they switched back and forth to give viewers a different type of sight. In the background, we could hear, at various times, a dull rumble, then the sharp sounds of what seemed like gunfire, and regularly the heavier sounds of explosions. This background of sound was constant, a source of information which told people of a city under attack, a city wounded. A few times the screen would switch to a map of Baghdad on which were marked the various 'leadership targets' that were presumably the objects the bombing was meant to obliterate.

'The tyranny of the visual, those nights where all that bombing was going on, was so spectacular, was so interesting to see that it essentially blows everything else out of your brain,' reasoned Robert Thompson, a professor from Syracuse University (PBS, 22 March). 'Whatever analysis, whatever background, whatever context in history might be being reported tends to be overwhelmed by the fact that you so focus on these images, the likes of which we've never seen before.' In fact the cameras gave two quite different views of what was happening. The night sight was fixed. Its image was composed of two main features, showing a cityscape and skyscape full of black with a row of green globes of light, of differing sizes. Sometimes we could see a flash of green, even a plume of green, sometimes a green globe would blink brighter, pulsate perhaps. The evening skyline might show an occasional pin prick of light. Very briefly the screen would brighten, presumably because an explosion had thrown light across the whole viewing area. It was, to use the analogy of art, like an abstract, or near abstract, painting, where actual objects had been transformed into geometric shapes. Because it was so incomplete, so flattened, the image required the viewer fill in the picture. You had to imagine what the globes were – fires, buildings, devastation. But for that very reason it could not so readily involve: we were distanced from the action by the images which represented that action. These pictures were similar to the kinds of images generated on computer screens in the early days of video games, as Goldstein had noted.

By contrast, the regular eye brought the viewer directly into the picture. This camera was highly mobile, sometimes frenetic, jerky, as it panned the scene, abruptly cut to another picture, zoomed in for a close-up, stopped on a panorama, then shot up into the sky, only to pan down after a few moments of black. Now you could make out buildings, clusters of light, fires, and even smoke; so Baghdad suddenly looked like a real place. Like a real place, yes, but a city afflicted by angry red boils, a skyscape full of the smoke of destruction. When the bombs or missiles struck, the immediate effect was a flash of white light, an evil blossom of devastation, normally with a shade of yellow, and surrounded by a red aura. That swiftly changed into a billowing, dark, reddish cloud before receding into the general background as smoke. But sometimes the screen itself would go white, perhaps because the camera had closed up on a site that was hit, giving the definite impression of a massive explosion. So the regular eye did bring people into the scene of destruction; it looked much more real, and thus much more shocking. What we saw, to employ once again the analogy of art, was something still fantastic but akin to the apocalyptic paintings of Hieronymous Bosch, full of dark smudges and flashes of light, depicting warring armies and the arrival of hell. Except, unlike a Bosch painting, we did not see any bodies.

Mansbridge seemed overcome by what he saw. He admitted, 'This is unlike anything we've witnessed before' and later, 'It's hard to know what to say when you watch something like this.' At times neither he nor the others spoke, letting the images tell the tale. But what tale did they tell? The demands of television compelled speech, an attempt to explain. Mansbridge briefly fell back into the official frame of reference, talking about the various declared targets of the assault. The admiral added, 'Talk about weapons of mass destruction.' 'Well, there's certainly mass destruction going on in downtown Baghdad,' replied Mansbridge. Struggling to explain again, to put the event in some sort of a context, he suggested to the admiral that the first hit on the city was reminiscent of 'carpet bombing,' because a row of buildings had apparently been struck by 'one bomb after another.' That analogy, however, broke with the script of the whole scenario. The admiral swiftly corrected Mansbridge: this was not at all like carpet bombing because satellite shots demonstrated the Americans had clearly targeted particular buildings. (While he spoke, the picture of the wounded city was replaced by the map of Baghdad with its regime targets carefully identified.) 'I would not say carpet bombing, I just could not envision carpet bombing.' Even though Mansbridge knew that, he said once again it all had the 'appearance' of carpet bombing. Then he too referred to the map which served as the master image to fix the meaning of the assault as concentrated on the regime, not the city. The third voice chimed in to talk about the precision munitions of the Americans, 'the multiple aim-point technology' of the B-2 bombers. The admiral agreed, adding that the whole scene demonstrated 'the technology advances' of recent years. 'This was not possible ten years ago.'

The experts had worked to bring the interpretation back into the official frame of explanation, explicitly denying the wild analysis of Mansbridge, which threatened to cast doubt on the war script. For if this assault were seen as carpet bombing, then what was being done to Baghdad might better be described as a war crime than an attack on the Iraqi regime. Then the assault would be placed in the context of a remembered Second World War, when Allied air raids levelled the cities of Germany, leaving behind, in memory at least, destruction, desolation, and death. In fact, the whole issue of the bombing of Germany and Japan during that war had become a matter of much contention in the 1990s. In Canada the controversy broke out over what was deemed an anti-bombing documentary on the CBC called *The Valour and the Horror* (1992); in the United States it focused on a planned exhibition about the *Enola Gay* and the A-Bomb at the National Air and Space Museum (1995). So the champions of 'clean war' had to downplay the context of bombing and affirm the idea of precision munitions, high-tech warfare, to fit Washington's propaganda. That sanitized the exercise, making it akin to all the explosions which graced, for instance, the Bond movies.

Ironically, the roles were reversed in another CBC broadcast of the assault on Baghdad. This time Mansbridge interviewed the Jordanian correspondent Tamara al-Karram, then watching the shock-and-awe show from a roof top in Baghdad. She was overcome with the extent of the assault: explosions everywhere, even if many did concentrate on targets situated on the west bank of the Tigris, so that the whole city was damaged. Mansbridge made reference to 'the forty-five leadership targets' that, according to the script again, were the object of the bombing. Al-Karram did not question, directly, this repetition of the official line. Instead, she said the targets 'are everywhere, they are among the civilian buildings ... It is a catastrophe.' Here again were two conflicting frames of analysis, one signifying and even advertising the power and sophistication of America's military technology, while the other expressed the plight of its victims.

Undeniably the broadcast had the potential to seize and to fascinate, as Thompson had suggested. But these images – an 'animated Cubist' collage though they may be – were swiftly interpreted and understood, though in quite different ways. Thus, one Canadian viewer railed against the horror of this real-time war in an e-mail he sent to the CBC a few days later. He had a great deal of 'trouble watching bombs dropping on Baghdad. CNN makes every flash of light look like the beginning of a Walt Disney movie. Behind every flash of light it is almost certain that we are witnessing an execution of innocent civilians by the American War Machine,' wrote Kent MacMillan. 'War is disgusting, but turning mass executions into an ABC afternoon weekly TV program is beyond disgusting and it must be stopped by any means.' It was exactly this kind of interpretation that raised a problem for the Pentagon. '"The images on television tend to leave the impression that we're bombing Baghdad," said Rumsfeld, clearly addressing international humanitarian concerns about rising casualties in the bombed-out city,' according to the *Toronto Star* (24 March). But then he denied what the eyes saw. '"The coalition forces are not bombing Baghdad," he said, insisting these are surgical strikes of military targets.' The British correspondent David Chater of Sky News, reporting live from Baghdad for CBS News during the course of that Friday evening, delivered the kind of message Rumsfeld preferred. Amidst all the bomb bursts, the flashes of white and red and orange, he observed that 'Baghdad,' the regime not the city, now 'knows what the Pentagon means by shock and awe.' And, he might have added, so did the rest of the world (see figure 4.2).

A lot of this real-time war, however, was composed of a more prosaic variety of images delivered by the embedded journalists. 'A little channel surfing will get you a lot,' claimed Nancy Franklin in the *New Yorker* (31 March): 'the tanks of the cavalry rolling north on that vast expanse of sand in southern Iraq (tanks and goats and sand was the specialty of the day on

Figure 4.2 War as ad (© Bruce Plante / Dist. by Universal Press Syndicate, *The Chattanooga Times*)

Plante's cartoon captured the idea that the war was one dramatic way of sending a message. Iran and North Korea were the two other members of that 'Axis of Evil' George W. Bush had denounced early in 2002. The presumption was that the leaders of these and other recalcitrant countries, like Syria for example, would learn what an armed and aggressive America could achieve. A swift victory might well deliver just that kind of 'shock and awe' necessary to intimidate these states so that they would prove more amenable in the future to American diplomacy. David Sanger wrote a story in the *New York Times* (6 April 2003) entitled 'Viewing the War as a Lesson to the World,' where he cited an anonymous official who pointed out, 'Iraq is not just about Iraq.' Washington, or at least some important part of Washington, and Sanger clearly implied the President agreed, looked upon 'the confrontation with Saddam Hussein as something of a demonstration conflict, an experiment in forcible disarmament.'

Thursday on CNN); the men of the 101st Airborne Division hunkering down near a bunker; Geraldo Rivera in Afghanistan, ringed by a handful of armed soldiers, who appear to be protecting him while he's on the air; and reporters in the oil fields near Kirkuk, on the road with the infantry, and in the desert in Kuwait, talking through gas masks.' Sometimes the correspondents became just a bit too sentimental. 'On Friday, a CNN reporter in Iraq talked about how the soldiers were professionals, saying, "They do what most of us can't do." He added that "they cause death, but then there's the human part" – at which point he handed the microphone to two soldiers so that they could say hello to the folks at home.'

One study of the first week of war found that roughly 80 per cent of the reports focused on the correspondents alone, who were not necessarily interviewing anyone at all. Witness the case of David Bloom, an NBC journalist (who later died, of ill health), part of the American blitzkrieg, who was stationed with a mechanized unit of the 3rd Infantry in its sweep toward Baghdad. His reports had recalled the movie *Three Kings* (1999), in which a few US soldiers search through southern Iraq, right after Gulf War I, looking for Saddam Hussein's stash of gold bullion, a quest that produced exotic sights and strange adventures. On the 21st of March he reported from atop a rapidly moving tank carrier, the desert sweeping by behind him: dressed in some kind of vest, presumably bulletproof, Bloom rocked up and down on the vehicle while he told viewers what the column, or 'we' as he said, had achieved earlier in the morning and what the rush northwards was like now. March 26 found him parked in the midst of a sandstorm, which made for very poor pictures; Bloom explained the sense of peril of the troops, fearful of the paramilitary forces who had adopted guerrilla tactics against the column. By the 3rd of April he was parked again, beside the road, guarded by a soldier who seemed to be playing with his rifle, as the column moved up along the road, on the outskirts of Baghdad. Once again, Bloom took the opportunity to talk about what had happened, in this case the collapse of the Republican Guard (or rather how the enemy had been 'degraded'), as well as to register the sense of anticipation among the troops over what they were supposed to do next. He made reference to the idea of a Baghdad hell, the prospect of entering the city in force, and so facing 'a much more deadly form of fighting than they want to engage in.' Bloom provided, in each case, a mediated version of what had or was happening. Almost the only images were of Bloom himself.

There were, of course, some scenes of combat. The unit that NBC's Bob Arnot was with were caught in a firefight near Kut, just south of Baghdad, on the 3rd of April. Arnot was clearly excited, even frenzied: he spoke quickly in short, clipped sentences, and moved swiftly, first one way and then another. He told of snipers, of 'in-bound mortars.' He pointed to 'our' machine-gunner, to the row of mortars ready to fire. You could hear the voices of the soldiers yelling something, something not clear, in the background. Bullets, Arnot said, were 'literally whizzing over our heads.' But the troops, 'even in the heat of battle, were trying to minimize civilian casualties.' The US Marines, engaged in what he termed 'a tremendous battle,' were struggling to get over a bridge – 'the action is really picking up here.' In fact, a viewer had to take Arnot's word for all the action, since the images were too distant for a viewer to make out easily just what was going on. The report was not at all like one of Hollywood's action movies, no Arnold Schwarzenegger massacring the enemy up close and personal. It did give an intimate view of the war, but what it focused on was the understandably agitated Bob Arnot, whose life seemed in danger from all the trouble going on around and on top of him.

'For reporters, it is a chance to convey the minute-by-minute reality of war in a way that no one has ever been able to do,' noted Franklin; 'and we at home have been able to watch history as it happens, instead of years later, after someone has pieced together footage for the History Channel.' This was a very sanguine view of the real-time war, for so many of the reports and images were mundane and repetitive, the very kind of material that would not make it into a documentary for the History Channel. The correspondents did provide a narrative, they did impose an order, but it was an order that reflected their personal views or experiences, the media's taste for sensation, and the overall script of the Pentagon. What they supplied, normally, was a representation of war, of bits of war, from which the action and the gore was largely absent.

III

The real-time war was itself embedded in a much more diverse package of news and views and stories about the Iraqi adventure. The satellite and cable news channels continued to offer a considerable amount of live war coverage. After the initial activity, however, the networks soon switched back to a more or less normal schedule, in North America anyway, leaving war mostly to early morning shows and the nightly news. About 40 per cent of American TV coverage, more in the case of Fox News, focused on the battles and strategy and tactics, according to the TVNewscan project. Newspapers never did supply real-time war, though they filled their first sections, and perhaps a special section as well, with all manner of war reports, some from embedded correspondents, incredibly detailed maps of the advance of coalition forces, and assorted commentaries on life and opinion in the war zone.

The accuracy of all the information provided by the Western media was in question almost from the beginning. The journalists, embedded or otherwise, got it wrong, especially in the early days. Military sources gave out stories too soon. News media were sometimes too ready to believe official sources, although reporters were quick to make corrections once they investigated. The port city of Umm Qasr was taken many times before it actually was captured. A major tank battle between British armour and Iraqi armour out of Basra evaporated into thin air. The surrender of a whole Iraqi division, something that would have confirmed expectations, never happened. An Iraqi commander who had supposedly surrendered actually turned up on Al-Jazeera. A much touted uprising against the regime in Basra, again an event that would have demonstrated that the Iraqis really were yearning for liberation, proved false when Al-Jazeera showed the streets were quiet. An embedded journalist, Walter Branigin of the *Washington Post*, first cast doubt on the military version of a shooting at a checkpoint near Karbala on 31 March, where soldiers blasted a car full of Iraqis – he claimed the solders never gave a proper warning to the Iraqis. A couple of atrocity stories by Blair and Bush were never substantiated, stories that had credibility nonetheless because of the odious reputation of the Saddam Hussein regime. Claims that the coalition had found a morgue full of torture victims yielded instead a warehouse full of corpses from the Iran-Iraq War of the 1980s. News media reported the discovery of a chemical factory, only to have the military deny this finding a bit later. The marvellous new technology of reporting was no sure cure to that legendary problem, the fog of war. Indeed, that technology seems to have allowed rumours and hopes to fly more rapidly than ever from briefings and interviews to newsrooms and then audiences.

Nor did the practice of embedding provide that understanding of the broader picture which audiences needed to evaluate the war. 'What we are seeing is not the war in Iraq; what we're seeing are slices of the war in Iraq,' Rumsfeld told the country, a quotation that found its way into many newspapers. 'We're seeing that particularized perspective that that reporter or that commentator or that television camera happens to be able to see at that moment, and it is not what's taking place. What you see is taking place, to be sure, but it is one slice, and it is the totality of that that is what this war is about.' Television, notably the cable news networks, again came in for the most serious criticism. 'They had the people with the big hair asking questions on television,' said Carla Robbins of the *Washington Post* (*Editor & Publisher*, 11 April). 'I would cringe whenever they asked really smart people really dumb questions.' The print media, at least, liked to believe their journalists focused on the story rather than the image. But a columnist in the *Washington Times* (14 April), a supporter of the administration, argued after the fact that a lot of the media, print as well as television, got the whole story wrong. James Lakey recounted a series of cases where front-page stories and television commentaries cast doubt on the wisdom of the war plan, predicting a quagmire, even a disaster, just before the American blitzkrieg swept into Baghdad. Of course, some of these errors of analysis were a result of accepting the myth that Iraq was a credible enemy, a myth that had been promoted by Washington.

The more interesting issue was the way in which marketing affected the presentation of the war on television. The American networks were infected with a bad dose of patriotism (see figure 4.3). This infection took various forms. Some were trivial, such as the American flags on lapel pins and on screen, the references to 'we,' the cheerleading tone of an embedded correspondent. Some affected only an individual, notably the way in which the veteran Peter Arnett, ensconced in Baghdad, was fired by NBC after he gave an interview to Iraqi TV where he suggested the war plan had failed 'because of Iraqi resistance.' His comment set off a firestorm of criticism at home: Arnett was playing Saddam Hussein's game, giving the regime a propaganda victory. NBC dropped him quickly, though he was soon hired by Britain's *Daily Mirror* and later Al-Arabiya. The infection was much more pronounced at one cable network, Fox News, which well before the onset of the war had adopted an America First position. Its early morning talk show *Fox and Friends*, for example, was blatant about its loyalties – Arnett was really a traitor, suggested one of the co-hosts. Especially telling was the impassioned admission of Neil Cavuto, a Fox anchor, after someone criticized him for bias. 'You damn well bet I am, Professor,' Cavuto said on air (*Time*, 14 April). 'I'm more in favor of a system that lets me say what I'm saying here rather than one who would be killing me for doing the same thing over there.' One survey of nightly

Figure 4.3 Media patriotism (© 2003 Tribune Media Services, Inc. Reprinted with permission.)

There was an attempt to brand war coverage, led as Horsey pointed out by the example of Fox News. The networks used sound effects as well as visual cues to differentiate their coverage and to set the right mood. Well before the war began, for example, Fox had already settled on its theme music, which Nicholas Engstrom later called a case of 'Metallica rehearsing Wagner, the guitar chords rising over thudding drums.' In practice, though, the heavy guitar sound was replaced with milder strings and more drum beats. A few days into the war other networks established their own soundtrack for war. CBS brought on its anchor, Dan Rather, with 'an aggressive drumbeat' and 'a reverberating bass guitar.' MSNBC used 'nerve-wracking strings, drums, and tolling bells' to announce its regular war updates. CNN's signature music was much the same, 'minus the bells.'

newscasts, the TVNewscan project, found that the coverage of Fox News boasted a decidedly more 'supportive' tone than did any of its major rivals.

Yet the patriotism, or rather the fear of not being seen as patriotic, of offending the public, could affect the way in which television news in general handled a story. So it was that the networks acceded to the Pentagon's wishes when they failed to air a video of American prisoners of war and American dead shown by Al-Jazeera early in the war. Edited versions did appear later, after the next of kin had been notified, but not the grisly pictures of the dead. Showing the whole video would have amounted to a propaganda victory for the Iraqis, or so Rumsfeld suggested. It was also a way of protecting American sensibilities from the gruesome consequences of war. The incident recalled the scenes of a dead American ranger being dragged through the streets of Mogadishu in 1993. In legend, a legend now doubted by scholars, these shocking pictures had led Washington to withdraw from Somalia.

American television developed something of a split personality because of the war. Some reporters and some programs remained committed to the assorted conventions of journalism: show the facts, tell the story, strive for impartiality. That was exactly why the veteran newsman Ted Koppel was upset by the network's response to the Pentagon over the Iraqi video. Some analysts criticized the Pentagon's war plan, wrongly perhaps, but that showed their independence if not their wisdom. Most other pundits did not: indeed, they became flacks for the military. Television news increasingly began to promote the Iraq War as a public good. Writing just as the war began, Sheryl McCarthy of *Newsday* (20 March), a New York City paper, cited gung-ho morning news shows, correspondents who parroted the government's line, the loving pictures of all the hi-tech weaponry the American forces had at their disposal. 'Their message is that the United States is powerful and righteous, that we're prepared to give Hussein a good whipping, and that anybody who opposes us is suspect.' What the networks decided to define as news, the 'reality' they manufactured, confirmed the Pentagon's ideal of a clean war. The news downplayed the issue of civilian casualties and the damage to Baghdad. According to Al-Jazeera (9 April), CNN's Aaron Brown defended the decision not to highlight the horrors of war on the grounds of good taste. The news worked to sentimentalize the American soldier, showing how they strove to help Iraqis in trouble: the troops became agents not just of liberation but of humanitarianism as well. The acceptance of the language of war put out by the Pentagon realized the aims of viral marketing. The obsession with precision weaponry and the features on bombers and warplanes had the effect of delivering a message that war American-style was clean. The celebration of victory, the pictures of cheering Iraqis that filled screens on 9 April, of course, confirmed the Pentagon's view that the war was just. This sanitizing of war stood out all the more because Arab TV, and especially Al-Jazeera, sold their audiences the supposed 'reality' of a dirty war. Reza recalled how striking was the contrast: CNN offered scenes of 'soldiers holding a baby ...'; but turn to Al-Jazeera and 'it's soldiers killing a baby.' (See figure 4.4.)

IV

When the war began, the media, and most especially the North American television networks, expected to lose huge sums of money, depending in part upon the scale of the effort they mounted to cover the action in Iraq. The difficulty was not only the expenses of covering the war, however. Past experience had demonstrated that when war came, advertisers got scared that the grisly footage would create an environment which was not congenial to selling their products. Besides, polls taken after 9/11 had shown that the American public believed advertising should disappear from television during a national emergency, and a third claimed they would disparage any advertiser who dared to disturb their anguish with a commercial. Procter and Gamble, the world's largest

Figure 4.4 The two wars (Steve Greenberg, *Ventura County Star*)

Greenberg captured the extraordinary contrast between the images of war purveyed by the two most extreme champions of the opposing causes, American and Arab. Al-Jazeera was not simply an organ of Iraqi propaganda. At one point, indeed, its journalists were tossed out of Baghdad because the network was deemed hostile to, or insufficiently supportive of, the Hussein regime – they were allowed to return a few days later. But what Al-Jazeera produced was evidence the invasion amounted to a very dirty war. It concentrated on showing hurt children, overflowing hospitals, dead bodies, devastation. It hyped any evidence of Iraqi resistance. It aired Iraqi videos. It doubted the precision of American weaponry, questioning the success of the coalition cause. It denied this was a war of liberation. The 'reality' Al-Jazeera created was infected by another brand of patriotism, Arab and Muslim anger at what seemed an imperialist adventure by two Western powers, the United States and Great Britain. The Iraq war became yet another example of the way the West sought to dominate the Arab and Islamic world.

advertiser, planned to pull all ads from television for the first forty-eight hours of the war. MasterCard intended to drop its campaign during the first week of war, Pepsi thought it would suspend most ads, and General Motors, the biggest advertiser in the United States, would only continue advertising on local and entertainment channels. The networks themselves decided not to run ads when the war coverage was most intense, partly because that might offend the sensibilities of viewers. War was one of those signal events that had the capacity to shut down the main business of commerce.

There certainly were losses, close to $80 million in the first week of war coverage. The four majors in the United States (ABC, CBS, NBC, and Fox) lost an estimated $22.4 million in the first full day of war, 20 March, claimed a report in the *Globe and Mail* (25 April). But thereafter the picture got much brighter. Revenues improved in part because, as the *Washington Post* (29 March) noted, the major assaults on Baghdad occurred when it was early morning in America, so the networks could generate revenue from the more lucrative prime-time advertising. Fox News, for example, had been able to sell all its evening spots on the top-ranked *The O'Reilly Factor*. It was also true, however, that the majors soon returned to a semblance of normal programing that provided the right milieu for commercial messages. And the fact that the war as presented was so clean meant many advertisers were not scared away for very long. According to *Advertising Age* (31 March), the major American auto makers were preparing to return, mounting new campaigns that would cost in the neighbourhood of $350 million. The magazine later reported how there was a substantial rebound in ad spending in weeks two and three of the war, sufficient to overcome the past losses. The exceptions were the chief purveyors of real-time war, the cable news networks, which had lost about $35 million over the three weeks of war because they scheduled fewer ads.

The underlying reason that advertising had returned was the public mood: the war was no shock, like 9/11. 'Back then we were in deeper mourning. Now we're on the attack,' Faith Popcorn, the noted market consultant, told *Advertising Age* (31 March). Nonetheless the American networks had not yet discovered how to make money out of war. Which did not mean that the war coverage was just a public service television offered on behalf of the nation, or the government. Rather network executives dreamed of using the war to capture a larger share of the viewing audience. Success might create a momentum that would carry the victor ahead of all rivals when normality returned. The immediate impact of the invasion was to send people to television to watch real-time war. The ratings of all news services jumped. NBC Nightly News, the market leader among the broadcast networks, posted its biggest audience totals, approaching twelve million viewers, in the first ten days of war. The most dramatic increase, though, was for the all-news channels, in the United States the cable networks CNN, Fox News, and MSNBC. Their audience totals exploded, up a whopping 651 per cent at the lowest-ranked MSNBC in the first week. Even in Canada the war benefited the all-news channels, much more the American CNN than the domestic services CBC Newsworld and CTV NewsNet: on 19 March (Canadian time), when the cruise missiles struck Baghdad, CNN pulled in an unheard of 1.1 million Canadian viewers. Similarly, Sky News drew a record share of viewers, about 1.2 million, in Britain during the fierce bombing of Baghdad on 21 March.

The numbers did not stay high. A certain amount of war fatigue set in among the general public after the first week of conflict, and that grew, especially when there were so few moments as intense as the bombing of Baghdad. A tracking survey conducted by Pew Research found that four in ten respondents in the United States believed the media had focused too heavily on the war. People wanted other news, they wanted diversion, a return to entertainment programing. The totals for the regular broadcast news were the first to fall away. The sizeable minority of news junkies – ironically Pew found that another four in ten 'can't stop watching news about the war' – kept the audience levels of the all-news services well above pre-war levels until the end of the war. By the third week of April, however, newspapers were reporting that cable TV totals were also declining toward pre-war levels.

Who won the media war? In the Islamic world the Arabic channels were clear victors, according to the reports of the Western news services and newspapers. People watched CNN and the BBC some of the time. They even listened to Radio Sawa. What they believed, though, was Al-Jazeera and the rest. *Time* (7 April) reported that students and professors in Turkey had burned a television set 'to protest CNN's "one-sided" coverage.' Time and again reporters found that Arabs were regularly watching Al-Jazeera at home or in cafés and the like across the Middle East. They also discovered that Al-Jazeera had found considerable audiences elsewhere in the Islamic world. According to the *Washington Post* (7 April), TV-7 in Indonesia carried the Al-Jazeera feed and added translators. 'We believe al-Jazeera more because what they said about the war is true,' said Suhendro, a mosque leader in Jakarta. 'I mean, they showed us how Iraqi civilians have become the victims of the war. Children, mothers, old people, civilians killed and injured because of the war. I see them losing their hands and legs and other body parts. Scenes I will never see on CNN.' Even if Al-Jazeera was as much the vehicle of illusion and propaganda as CNN, still this Arab channel had won fame as a maverick brand in the world of global television where North American and European sources once dominated.

The war coverage in North America did not change the rankings among the broadcast or the cable networks. Neither CBS News nor ABC News were able to capitalize on the opportunity. NBC remained on top in the United States. So too, in Canada, did CTV, which dashed the hopes of the public broadcaster. CBC executives had long believed that they managed the most trusted news source in times of crisis, and viewers did give the network higher marks for the quality of its war coverage. CBC totals increased, but not enough to overcome the existing CTV lead. Likewise, among the cable news services there was little change in standings. CNN was unable to replay its victory of 1991. Fox News had taken the lead from CNN over the past year, and it maintained that lead during and after the war. Indeed, Fox News managed to keep its viewing levels high even after the middle of April. It averaged 3.11 million viewers at night in the week ending 20 April, which put it ahead of all cable networks, including the entertainment channels, which once had won in the prime-time hours. By contrast, CNN had slipped to 1.77 million.

That was too much for Ted Turner, founder of CNN. Asked about Fox News, Turner replied, 'It's not how big you are, it's how good you are that really counts.' According to the *Guardian* (25 April), Turner lambasted his long-time rival Rupert Murdoch, the owner of Fox, calling him a 'warmonger' who had 'promoted' the war. Turner's outburst was just sour grapes, suggested Bill O'Reilly, the host of the top-ranked Fox show, already something of a national institution. O'Reilly had a point: it must have been galling for Turner to see the other network a clear winner – when Fox News appeared in 1996, Turner said he was 'looking forward to squishing Rupert like a bug.' But Turner also had a point. Murdoch had been fervently pro-war and his vast media empire had followed the owner's lead. There were rumours that Murdoch's strong support for Bush had something to do with efforts to get the rules of the media game changed so that Fox Corporation could acquire more properties in the United States. But the type of journalism Fox News practised had been set from the beginning. Although it might boast of its fair and balanced coverage, Fox News had never been known for its impartiality: most of its program hosts freely mixed opinion and news. In times past the cable network had won favour with conservative politicians and viewers because of its definite right-wing sympathies. Now Fox News had proved that its brand of war coverage, full of bombast and vigour and patriotism, was a crowd pleaser. The mix suited the militancy of an increasing number of citizens in a post-9/11 America. The success of Fox News was a marketing triumph, despite the blow that delivered to the traditional standards of journalism.

IV

No matter how extraordinary the coverage, virtually no one was satisfied with it, outside the media anyway. That was the nature of the news game. The main players were never likely to think their interests were adequately represented in the news. When the subject was as important as war, when in effect the news packaged war as a commodity, then everyone became a critic. The complaints were legion: about propaganda, war porn, crummy journalism, too much speculation, incomplete and inconsistent coverage, lots of repetition, and on and on. Not even, or rather not all, the military leaders whose brilliance the coverage ultimately advertised thought the media did a decent job. Consider just one outburst, this from Air Marshal Brian Burridge, the commander of the British forces in the Gulf, reported in Britain's *Telegraph* (7 April):

> The UK media has lost the plot. You stand for nothing, you support nothing, you criticise, you drip. It's a spectator sport to criticise anybody or anything, and what the media says fuels public expectation. That may sound harsh, but that's the way it feels from where I sit.
>
> If you look at what fills newspapers now, it's the equivalent of reality TV – it's superficial, there's very little news reporting, there's very little analysis, but there's a lot of conjecture. The media thought they were going to get a one-hour-45-minute Hollywood blockbuster, and it's not like that. War is a dirty, disgusting, ugly thing, and I worry about it being dignified as infotainment.

Burridge thought that the British press purveyed a kind of reality TV. In North America observers claimed the same about the broadcast and cable networks. The analogy had some merit. Reality TV was one of the hottest entertainment properties on American television: it referred, in particular, to programs like the *Survivor* series, *Fear Factor*, or the various *Big Brother* shows where 'real' people as contestants sought to overcome challenging or unpleasant situations to win a prize. Their style was borrowed from news and documentary shows to highlight the thrills, to interview contestants, and to spin out the conjecture about who might win, all for the pleasure of viewers. Sometimes viewers could even vote on how these individuals performed, notably in the case of the extraordinarily popular *American Idol*. Like such shows, the design of the real-time war was largely set, but the actual incidents – the thrills and the disappointments – were unscripted. So the extensive television coverage offered viewers a chance to share the anxiety, the anguish, and the excitement of soldiers, sometimes as it happened, and again from the comfort of home, thus turning citizens into voyeurs. There was even a bizarre moment when some viewers 'voted' on one performer: NBC received a flood of angry e-mails damning Peter Arnett before its decision to fire the veteran reporter. Of course, unlike *Survivor*, the final outcome was never really in doubt. Nor were viewers able to share the anguish of the Iraqis, at least not very often. The match was not perfect: the war against Iraq was hardly a contest among equals. But the analogy does capture some of the flavour and the appeal of war news.

There was no permanent solution to the problems of the TV war. The answer might seem to lie in building more diversity into the media system. Encouraging Al-Jazeera to enter North America would afford the public access to an alternate view of events in the Middle East, though the impact would be very muted if the service was not available in English. Besides, the availability of Al-Jazeera would only have heightened the concern over war porn, given the Arabic focus on the dirty war. Hiring more 'unilaterals' offers the prospect of a different perspective on the war, as would the spread of the practice of embedding, should a future enemy allow 'embeds' in its own forces. But the downside would be even more attention to the bits and pieces of battle, another wave of news fragments, only made coherent by the analysis of the journalist. Television could borrow more from the example of the print media, where columnists might adopt a different line, on the right or the left, than the editorial slant of the newspaper. Except these licensed dissenters would have difficulty securing much air time, especially when a network goes to war as well, which happened all too quickly in the United States. The patriotic imperative was difficult to resist when the political elites and so much of the public, the market of consumers, was already committed to the war, and eager to rally to the flag in support of its own troops.

The only effective defence against this real-time war lay, as always, in the hands of consumers. They could resist the full impact of marketing by seeking out alternative sources of news, especially on the Internet. They might rely upon newspapers, more than one of course, which often did a better job of providing a more rounded appraisal of events. They could use cable or satellite to surf through a greater range of television signals, the BBC as well as CNN, PBS and the CBC. The last two networks, committed more to public service than corporate profit, had at least maintained a higher standard of journalism. Best of all, consumers should avoid the real-time war, one of the obscenities of this television age. It was hardly necessary to experience the bombing of Baghdad or a firefight somewhere on its outskirts to understand the importance or the nature of the war. The print media supplied more than enough material. Radio offered the immediate updates a news junkie needed to stay abreast of what was happening. Television cannot but turn war into a spectacle and a story that employs the styles of pop culture to fashion the infotainment even Air Marshall Burridge found distressing. Consuming live war amounted to a form of submission to the dictates of its co-producers, the Pentagon and the newsrooms. The moving images of television are the most seductive, the voice of television the most authoritative, the content of television the most difficult to critique. TV news is always a threat to democracy, as Postman and Bourdieu said, but most especially

Figure 4.5 The evil eye (Francisco José Calderon, Cartoonists &
Writers Syndicate/cartoonweb.com)

The war against television has gone on for roughly half a century,
beginning in Britain and the United States, where television was
first introduced on a wide scale after the Second World War. At its
most extreme it has amounted to a kind of neo-Luddism, a rejection
of what has variously been called 'the boob tube,' 'the idiot box,' a
kind of 'moving wallpaper.' More often the critics have sought to
reform the medium – PBS was one such venture in the late 1960s –
or to retrain the public – Postman urged schools to take up the cause
of media literacy. The trouble is that the spread of commercial
television and the popularity of its offerings everywhere has ne-
gated whatever gains were made in this endless struggle to limit
the cultural harm of the medium. Recently the arrival of the Internet
brought new hope, though it too may become yet another source
of the television signal – CNN, among others, was selling its video
clips on its website during the war. Calderon's cartoon is just a
clever restatement of the Luddite position: blow up the box.

when harnessed by the discipline of marketing. The answer is simple: turn off the TV (see figure 4.5).

That might seem a hopelessly naive solution. Yet one of the findings of Pew Research (9 April) illustrated that some people, especially mothers, were already aware of the potential harm of TV news. During the war many American parents did restrict the use of television news to protect their children. About half of the sample reported they were monitoring and limiting kids' viewing, up from roughly a third back in 1991. They did so chiefly because of the way the images of war could produce fear (say, about the safety of a relative) and anxiety (as one child asked, What happens to the kids there?). A focus group revealed that some parents were even denying themselves TV to make the prohibitions stick. 'I'm out all day in my job, on the road, and I listen to the radio,' said Victoria, a mother of two preteens. 'I can get the information I need when I'm by myself. That way when I go home, I don't need to put it on. I am trying to give [my children] a normal life.' Real-time war was just too dangerous for the minds of innocents.

FIVE

Consuming War

A familiar theme in the criticism of the real-time war was the lot of the overwhelmed viewers, caught in a media storm and unable to find their bearings (see figure 5.1). How could anyone make sense out of such a profusion of information, analysis, speculation, rumour, and contradiction? That kind of question, though, spoke more to the naiveté of the critic than the life of the consumer. Except for new arrivals or the hopelessly distracted, adults in North America are veterans of innumerable media storms, the result of growing up in the age of unlimited media. They have had to develop what Todd Gitlin called 'styles of navigation' to cope with the torrent of advertising, entertainment, and news that has always surrounded their lives. They have to make meaning on a daily basis to function effectively in the wider society. The skills born of the experience of understanding ads or sports, music or movies, the financial pages and the political news – these skills they could readily apply to war coverage.

The ability of people to swim through the sea of communications is of crucial importance to the functioning of democracy. Democracy is, at bottom, about talk, it is first and foremost a 'discursive' phenomenon, to borrow from the jargon of cultural history. Before voting, before polling, even before what we call human rights, democracy requires a dialogue among the citizens and between the citizens and the gover-

Figure 5.1   Making meaning? (© 2003 by John Trever, *Albuquerque Journal*. Reprinted by permission.)

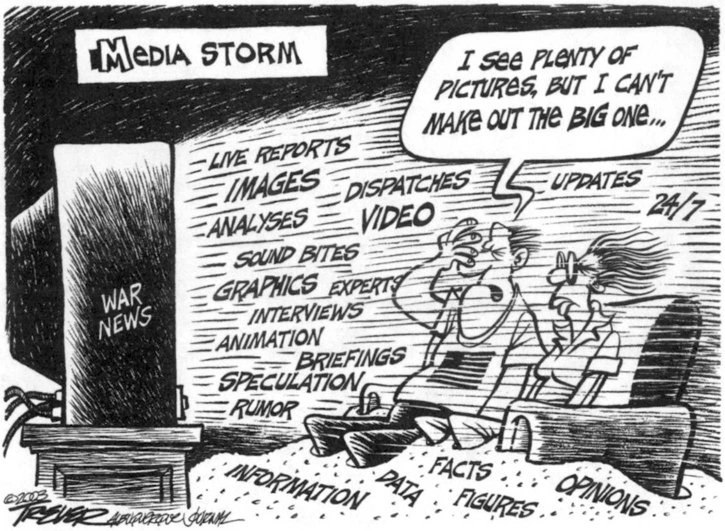

nors. The health of that talk determines how democratic the public sphere can be, which is the reason why the news media that inform the public and debate issues are at the foundation of civil society. The trouble is that the task of governance has fostered techniques to manage and shape public opinion in order to ensure the legitimacy of political action. Now the state and the various elites, bureaucratic as well as political, business as well as moral, employ the images and the rhetoric of advocacy and public relations to secure the success of their public goods. Citizens as consumers must learn to evaluate, to weigh, to discount, and so they approach the media with a mix of belief and disbelief.

This chapter explores how consumers of the Iraq War made meaning and what some of those meanings were. It relies almost exclusively on the findings generated by the interviews I carried out with a small group of people living in and around Toronto during the three weeks of war. They were asked to talk about propaganda and marketing, where they went for news, the ways they came to understand what was happening, and what they made of the war. These interviews occurred in early and mid-May, so the responses were conditioned by the emerging difficulties of the occupation. Not that this negates the value of the opinions people expressed; rather, it underlines how these opinions were the fruit of a moment in time. Much of their experience is told in their own words, although obviously I have organized the quotations so as to explore how war took on the guise of a commodity.

I

You are what you read. It is an old saying, and it has more than a grain of truth. But what would you make of this young man? He swore by the *Financial Times*, a London financial paper meant for investors, managers, and owners, the capitalist class in short. The best paper for 'non-propagandized news,' Geoff said, more 'straightforward' because it was meant for the elite, not the rabble who consumed CNN. Yet he was an activist who supported a variety of different causes associated with the anti-capitalist movement. Then there was a literary type, who on the weekend read the *Toronto Sun*, a downmarket tabloid, hardly a source of much intellectual fare, but he read it partly because he liked the editorial cartoons. Or consider the case of Richard, a retired professor, who never watched the CBC – 'It's a fetish with me' – because the public broadcaster seemed so anti-American and so anti-Israel, 'verging on anti-Semitic.' He was much more taken with the news and views of the *Economist*. By contrast, a pair of left-of-centre nationalists, Glenna and Bruce W, preferred the CBC because of their 'political bent,' and their choice seemed to fit better the 'truth' of the old saying. Little wonder they avoided CNN 'like the plague.' One teacher listened to 680 News, an all-news radio station, in the morning which offered a quick start to the day; a businesswoman, Irene, preferred 96.3 FM, a classical-music station, since its news was 'precise.' All of these people had fixed tastes in the media they preferred to consume, definite likes and dislikes, and these tastes determined what they would use to learn about the war. They may have read or watched or listen more carefully ('I was reading much more closely than I would normally,' recalled Sam, a commuter who surveyed his papers on the way to and from work), but these patterns did not change much, with one significant exception.

Most members of the citizens' panel were regular readers, some heavy readers, of newspapers and magazines, making them part of a bare majority of Canadians. One estimate of media habits in 2002 found that only 54 per cent of adults eighteen and over read a newspaper on an average weekday, spending about forty-five minutes with the newspaper, though 81 per cent had read at least one in the previous week. All three of the major Toronto papers, the *Globe and Mail*, the *Star*, and the *National Post*, supplied copious amounts of war news, much of this of a high quality, some written by their own correspondents (Rosie DiManno, a *Star* columnist, was one of the standouts). The *National Post* was especially interesting because it constituted the loudest voice of neo-conservatism in Toronto: it displayed an extraordinary effusion of triumphalism on 10 April when it gloated over the coalition victory signified by the fall of Baghdad the day before. Bob perused the three major papers every day, even though he did not agree at all with the *Post*. He also read faithfully the *New York Times* on the Internet; indeed, the *Times* site was his default web page. Occasionally he looked at the *Washington Post* and, when in Ottawa, as he was at one point during the war, some French-language papers, *Le Devoir* and *La Presse*. The group of teachers I interviewed were inveterate *Star* readers, whatever else they might sample. In fact, most people read the *Star*, the paper with the largest local circulation, although Mike was not interested in its war coverage, preferring instead that of the *National Post* and the *Globe*. A number of consumers used the Internet to reach newspapers outside Toronto: Oscar read the *Guardian* as well as the *New York Times* and Reza read the Pakistani and Egyptian press.

All this reading marked these people as members of the public sphere. Newspapers remained the most significant source of political information and comment, as well as a diversity of opinion, at least in the case of Canada, not just because of what they offered but also because of the medium itself. Reading is a mode of communication far more congenial to reflection than either listening or watching: reading requires more thinking and it allows the individual to control the pace of communication. You can mull over a column much more readily than a televised news item. Words engage the mind, images stun the mind.

Yet television has long been the main purveyor of news to everyone, and most especially in any time of emergency, such as the Iraq War. According to Statistics Canada, Canadians watched television for 21½ hours a week in the fall of 2000, though much of that time was devoted to viewing entertainment. The figures had declined from the early 1980s, and the Internet played a part in that decline, since people had shifted some time to surfing the web. But this was not yet an Internet war, at least not generally: most of my consumers still turned to television to get the news, except for a couple who were inveterate surfers. (That said, my main source of war coverage was a series of websites, mostly those set up by television networks and newspapers in North America and Britain.) Toronto was served by the three major television networks in English Canada, the CBC and the two private services, CTV and Global, as well as a provincial channel, TV Ontario. The CBC offered radio, over-the-air television, as well as an all-news cable channel called Newsworld, both English- and French-language services, and a comprehensive website full of war news. The CBC provided the most Canadian coverage of the Iraq War, although the corporation had refused to embed any reporters, using instead unilaterals and freelance journalists, in addition to material it borrowed from other services. Its performance in detailing what happened and

exploring why it happened proved excellent, a view confirmed by some, but not all, of the members of the panel.
Cable brought in the major American news channels, including Fox News and CNN. A satellite dish and some cable
packages could provide more exotic fare, such as the BBC and
even Arabic television, include Al-Jazeera.

The whole of the citizens' panel watched some television
during the war. One busy man, both a student and a white-
collar employee, used TV more than any other medium to
keep abreast of the news. A retired professional, who was
mostly at home, had the set on almost all the time, though he
might well be doing something else than just watching. By
contrast, another panellist only recalled some regular viewing
of *Studio 2* on TVOntario to see a panel of experts debate the
events of the war. Similarly, Irene made a practice of watching
the BBC in the morning and the evening, but otherwise had
little time for regular television viewing. Nearly all (excepting
Richard) had tuned into the CBC, both Newsworld and the
broadcast news, at one point or another during the three
weeks, and some made a practice of watching CBC's late-
evening newscast. Less often people mentioned CTV or Global. They did view a wide range of non-Canadian channels,
however. Irene was not the only person to view the BBC – a
retired couple, who normally watched a lot of television, had
the habit of tuning in to the BBC. Reza had a satellite dish that
enabled him to pull in Al-Jazeera and Al-Arabiya. Since he
also watched the CBC, CTV, and a variety of American channels, he spent a lot of time just surfing, usually until the wee
hours of the morning. One teacher, Melissa, also used the
evening hours to sample a 'range of perspectives,' including
BBC News. The most common foreign channels, though, were
the various American networks, including Fox News, but
especially CNN.

Watching CNN was the one significant change in the habits
of the panel. Some people were almost apologetic – Dennis
said he watched 'against my better judgment' – because they
regarded CNN as so American and, as another added, so full

of repetition. But watching CNN seemed unavoidable. It still had the reputation as the best 'live' channel: 'When you wanted to be live,' you went to CNN, claimed Michael. Stephanie turned to it for the initial wave of bombings of Baghdad. 'It was there, it was live, and it was constant,' recalled Bruce R, 'so I could punch in any time and find out where we were, kind of thing.' Whenever he wanted to sample some of the images of war, Chris, who listened to CBC Radio a lot, tuned in to CNN, though he found its 'gung-ho' attitudes upsetting. Even Geoff, so critical of the American media, was sucked in by what he called the CNN effect. 'So I would watch it for about, you know, fifteen or twenty minutes until I was too enraged because I found it, I mean, as I think we're all going to say, total rubbish ... I didn't watch it for news, I watched it to understand what was being told to Americans.' Reza said much the same thing: 'They give you the government line when it comes to at least US foreign policy.' CNN, for these Canadians, was the main purveyor of the real-time war, in all its American splendour.

The war was something of a blockbuster, a must-see event, no matter what people's views about its justice. True, some people were not engaged by the war. Savino avoided much of the coverage: he had overdosed on too many crises, too much media hype, over the years. Sam admitted to irritation because this American story dominated the media, even if he did follow what happened. Mike was more interested in finding the rationale for the war than in war reporting, so he was never glued to the TV. All these individuals, call them distanced consumers, thought there was 'an information overload': 'I didn't think enough new material was coming out every hour,' recalled Sam, 'to justify that kind of coverage.' But the others were, at various times, intensely interested in events. 'I remember being in the kitchen,' Jennifer claimed, 'and my sister saying to me, "Come quick, you've got to see this." And it was the bombs exploding right away. We just sat there and watched it.' Nearly all of these consumers spent more time than usual, sometimes a great deal more, reading and watching news. Occasionally the intensity was just too much: 'I found that for mental health reasons there were times when I just blanked out' (Dave). Another found the coverage both 'depressing and exciting' (Bruce W). 'It was a scary time,' remembered Michael. 'I don't think there was any doubt at all that the US was going to win. It was just a question of how nasty and bloody it was going to be.' This war buff lost interest when it became clear how effective was the American blitzkrieg. But a few consumers were absorbed by the war news throughout the three weeks. Richard was addicted to international affairs, so he was bound to stay tuned when an event of such magnitude was happening. Bob watched with a certain 'dread' because this event presaged, in his mind, the deep disorder of 'the international system.' Reza, born in Pakistan, was obsessed because of his own background: here was yet another Western invasion of the Muslim world. What seemed to count most were the fears and expectations of these heavy consumers, or rather their response to the ways the commodity had been presold.

II

'Washington was clearly, you know, cranking out propaganda,' claimed Mike, speaking here for just about all of the panel. Everyone was aware of the marketing offensive mounted by the White House and the Pentagon in the months preceding the invasion as well as during the war itself. Even Richard, a solid coalition supporter, recognized that Washington had vigorously promoted the war. 'Would you call a President who makes, I don't know, at least two or three trips a week pushing his particular agenda, would you call that propaganda, if you do, then, yeah, ok, it was propaganda.' Others were not so reticent. One talked about the selling job of the administration. Another thought the 'claims about civilian resistance and uprisings and cities falling when they hadn't fallen' was 'pretty classic propaganda,' directed both at Iraqis and Americans (Mike). A third commented on how Washington had clearly set out to manage the news. 'The White House slime machine belches and there are people there with their buckets ready to cart it off to their local newspaper,' claimed Bob. Even 'the choice and nature of the images being shown,' added Bruce R, 'had a strong propaganda purpose, and very much geared to maintaining support in North America.' The fact was that Washington had proved extraordinarily effective, and that was sometimes a source of rueful admiration. 'They wore down the American people,' asserted Irene. 'I think they are masterminds,' said Geoff. 'I think they've triumphed in accomplishing their real goals.' The panel was ready to give the devil his due, an attitude reminiscent of the response consumers often have to a particularly clever piece of advertising or a novel brand of promotion.

My citizens' panel knew they were being manipulated by the language of war the Pentagon had manufactured. Both Glenna and Reza found 'shock and awe' a horrible term, 'disgusting' and 'disgraceful,' because it sanitized the bombing of Baghdad. The very phrase 'Operation Iraqi Freedom' struck some peace activists I interviewed as especially odious, since they thought what the Americans really wanted to 'free' was Iraqi oil. Stephanie got angry, so she said, every time she saw the phrase at the bottom of the TV screen, in itself a sign of how ubiquitous it became. But awareness did not necessarily produce disdain. 'Every war needs a brand, you know, we need a name, we need an identifiable brand,' mused Geoff. 'And that was the brand name for that war.' Both Bruce R and Mike believed 'coalition of the willing' was 'a lovely phrase' that made sense: 'In Canada it nicely skewered us as being not among the willing,' added Mike. Chris felt 'shock and awe' 'sort of makes people feel really good about the American military.' There was, in other words, a sense that Washington had demonstrated its marketing genius.

When propaganda was so rife, what or who could you believe? 'We were very suspicious,' noted Bruce W. 'I would say that I believed about one in two hundred words,' added Glenna, laughing. Sam expressed a similar kind of cynicism about 'what I'm hearing or reading, headlines that are reflective of what I would consider American propaganda, the whole use of new euphemisms for war that haven't been seen before, always sort of doubting what was new or being reported [about] what was going on.' The most common response to Washington's endeavours – the speeches, the briefings, the news conferences, the documents – was scepticism: the claims all had to be discounted.

But not necessarily discarded: people still tried to evaluate the merit of the arguments. I asked what was the 'Big Lie' of the propaganda campaign, a leading question as one panellist pointed out. The purpose was to identify what these consumers thought was the central falsehood of Washington's case. One portion of the panel, obviously those who had opposed the war, believed the 'Big Lie' was the threat to the world posed by the weapons of mass destruction in the hands of Saddam Hussein, a lie revealed as such because of the Iraqi failure to use biological or chemical weapons plus the inability of the American teams to find any sign of his weapons program. Indeed that seemed so obvious it provoked mirth: 'The poor things still haven't found their weapons of mass destruction.' That failure surprised Bruce R because he presumed they would manufacture the evidence to suit the need: 'I actually did think they would find a way to find them.' Others talked about the myth of liberation (why choose Iraq?) or the demonization of Hussein (was he really worse than other Middle Eastern despots?) or the connection between al-Qaeda and Hussein. 'That this is about liberating Iraq,' that was the Big Lie, decided Reza. 'Yes, you can have democracy, but not of the type you choose' – a reference to the American opposition to a theocratic republic, rule by the mullahs, even if chosen via an election.

However, the probe also revealed a much more complicated mix of belief and disbelief. A peace activist was briefly seduced by the cry of liberation. Maybe America did have a responsibility to spread democracy. Though he doubted much of the propaganda, Chris also found it difficult to dismiss out of hand the argument that invading Iraq meant liberating Iraq, even after the fact: 'Suddenly there are all these people who are going to be free now.' A case of truth in marketing? Though Mike had doubted Saddam Hussein possessed any weapons of mass destruction, since Iraq had been so badly 'battered' in the previous conflict and during the decade after, he thought Washington was probably sincere: 'Apparently they took a lot of precautions with their troops, so they were genuinely worried.' Two others recalled the nuclear threat, one of the motifs of war publicity, was a plausible justification for war. Savino was never able to make up his mind about the justice of the war – 'I was waffling.' Mike too admitted he was thoroughly 'confused about the war. I changed my mind about it often.' That was not the only sign of the influence of propaganda. Only two people doubted the fundamental villainy of Saddam Hussein. A number of consumers were surprised by the speed with which the Iraqi army had collapsed: they had accepted the idea of Iraq as a credible enemy. Mike's expectations of what might happen were similarly conditioned. 'Where I was misled, I heard all this expert commentary on ... how dangerous street fighting would be and how this was going to be Stalingrad all over again and I heard immensely learned people [speaking] on the impossibility of street fighting and how this was going to be awful for the Americans, so I was surprised as everyone else when these cities just folded up, the Iraqis folded up.' The propaganda barrage, the sheer force of repetition had an impact.

Decoding the propaganda meant work, sometimes hard work. Mike read widely before the war to sort out the merits of the American case – he cited Kenneth Pollack's *The Threatening Storm: The Case for Invading Iraq*. Others tested the official claims against personal views, putting these claims in some existing or wider context, whether the result of past experience or present knowledge. An opponent of the war relied on his understanding of the Middle East, where he once had business dealings, to fashion an argument about Washington's ignorance of the Islamic world. People on the left, both old and new, drew upon their knowledge of America's misdoings. They made reference to Vietnam or Latin America or Israel to justify doubts about American virtue. They talked about the decade-long assault, the sanctions and the air assaults, mounted against the Iraqi people, which had caused a huge number of deaths and a general decay. When I asked such people what they thought was the chief cause of war, the ordinary response was oil, variously portrayed as an engine of prosperity, the fuel of empire, and the prize sought by the energy industry. They were also more inclined to believe in a conspiracy of hawks or neo-conservatives who had captured control of the American agenda. Always their views bore the signs of that culture of anti-Americanism that had flourished for roughly half a century.

Let me now consider in more detail a few cases that illustrate how individuals built a case for or against war. Each person worked with, or worked through, the vocabulary of morality. Consider first the views of Richard, who had a wide knowledge of international affairs based upon his years as a scholar and teacher. He strongly supported the coalition cause and the American case. 'I derive enormous comfort from the idea that there is a Pax Americana.' That was not because of any great love for Bush or the hawks, all of whom he found a bit distasteful – 'I'm not bothered by their strategy, I'm bothered by their tactics.' He found Rumsfeld and the boys much too loud, too antagonistic. He was no fan of unilateralism. Yet he had nothing but contempt for France, Germany, and the United Nations, which all too often he found 'pathetically ridiculous.' Nor did he have any respect for Jean Chrétien, 'an insult to this country,' whose opposition to the war 'did this country horrendous damage because he made us look like idiots, a laughing stock.' Rather, he adopted a realist posture which assumed a world that must be ordered by the only remaining superpower. The United States had every right to wage a preventive war to protect American lives and world peace against an obvious menace. Richard had believed Saddam Hussein commanded weapons of mass destruction, and so admitted he was puzzled because the regime never employed these in combat. Equally, he thought the United States should act to bring down a despot, to liberate a people and spread the idea of democracy. 'I'm not suggesting that one should go about removing all tyrants because it's too complicated but when it's possible, by all means.' He was not surprised by the speed of the coalition victory: the Americans had 'the best army in the world' and the Iraqis had proved they were 'duds' back in 1991. He thought this massive demonstration of American power would serve to make a better world. 'The Arab Street actually respects power. And I think the Americans demonstrated very clearly who has the power.' Even though Richard had no liking for war, and who did these days, that last comment made clear how he had accepted the virtue of war as a promotional commodity.

Not so either Bob or Reza, both of whom viewed America through the lens of anti-imperialism, but in very different ways, one a champion of the West and the other of the East. Bob, admittedly pro-American, was aghast at how Bush and the hawks, 'a group of clowns,' had dishonoured the United States. He had come to disapprove of war when it became clear how phoney was their case: he was particularly angered by the 'disgraceful' address Colin Powell made to the UN in February. In fact there was no 'imminent threat,' no proof of a nuclear peril, no link to al-Qaeda, nor was Iraq of much real significance to the United States. 'As a historian, of course, you know, you are aware of what's become of lies in the past; they will come back and bite you in the ass.' But Bob's wider views were heavily influenced by the pro-war arguments of the *National Post* and, to a lesser extent, the *Globe and Mail*. These reminded him too much of Canada's own imperialist past a century ago when so many papers supported the British cause during the South African crisis: it was an 'absolutely perfect parody of the imperialist claptrap of the 1890s.' All the discredited views of that sad past resurfaced, including even the notion of 'racial solidarity,' now expressed as 'the Anglo sphere.' The Iraq War became yet another case of 'an imperial democracy overreaching itself,' and the consequences of this ghastly error would endanger the stability of the world order for years to come.

Reza found himself reliving not the Boer War but the Indian Mutiny (1857), when Britain had put down a major uprising to ensure the integrity of its empire in Asia. On the American side were 'imperialist designs' and 'strategic initiatives' justi-fied in the name of 'democracy and civilization and liberal-ism'; on the other side, the Arabic and Muslim world, 'I see despots and people resisting in the name of god, jihad, the same rhetoric exactly.' Saddam Hussein's regime was no more than an oppressive state, once an American client, now the object of a lesson to all the 'proxy governments' in the region. The war left Reza with a feeling of shame and hopelessness. 'Where has the Muslim world in general gone so wrong? You know ... the powers can just walk in and take over a country and decide which way it goes, on the one hand. On the other hand we're, you know, under the yoke of really despotic regimes. And then the third is that the option, even the anti forces,' and here he referred to bin Laden and the jihadists, 'represent such retrograde ways of seeing that, well, you're just left with the feeling that there's nothing left – what do you do now?'

Both Bob and Reza expressed admiration for Chrétien's antiwar stance – it was both right and righteous – which had kept Canada out of so sordid an adventure. Irene, by contrast, thought Chrétien 'an idiot.' Why? 'If you bite the hand that feeds you, then he's going to go home with the paycheque and we're going to be standing there holding the bag.' Canada, a dependent state, a part of the American sphere, should have backed Washington. Her opinions shed light on how facile was the division of the public into pro-war and antiwar camps. Irene called herself antiwar: 'I hate violence, but the point is, putting that aside, there was no other way out for the US.' Irene was never impressed by the antiwar movement. Yet, ironically, she accepted much of the rhetoric of that cause, the emphasis on oil, the belief that Washington had a secret agenda, the feeling that America would never leave Iraq. Washington wanted it all: it was, indeed, going for empire. Yet Irene counted herself 'a realist' who looked upon the world as a paranoid domain in which the struggle for power and money determined all affairs. She had accepted the idea that Iraq was both an imminent threat and a credible enemy: after all, 'the Americans sold' the weapons of mass destruction to Saddam Hussein when he was their client. 'They had us programed to believe – look what they did in New York City.' Washington had to deal with 'Talibans all over the world.' It had to boost the American economy. It had to teach other renegade states a lesson, and she thought Iran, North Korea, and even China were next on Washington's list. So here was a case where the antiwar propaganda had fed a person's conspiratorial frame of mind about a future dominated by perpetual warfare. Irene had rejected the vocabulary of morality to espouse a view of a world order organized according to the nasty laws of Thomas Hobbes.

III

The panel wanted news it could trust. Despite all the talk in recent years about how impossible it was to find 'truth,' consumers of journalism still desired an interpretation of reality that was complete, impartial, balanced, and objective, the traditional virtues. The words 'objective' and 'objectivity' kept cropping up in people's conversation, both as accolade and as property. I had individuals tell me about the excellence of the *Guardian* or the *Economist* or the *Financial Times* (all British publications), about the wisdom of Paul Wells of the *National Post* ('intelligent and balanced stuff') or CNN's Aaron Brown (he asked 'hard questions') or Lewis Lapham, editor of *Harper's Magazine* (a source of 'objective opinions'), about the merits of TVOntario's collection of experts ('they were detached'). The CBC, BBC, and even CTV struck a number of consumers as more trustworthy than the American networks. In general, Dennis thought the 'outsider perspective' of Canadian sources meant they gave a more balanced appraisal of what was happening.

Finding much of this sort of product, though, proved very difficult, especially in the era of real-time war. One problem was endemic to the dominion of television. 'It is now, I think, virtually impossible to distinguish whether what you are watching on television ever occurred in the real world or ever occurred in the real world in that particular combination,' mused Bruce R. 'You just don't know, you can't know.' Another problem was the constant influence of propaganda. Irene would only count 10 per cent of what was said or shown as credible. A third problem was war itself, where traditionally the real story was hidden from view. 'Once the shooting starts you sort of have to wait until its over to find out what happened,' remarked Mike. Thus, it should not surprise that the panel was upset with the performance of the news media.

Consumers objected to the style and the character of reporting, most especially on television. True, the real-time war did bring lots of 'interesting things ... you don't get anywhere else,' mused Mike: he mentioned how all the statues and portraits of Saddam Hussein were 'a kind of visual proof' of the dictator's megalomania. Even so, the complaints were endless. TV news was always 'shallow': only 'limited footage,' played over and over again, 'often pretty stupid and pointless conversations with people,' so 'hugely repetitive and boring.' According to Chris, the questions reporters asked at briefings were not 'pressing,' they were all too kind, perhaps because they were afraid of being banned from future briefings. Correspondents never provided an effective coverage of the military operations, neither the overall strategy nor the details. Even CBC Radio had indulged in a bout of 'just total cheerleading for the Americans' (Geoff) when Hussein's statue fell in a Baghdad square on 9 April.

Nor was the panel much impressed with the practice of embedding journalists, especially when those correspondents seemed so enamoured of their own virtues. Stephanie found one such embed 'fairly amusing': there he was, dressed up in his battle garb, rushing around, sounding self-important, but actually saying very little about what was happening. 'The reporter ... was so high on the moment,' recalled Dennis of another such incident: '"This is the first time we've ever seen this, people, you have to realize this, this is cutting edge, we're breaking ground here, no one has ever seen a war happen as it happens like this, real live time." It was a live picture. And I thought to myself, who cares, we don't want it.' A critic of the invasion thought these correspondents were little more than puppets of Washington: 'They were soldiers,' said Jennifer. A champion of the coalition found they were too negative: 'They practically rejoiced when they thought the Americans met with a failure,' argued Richard. No one believed they provided much understanding of the broader picture of the war.

The panel was no more pleased by the array of experts and generals who were supposed to analyse the war for the viewing public (see figure 5.2). People might make exceptions, expressing a liking, or a particular dislike, for one or another talking head. Among the Canadians, Janice Stein, the director of the Munk Institute for International Studies at the University of Toronto, came in for kudos and brickbats from a number of individuals. She clearly had established her celebrity status, in fact long before the invasion. Two individuals found appalling the way the hawks had dumped upon the retired generals in the United States who had dared to criticize the war plan. Another thought these generals were just pushing a personal agenda: 'Sometimes it was quite pathetic to watch these people' (Richard). Still, the panel was agreed on its overall dismissal of the merits of this type of TV personality. 'I got very tired of them, to be frank' (Sam). 'We turned them off' (Bruce W). 'First of all a waste of time' (Oscar). 'It was just straight up propaganda' (Dave). 'I definitely blocked them out because they were total rubbish' (Geoff). The trouble was that the experts did not offer the kind of insights into military operations, the Iraqi situation, and above all the big picture that the panel was looking for. Here the character of the panel

Figure 5.2 The pundits (Gary Clement, Cartoonists & Writers Syndicate / cartoonweb.com)

Military analysts, one-time generals and colonels, foreign-policy scholars and the like, pundits the *National Post* called 'the talking warheads' (27 March), all were a staple on television networks in North America during the war. Their task was to fill the gaps, that is, to explain what was happening as well as to occupy airtime when the news itself was less than exciting. Some of the most celebrated in Canada were Major-General Lewis MacKenzie (CTV), the journalist Gwynne Dyer (CBC), and the academic Janice Stein (CBC and TVOntario). In the United States the ex-generals Barry McCaffrey (NBC) and Wesley Clark (CNN) earned notoriety for criticizing the war plan because the troop strengths seemed inadequate to the task of crushing the Iraqi military. That brought down a truckload of abuse on their heads. It was ironic that the strongest attack on the Pentagon should come not from the Democrats in Congress but from a few pundits on television.

played a role: all were opinionated consumers of public affairs who looked askance at the credentials of these analysts. 'How are they experts?' asked Chris.

Time and again these consumers commented on the most glaring absence in all the coverage of the real-time war: what was really happening in Iraq. 'I don't have any concept of what the casualties were,' said Stephanie, 'of what Iraq looks like right now, of the situation of women and children, of the people who are in poor health – I don't know any of those things, so I don't think I know very much about the war.' The trouble was that the journalists, excepting a few stationed in Baghdad, were concentrated with the coalition forces. 'The real on-the-ground reporting was not coming from the Western press,' noted Reza, who had watched the Arab media. 'While on CNN you'd be watching tanks firing into the outskirts of Karbala, on Jazeera you'd be watching them [the shells] coming down.' Consumers heard a lot about American casualties and coalition victories. They heard about the surrender of Iraqi troops. They saw some pictures of happy Iraqis, some of disgruntled or angry Iraqis. Occasionally, recalled Chris, you would hear on the CBC or BBC about overflowing hospitals in the embattled cities of Iraq. But they did not know the number of civilian deaths, a crucial statistic because it was the measure of the truth of the Pentagon's claim it was waging a clean war. 'One of the things that bothered me most ... [were] the daily tallies of Americans captured or killed,' said Sam, but 'never the daily death rates of civilians or Iraqis killed ... [which] kept any sense of impact of what this really was doing to the people there, in Iraq, from those of us in the West watching.' When I asked how many civilians had died, the answers ranged from a few thousand to thirty thousand, depending in part upon the attitude the person had toward the invasion. Much later, the results of a study published in the *Guardian* (29 October) estimated a total of between 3200 and 4300 civilian deaths.

The most vociferous complaints, not surprisingly, were directed against the American television networks, and in particular CNN, deemed the voice of America. 'I couldn't trust what I was hearing from the American sources to be true,' lamented Melissa. CNN had 'just picked up all of the Pentagon's terminology,' thought Geoff. 'Like when you talk about "degrading" the forces around Iraq, which is not called "mass murder" when we do it.' Reza recalled a battle in which there were four American casualties, and perhaps four or five hundred Iraqis slain: the reporter, apparently, was both happy and amazed, excited by the accuracy of American fire-power, the dead Iraqis a matter of little moment except to demonstrate American superiority. The military types on TV were just a joke, 'preaching the Pentagon line' (Michael). The antiwar cause disappeared from the picture, so I was told. It seemed to most consumers that US television largely served as the vehicle for American propaganda. 'The problem with the media this time was that it was hard to take anything the Americans said seriously because they were embedded in the military, and that bothered me so much,' recalled Jennifer. 'You know ... they weren't being objective, the whole point of journalism is to be objective, and they couldn't be, how could they be when they were with these other soldiers day and night?'

But even Richard was not pleased. 'I think all the media with the exception of the *Economist* had a peculiarly anti-American touch.' That epithet he applied to US networks like ABC because they always searched for what was going wrong. In fact, newsrooms did play up stories of friendly fire, evidence of setbacks or foul-ups, the worries or disenchantment of ordinary soldiers, the anger of Iraqis, apparent failures like the early efforts to distribute humanitarian aid, all of which cast doubt on the wisdom of the war plan. Why, he was not sure: 'Whether they thrive on failure ... it's easier to dramatize than success.' The news had always had a taste for upset and sensation because that produced the kind of drama that attracted attention – and, in this case, clashed with the marketing strategy of the Pentagon.

The point is that no one on the panel, whatever their position, admired the practices of American television news, an ironic counter to the self-praise the embedded journalists indulged in after the conclusion of hostilities. 'We know little, very little actually of what is really going on,' asserted Irene. 'We'd probably lose our hair if we knew the rest of it.' All but one of the panellists concluded there was a missing, indeed a hidden, story despite the welter of opinion and news. Michael admitted to 'a low level angst' about 'things I wasn't being told,' no matter where he looked for the information. That story might be the whole issue of Iraqi casualties. Perhaps it was the 'screw-ups that we didn't hear of as well, in terms of friendly fire.' Could it be the true effectiveness of American weaponry? Or was it the real motive behind the war, oil, Washington's secret agenda ... whatever. 'America is so powerful they managed to keep amazing things hidden,' commented Glenna. War journalism was deemed something of a failure, a much-hyped commodity that did not satisfy: the media, again especially television, had not supplied the kinds of news and insights that people thought they needed to understand the war. Above all, it was not complete. Unintentionally, perhaps, the meaning of that overused phrase, the fog of war, was brought home to the consumers. 'I thought the sort of macro coverage of the war, and this would apply to virtually everybody, was dreadful,' argued Bob. Instead, what we got was 'Buck Rogers goes to Iraq.'

IV

And that was the point of the whole phenomenon: real-time war was as much a kind of pop culture as it was an exercise in journalism. The Iraq conflict had the appearance of a war made in Hollywood. The translation of war into a form of infotainment was the great novelty, although in some measure it had been presaged by the coverage of the first Gulf War a decade before. Talking about Iraq the movie proved more difficult than evaluating the issues of propaganda or journalism, because war is not supposed to be a category of entertainment. No one claimed the real-time war was enjoyable – repugnant or depressing, yes. Only Glenna admitted that she 'found it kind of exciting.' Some individuals resisted the idea of treating war as spectacle and story. Mike insisted he interpreted the event in terms of past wars, not in terms of movies and the like. Irene found this topic a bit sick: war was a serious business. But even these doubters perceived there was a dimension of the real-time war that the context of journalism could not capture.

The panel realized that television had crafted the coverage to ensure the audience was engaged in familiar ways. 'The media ensures that all those elements are there now,' claimed Savino, the cynic on the panel. 'Normally the elements that you're talking about in a story, they're there, the adventure, the spectacle, they're there, they occur naturally. Here they either occur naturally or we will ensure that it occurs.' Underlying Savino's comment was the presumption that this action on the part of the newsrooms was wrong, though not surprising given the moral freight attached to the discussion of war. Yet these consumers consistently used the repertoire of popular entertainment, and did so often without any prompting, in order to understand or to express the meanings of the war they had only experienced at home. They acted out a double role, as critics and as fans, shifting from what stories they thought television was telling to how they felt about these performances, although none would have relished being called a fan of war. 'This war is like watching a movie,' said Irene. 'It's a soap opera.' Others made comparisons to sports coverage, to westerns and war movies, or to video games. (Missing from this list was one genre that caught the fancy of journalists, namely reality TV, perhaps because most panellists disdained such sensational shows.) Their accounts of what they saw were peppered with specific references, usually to recent movies: *Wag the Dog*, the forthcoming *Terminator 3*, *Three Kings*, *Star Wars*, *Star Trek*, *Blade Runner*, *Saving Private Ryan*, *Independence Day*, *Bowling for Columbine*, *Dr Strangelove*, *Lawrence of Arabia*, even Charlie Chaplin's *The Great Dictator*. The varied list of titles illustrated how Iraq the movie was actually a series of stories, some tragic, some comic, some triumphant, appealing to a range of tastes.

1. Tragedy: Calling war a tragedy nowadays is trite. It is so easy a comment. Everyone could accept that judgment. Even asking the question of how war was a tragedy seemed redundant. Look at the dead bodies, the hurt children, the looted cities. The incessant bombing of a capital that had few defences was both obscene and outrageous. 'The whole thing of overwhelming a civilization in that way, I felt very ashamed that a western, civilized nation would believe that crushing any nation, bad or good, in that way' was a necessity, said Bruce W. Consider what had happened to the United States this also from an antiwar perspective – where a republic of virtue had been captured, in Bob's words, by a group of people 'overcome with ambition.' Think of the discovery of the mass graves of Saddam Hussein's victims – this from a pro-war perspective. One person showed me a newspaper picture she saved of a dead child, only its tiny feet showing from underneath a piece of tarpaulin. 'Nothing, nothing justified that,' Glenna said, almost weeping. 'I think of our grandchildren's little feet ....' Irene had dreamed a scene of a crying woman looking out a window as the bombs fell, her version of the nightmare of attack. 'That's the absolute framework within which you view all of it,' Mike told me, as 'a huge tragedy, a vast tragedy.' (See figure 5.3.)

But that was not how the war played out on television screens in North America. Consumers were aware that there was a different product, the dirty war, available on Arab television, although only Reza was able to sample this vision of tragedy. Michael: 'I'm told that the Arab media had a kind of obsession with the grizzly civilian stuff that could be seen to be obscene, but you understand in a sense why they're doing it and our media didn't.' Sam: In North America 'there was either a resignation or an actual affirmation that this needed to be done, that there was no other alternative.' Real-

Figure 5.3 Looting (Roy Peterson, Cartoonists & Writers Syndicate / cartoonweb.com)

One post-war tragedy was the explosion of looting that raged through the cities of Iraq after the regime collapsed. What most disturbed observers was the systematic pillaging of the country's museums, some of which seemed the work of professional criminals intent on getting hold of the nation's treasures. The Americans, at first, seemed almost nonchalant about the disaster: 'Stuff happens,' Rumsfeld said. Peterson's cartoon expressed that old notion of the American as barbarian that had done service in Europe throughout the twentieth century. Here was the young soldier, uncouth, unconcerned, all dressed up in his gear, the image of the action hero, looking down on the sophisticated older man, the representative of an ancient civilization, cleaning up its remains.

time war was sanitized, cleansed, the dead bodies and the devastation kept at the margins of the story. How difficult, how necessary it was to remember this as tragedy 'when you're seeing these people sort of getting gung-ho about technology and what it achieves' (Mike). Watching hour after hour of bombs falling and mushroom clouds – 'you're not really thinking of the people' (Reza). Some panellists felt guilty about that. Others were deeply suspicious. 'That's it with war, if you just think of it as an exciting game, with machines, it's one thing,' said Glenna, 'but if you let yourself think about the people, as individuals, then it's a whole different thing, and I think the whole program is to keep you from thinking about that.'

2. Adventure: The media had resurrected the old nineteenth-century notion that war was, at bottom, an adventure. 'A lot of the coverage, print and TV, radio, [was] constructed around adventure,' said Bob, 'or things that are components of adventure, peril, personal peril, danger ..., the idea of daring do ...' The panel found the signs of this narrative everywhere. The very notion of sending 'these armadas and flotillas and whatever it is we call them these days going so far away and across the seas and landing,' argued Bruce R, 'I think that's the biggest adventure.' The build-up of forces in Kuwait, before the war, the way the troops 'would sort of hang around in the desert and do war games and stuff,' claimed Geoff, 'that was presented like a preview to the *grande* adventure.' The embedded reporters seemed to be caught up in their own adventure of journalism, reliving the experience of the famed war correspondents of times past – 'their heart-pounding renditions of what's going on in front of their eyes: look at that blow-up, look at them shooting over there ...' (Reza). One panellist made a specific reference to a journalist (perhaps David Bloom's report?) atop a tank: 'Very exciting, just like a Hollywood movie' (Geoff). There were all the stories of the special forces who performed 'the most dramatic deeds,' particularly their rescue of Jessica Lynch: 'It looked awfully

good' (Richard). The ordinary soldier was mythologized: people like us, or our children, but heroes now facing imminent peril. 'Adventure meets the media's fascination with the common man: the legacy of Ernie Pyle,' decided Bob, who personally found that it 'became incredibly trite within the first half-hour.' But then this was not intended to appeal to the professorial mind. A bit more acerbic was Geoff's comment, drawing on the extraordinary popularity of Hollywood's style of action/adventure over the past thirty years: 'This is appealing to what I'll call the Joe Lunchbox type, the type of men primarily who are into video games, war games, shooting, all those stupid Bruce Willis movies, all that kind of stuff.'

3. SciFi: This real-time war took on the guise of science fiction, a particular type of adventure film. There was the requisite monster, Saddam Hussein, purportedly armed with hideous weapons he might soon launch against the coalition forces – 'the great unseen, unknown peril that lurks on the other side of the sand dune,' as Bob put it. The 'green flashing lights and all that wonderful stuff,' asserted Bruce R, gave some of the coverage 'that aura of a "Blade Runner" kind of thing.' More consumers marvelled at all the amazing weapons, the huge tanks, the precision munitions, the extraordinary warplanes, that the Americans had at their disposal. The images of these machines of war lingered on in the mind. 'Unbelievable' was a word often repeated. Those hulking tanks, so strong that Iraqi rockets just bounced off them, could smash through any defence. The MOAB, sometimes called 'the mother of all bombs,' a conventional weapon packing an enormous load of firepower, was talked about a lot but never used. The smart bombs and missiles 'are all linked with satellites and with ground computers ... I mean it is Star Wars, no question about it, this push-button warfare,' said Richard. 'It's quite unbelievable.' All the weaponry raining down on Baghdad reminded another person of the second Star Wars movie in which the Empire sent its drones down to patrol a hapless planet. Then there were the instruments of real-time war, the

videophones, minicameras, satellite phones, and portable computers. 'I was probably most impressed with the broadcast technology,' recalled Bruce R: 'the real-time-ness of the whole thing, and the lovely pictures, the things you can't normally get pictures of.' All that was necessary now was to put a minicam on the helmet of a soldier. 'This is the war of the future,' mused Reza, 'how it will be covered and how it will be fought.'

4. Action: What struck these consumers, however, was how little action the adventure had produced. Perhaps that was because the American weaponry was so formidable. Mike, in particular, was struck by the American determination to fight a clean war that minimized civilian casualties. Just as impor tant, the Iraqi armed forces proved so feeble, thus giving the lie to the claim of a credible enemy. People did witness scenes of battle, other than the bombings, and these could be engag ing: one struggle to control a bridge south of Baghdad was mentioned a number of times. But such scenes were rare. Hence the common refrain that this was a war without much combat. Richard: 'There was absolutely no fighting worthy of the name.' Bruce R: 'I guess my big surprise was that all this yakking about firepower and shock and awe and stuff, let's go in and blast them, the one thing that struck me several times was how little actual hitting and damages' there was. The most succinct judgment on Iraq the movie came from Irene: 'It was a dud.' Such complaints gave rise to a sneaking fantasy about any future war in which America might face a worthwhile enemy, similarly armed to the teeth, and able to wage a real battle.

5. Human Interest: According to the panel, the networks filled a lot of time playing up the human side of the war, out of which came the impression they treated war as a social drama, full of anxiety, heartache, and happiness. Reporters interviewed soldiers or their family back home to convey how people felt about the sacrifices of these young men and women. There

was the explosion of happiness over the freeing of Jessica Lynch, which in itself appeared staged to raise morale after the American advance had stalled. There were the reports of coalition forces helping injured Iraqis or giving goodies to children or distributing aid, as if the invaders were humanitarian agents. Reporters always seemed on the lookout for the signs that, yes, the Iraqis were eagerly awaiting liberation. 'There were a couple of shots – I don't remember at what point of the war – of villagers, people, I don't know where they were, but coming out of their houses, either with hands outstretched or hands up,' said Bruce R. 'There was that flash every once in a while of people coming out, usually to convince us how welcome we were, but occasionally to do a little heart string tugging about how brutal life had been.'

Most consumers were not especially pleased with this kind of story. 'I don't find there is a lot of human interest in war ...,' and Mike specifically said he had not liked the handling of the Jessica Lynch rescue. Irene got 'sick and tired' of the Lynch story. Why? 'Because they sensationalize it to death. One person and they make it sound like God died.' The passion for the human-interest story, claimed Bob, was 'one of the worst things about public affairs coverage in the modern age. Human interest indeed, it's creature on the street stuff. And it's crude, and it's mishandled.' More blunt was this complaint by Geoff: 'Human interest was the extended interviews with the families of these POWs. Like I give a shit.' The emoting, or at least the invitation to get sentimental, was a silly diversion that masked the horrors going on in Iraq.

6. Mystery: Stories need ongoing puzzles and enigmas to feed the speculation machine and to hold the interest of audiences. The Iraq War had plenty, some big and some small, which were constantly reproduced by newspeople. Reza told the story of his wife, working then for CTV, who interviewed an Iraqi doctor working in a hospital. She was required to ask him where Saddam Hussein was. He yelled at her, 'Who the fuck cares? We're dying over here.'

In fact, audiences did care. The technique worked. Just about everyone on the panel found one or another of the puzzles intriguing, though they also thought some of the mystery was contrived. Did the regime have weapons of mass destruction and, if so, when would it use them? Richard wondered why Saddam Hussein had not used his terror weapons: 'It is a tremendous puzzle to me.' Would the invasion cause an Arab backlash and release a wave of terrorism in the West? Both Glenna and Bruce W expected there would be 'a lot more terrorism in the United States.' How long would the Iraqi forces, especially the Republican Guard, hold out? 'Everybody talked about [how] Baghdad was going to be really hard to take ... That's where all the hardliners were who had nothing to lose,' Chris noted. Would there be a Baghdad Hell, another Stalingrad? 'The motif of Stalingrad came up many times,' remembered Dave. 'I was waiting for the last stand, that they were going to have all these weapons, as if it were a movie, ready to go, and they were going to hold them off for a little longer,' recalled Savino. Where was Saddam Hussein – was he dead, was he in hiding, how had he escaped? 'Everybody still wants to know,' claimed Jennifer. 'Is he with Osama?'

7. Comedy: Stories need moments of comic relief, characters who can break the tension, which furnish the necessary contrast to the intensity of the struggle or the actions of the hero. Newsrooms managed to manufacture only a few ongoing comic subjects, notably the behaviour and the sayings of the Iraqi minister for information, Mohammed Saeed al-Sahaf, otherwise widely known in the Western media as 'Baghdad Bob' or 'Comical Ali.' Al-Sahaf had soon become notorious because he made outlandish claims about Iraqi resistance and American failure, even as events proved the opposite. He was something of an Internet favourite: websites collected his ludicrous claims and published cartoons mocking his style. In addition, my consumers detected specific instances where the media treatment of a person or an event was intentionally

funny. So Stephanie recalled how the CBC treated the Iraqis who celebrated the dictator's downfall by whacking his statues and portraits with their shoes. 'They totally made it into a joke ... These weird foreign people doing crazy foreign things – ha, ha.'

The panel had more difficulty admitting it enjoyed any of the planned humour because of the prevailing belief that war must be a tragedy. 'That's in bad taste' (Irene). 'I was without a sense of humour' (Reza). 'Oh no, I saw nothing comic about it at all' (Michael). It seemed almost immoral to laugh. Even so, the very same people might also admit that the antics of Comical Ali had supplied a small dose of humour. So Mike concluded there was nothing comic about the affair, 'Except [and he laughed] for that Iraqi propaganda minister who became, obviously, like the knight in the Monty Python skit who continues to fight on when he's lost all his limbs.' Richard 'loved' Comical Ali. He still found funny the claim the man made that there were no Americans in sight when in fact 'they were 200 yards away,' this at the time the tanks were entering Baghdad. 'I tell you that many American producers would love to give him a job.' 'It was hilarious.' 'I think also that it was very typical of the regime.' Throughout 'they were the most unbelievable liars.' 'They put Goebbels to shame.'

8. Farce: The panel was much readier to admit how they had made their own moments of fun out of the story. This amounted to a subversive act, a conscious misreading of what television might show or Washington might say, demonstrating a spirit of resistance, an ability to see through all the propaganda. 'Very occasionally the Americans seemed farcical in their reaching to try to make their case,' said Mike. 'You could see where they were trying to defend difficult positions.' George Bush was the butt of much humour because of what he said and how he said it. Oscar recalled receiving and sending many e-mails that rendered Bush a clown. Other leading figures, Ari Fleischer and even Donald Rumsfeld, were also mocked. 'It is kind of slapstick,' Bob thought. 'You

know, Rumsfeld should have come out with big feet and a red nose.' The failure to find the 'smoking gun,' the weapons of mass destruction, struck some in the antiwar camp as a source of mirth. 'People who were mouthing that phrase looked like they were about to break out laughing,' said Bruce W. 'It was like, in previous times, "the Evil Empire."' Indeed, there was a sense in which the whole war was something of a farce. 'If it hadn't been built up by media and by the necessities I suppose of international politics, it was really a relatively minor conflict, bluntly, with a whole lot of a whole lot being thrown at a whole little of a whole little, and made to seem like this glorious adventure,' argued Bruce R. 'It just wasn't.' I suspect that final judgment on Iraq the movie expressed the sentiments of many on the panel, whatever their views on the war as an event.

V

In a way these 'consumer voices' were practising democracy à la Habermas. Many years ago, at the beginning of what would be an extraordinarily distinguished career as a philosopher, Jürgen Habermas published a deeply pessimistic tome where he charted the rise and fall of a liberal democracy grounded in networks of political discourse. Much later, after its translation into English in 1989 as *The Structural Transformation of the Public Sphere*, the work proved newly influential in North America because of the revived interest in the nature of civil society born, in part, out of the liberation of Eastern Europe, an event that had lifted some of Habermas's gloom about the fate of democracy. The key to his democracy was the quality of debate and dialogue, what he called 'rational-critical' discussion, about matters of common interest among the public. That, in turn, depended upon the prevalence of many different virtues: the autonomy of the citizens, access to information, a commitment to rationality, a willingness to participate, an exchange of views, the ability to exercise some influence on the actions of the state. Publicity – political news and partisan rhetoric – had once helped fashion the necessary public sphere where citizens might debate at will; but publicity in modern times, really propaganda, had become an instrument that authority used to organize public opinion.

The people I interviewed were voracious consumers of the news media. I did know one person who never watched television; indeed, she did not bother to read much about a war she found abhorrent. She had opted out. A few members of the citizens' panel certainly limited their consumption of the real-time war, plugging into TV mostly for the nightly newscasts. Nearly all sought to find alternatives to CNN and live coverage, whether other TV stations or newspapers and magazines or the Internet. In effect, they had fashioned their own sets of defence mechanisms against the onslaught of propaganda and infotainment. Such people were neither 'dopes' nor 'dupes' of all the marketing. They acted more as free agents, playing a game with the product's sponsors to discover their own truths and their own pleasures. The impact of the war marketing was always mediated by their views, their prejudices, their tastes, the ways they navigated through the torrent of images and sounds. The particular experiences of these consumers ought not to be treated as typical. Nothing is. Recall the importance of location. One crucial difference between these consumers and, say, a similar American group was how patriotism operated to draw Canadians toward the antiwar position. Besides, no equivalent to 9/11 had yet struck a city in Canada. Still, the ways the individuals extracted meaning from the welter of infotainment and propaganda showed the very kind of competence essential to a democracy.

The trouble came at the next stage: how people might act on their knowledge. There was no channel to communicate with any of the governors who counted. The war experience accentuated Mike's wish, still occasional he admitted, that he could just phone up 'his' senator or congressman to express an opinion, rather than be sidelined in an irrelevant country. That was an extreme view. Nonetheless, other consumers expressed a similar kind of frustration, much of this focussed on the incapacity of the UN to work as an effective world parliament – 'pathetic,' 'dysfunctional,' 'totally ineffectual,' 'the biggest casualty.' In short, the hollowness of present-day democracy resulted from an institutional failure, the fact that citizens, no matter how well informed, how thoughtful, were unable to affect the course of global policy, even when they flooded into the streets. Put another way, the people who had betrayed democracy – the very politicians who sought to manufacture public opinion – belonged more to the elites than to the public.

SIX

Perceptions of War

The real-time war was a global phenomenon. It had the same sort of appeal to people in London or Tokyo as it did for any of the individuals I interviewed in Toronto. 'It's just like a Western,' said Aras, a 20-year-old student in Tehran (Reuters, 27 March). 'I sit in front of the television with my bowl of popcorn and watch the movie of the war.' It had the capacity to provoke both intense interest and intense emotions. 'It's just so horrifying,' said Ingeborg Boenigk, a teacher in Berlin (*Washington Post*, 2 April): 'When you see a body suffering, you feel for that person. I feel it even for the American soldiers, being away from their families.' And, eventually, it turned some people off, exhausted them, so they sought pleasure, relief, doing or watching something else (see figure 6.1). 'I got bored,' said Hassan Abdo, a tailor in Cairo, and he gestured toward a TV set in his shop now showing Arabic music videos (Reuters, 4 April). In the first days of the conflict, he had watched nothing but the war. 'I got sick of the same gory pictures and the same depressing news. The only news I want to hear now is that this war is over.'

The significance of the Iraq War was not the same in every place, however. People interpreted the war in different ways, in some measure because local television and print produced particular sets of images and rhetoric geared to suit the presumed interests of their nations and their audiences. It was

Figure 6.1 The exhausted viewer (© 2003 Tribune Media Services, Inc. Reprinted with permission.)

yet another demonstration of how the term the 'global village' masked the persistence of locality: the so-called global product could have very disparate meanings depending on where it was consumed. Apparently some large portion of the Japanese public saw the Iraq War through the prism of the Second World War. 'Military power is still feared here as a dark drug that poisoned the nation's mind and led to disaster in the last century,' claimed the *Washington Post* (7 April); 'Japan views its lure for other nations with the alarm of a recovered addict.' In Latin America, the *New York Times* (20 April) reported, the American triumph had set off 'a burst of anti-Americanism more intense than any in recent years,' stirring memories of past interventions in the affairs of supposedly sovereign lands. What follows looks closely at how the meanings of the war evolved in Canada, the United States, and the Middle East. I will pay special attention to the views expressed by ordinary folk, as represented in polls and the media.

I

In Canada the CBC made a conscious effort to cast Iraq as 'not our war': it provided extensive coverage of what was happening, using its own correspondents, a range of analysts, and TV feeds from a variety of sources, to build a Canadian perspective on the war. Speaking on the radio program 'Dispatches' (13 August), one reporter in the war zone explained how that approach affected her conduct:

> You do try hard not to do what the Americans are doing because watching coverage from afar it was their war. You know, anybody who watched Fox News and saw Oliver North come in as a reporter, you know, they were so jingoistic ... you knew you were doing something completely different from that. But because Canada didn't have an agenda you felt at least a little more loose to cover things that might not have been, the tone might not have been set by the US administration ... But at the end of the day, you know, did we all go out and do the hospital story, yes, did we all go out and do the education story, yes ...

That proved a difficult strategy to sell. There were citizens who believed Iraq should have been 'our war' as well as others who thought Iraq was very definitely the 'wrong war.' A wealth of e-mails sent to the CBC and posted on its website revealed its troubles. Right away the CBC got attacked for dropping its regular radio and television schedules to feature wall-to-wall coverage of the war. Why so much war, why show live the horrors of bombing, 'yet another media circus glorifying violence,' when Canada was not directly involved in the conflict? The pro-war side weighed in with complaints that the CBC analysis was anti-American, its journalists and analysts never missing an opportunity to condemn the coalition campaign. One writer, for example, expressed his disgust over the fact the CBC had aired the Iraqi video of the captured American POWs, when other networks – presumably meaning the American networks – had not done so: how 'distasteful and un-Canadian.'

Before very long, however, the war itself took on a new significance. Prime Minister Chrétien had declared just before the invasion that Canada could not participate in a war which lacked the sanction of the United Nations, a stand that according to the polls was endorsed by roughly two-thirds of the electorate. At the same time, he was careful neither to condemn the actions of Canada's traditional allies, the United States and Great Britain, nor to compromise Canada's existing military involvement in the war against terrorism. Officially the country seemed both neutral and friendly, on the sidelines yet hoping for a coalition victory. This in-between position struck many citizens, even in the antiwar camp, as just too complicated and indecisive to satisfy, and was one reason Chrétien received a large dose of criticism from the citizens' panel.

On 25 March Paul Celluci, the American ambassador, spoke to the Economic Club in Toronto. Toward the end of a relatively mild address about how happy Canadian–American relations were, he dropped this bomb: 'There is no security threat to Canada that the United States would not be ready, willing and able to help with. There would be no debate. There would be no hesitation. We would be there for Canada, part of our family. That is why so many in the United States are disappointed and upset that Canada is not fully supporting us now.' He had identified Canada as a 'free rider,' benefiting from the war on terror but refusing to share the burden of battle. Just a few sentences expressing dissent, but a kind of 'shock and awe' assault in its own right: the Canadian media publicized these words of hurt everywhere, taking them as sent directly from the White House.

The intervention coincided with, indeed fuelled, a growing anxiety over what might be the impact of the Americans' upset on the Canadian economy, an anxiety particularly evident in business circles. It also fed a deep sense of betrayal among some Canadians, furious that their country had rejected its traditional allies. Stephen Harper, leader of the Canadian Alliance, the country's official opposition, was already on record demanding a change in the country's foreign policy.

Two provincial premiers, Ernie Eves of Ontario and Ralph Klein of Alberta, announced their horror at Canada's stand and their support for Washington. Ordinary people started mobilizing friends-of-America rallies to push Ottawa to join the Iraq War.

Even before Cellucci's bomb, the e-mails to the CBC had reflected the split that had emerged between the antiwar and pro-war camps. What happened was the repositioning of the war issue so that it became a question that touched the core of the Canadian experience. The underlying concern was a fear that the United States might retaliate against Canada in ways that would damage the economic health of the country. Both sides talked in the language of morality, about rights and wrongs, duties and obligations. The antiwar champions had their own brand of nationalism, drawing upon a long-standing tradition of anti-Americanism to depict the United States as ogre and Canada as victim. Bush became the warmonger, a threat to world peace. These folk were proud that Ottawa had taken an independent stand in opposition to an unjust invasion. The friends of America expressed their feelings of embarrassment and shame over the stand of the Chrétien government, a bunch of wimps and cowards who harboured anti-American sentiments, a view supported by various casual comments that cabinet ministers had made in the weeks before the invasion. The pro-war rhetoric reflected the success of Washington's marketing campaign: writers looked upon Saddam Hussein as both evil and dangerous, yet another Hitler whose aggression menaced the world, just as in 1939, and they saw America and Britain embarking on a just war to free Iraq of his brutal tyranny.

On 28 March CBC Radio in Ottawa carried an interview with Debbie Jodoin, 'one dedicated yankophile,' who was organizing a friends-of-America rally in the city. Her's represented, as she put it, 'another voice in Canada.' That voice was a bit harsh, certainly earnest, not especially cultivated, a kind of voice not often heard on the airwaves of the country. Yet she too spoke in the lingo of marketing. She underplayed the possible size of the rally; she would be satisfied with 500 people, but it could be 5000 or, who knew, maybe over 100,000, all to register support. The problem was that the price of compliance was high: going to a meeting on Parliament Hill – but that price was necessary to compete with the previous successes of the antiwar movement. She repeated what were already shibboleths of the cause: a war of liberation, stand with our allies, American retaliation. Canada was 'a laughing stock of the world.' But what made the interview intriguing was the animosity Jodoin expressed toward the masters of the country. She spoke for 'the silent majority' whose opinions had not been considered by the Liberal government. All kinds of people were 'coming forward.' This was a movement to restore democracy to the country. She was no more than an instrument of the public, 'the people had empowered themselves.' She even lashed out at the polls, which at that point still showed an antiwar majority: 'I don't believe in the polls,' 'I have never been polled in my life' – leaving the impression that the polls were fixed, manipulated, and certainly no expression of the popular will. Her comments embodied the anguish of a bloc of citizens for whom the decision to stay out signified their exclusion from the political system. She had re-marketed the war issue in the language of populist revolt.

The anxieties and the shame had an impact on public opinion. So too did the real-time war, the images of American might viewers absorbed from the US networks as well as via their own channels. An Ipsos-Reid poll released on 6 April revealed a dramatic shift in favour of the war in English-speaking Canada. There, bare majorities supported the war and favoured Canada joining in on the coalition side. In Quebec, by contrast, less than a third supported the war, suggesting that the long-standing French-Canadian animosity to involvement in foreign wars, especially one sponsored by the so-called 'Anglo sphere,' was alive and well. The issue of war had the potential to cause one of those severe national crises between French and English which occasionally but dramatically shattered the calm normal in Canadian politics. The swift end of hostilities a few days later aborted that possibility, leaving Canadians to wonder what if any consequences the noncompliance of Ottawa might have on Canada–US relations. As to the war, a further Ipsos-Reid poll released at the end of May showed that 45 per cent of those surveyed now justified the American action in Iraq (49 per cent did not), a number significantly larger than in the European countries whose governments had also opposed the war. In short, the experience of war in English Canada had promoted Washington's vision of the war.

II

The American population went to war in the shadow of past disasters as well as triumphs, disasters such as Vietnam thirty years before and Somalia a mere ten years earlier. One of the great concerns, and a matter of much discussion in the higher circles of the government, was the willingness of the American population to accept casualties, particularly the deaths of their own troops but also the loss of life among civilians. There were studies suggesting the populace was much less casualty-averse, to use the military jargon, than leaders thought, a tolerance that the experience of 9/11 might well have increased. Washington's propaganda, however, had emphasized not so much the potential sacrifice as the prospects of a speedy and clean war, a war with minimal American and civilian casualties, indeed a war of liberation in which the Iraqis themselves would stop fighting and welcome the coalition forces. The evidence of Iraqi resistance, the anger of Iraqi civilians, the showing of American casualties and POWs, these signs questioned the expectations cultivated by pre-war propaganda.

During the first two weeks of war, just before the success of the American blitzkrieg, CBC Radio ran a remarkable series of radio documentaries which explored the views of ordinary Americans in a number of towns and cities along the border between the United States and Canada. One purpose was to discover just how upset Americans were with their northern cousins – the answer was not very. But more interesting were the efforts to probe the American public's response to the realities of war. 'I think we're doing the right thing. I wish it had got over in five days but ... that's not going to happen.' 'Day to day I sit and watch it [war] and it just seems like it's the same thing over and over, like we aren't moving as fast as we should.' 'I thought they would just roll over Iraq. I think in the end we will definitely be victorious but, um, you know, I'm sure we'll lose, um, a little more people than I'd expected.' However disappointed these people might be, they had remained committed to the war. Indeed, there was a rallying effect, a desire to support the troops now that combat had begun, and that influenced antiwar protesters as well. 'I wasn't for it, but now that we're in there, we got to do it. Not much we can do about it.' 'All the soldiers are over there now, ... we need to support 'em, we don't need another Vietnam. When they come home, we need to let 'em know they did their best.' People in Calais, Maine, were putting one white light in their windows that would not be removed until the troops came home. A schoolteacher was making yellow ribbons. If you could believe the documentaries, the American populace was coming together behind its armed forces.

In fact, a wide variety of poll results bore out this conclusion. A tracking poll released by Pew Research on 10 April showed how much the opinions on the course of the war had bounced up and down. The vast majority of respondents were prepared to say the war was 'going well' when the shock and awe campaign struck Baghdad. But a few setbacks (some casualties, the capture of American soldiers, the resistance of Iraqi fedayeen), not to mention the absence of happy Iraqis, all of this emphasized by war coverage, brought the totals down to roughly 30 per cent by the end of March. That is when the public began to fear the war might go on and on. Spirits improved in early April, especially after the rescue of Private Lynch on the evening of 1 April, which seemed to demonstrate the fortitude and skill of America's fighting men and women. That effect wore off after a couple of days. Then American tanks entered Baghdad and any fears were soon dispelled by the lack of significant opposition from the Republican Guard. The yo-yo effect showed first how unrealistic were public expectations of a quick and clean war. Even more, it demonstrated the impact of real-time war on public opinion: the never-ending flow of data made for extraordinary mood swings among the viewing populace, especially when nearly every event was constantly repeated and analysed in an orgy of speculation, sometimes gloomy speculation. These mood swings, however, did not shake the public's commitment to war. A Gallup poll found that support for the war had remained at the 70 per cent level throughout the three weeks of combat. The public was responding in very different ways to the real-time war and to the policy of war.

The public was surprisingly happy with the product television and the press had supplied. Admittedly, as war fatigue set in there emerged a clamour about too much war news. Throughout the war, roughly three of every four Americans rated the performance of the media as either excellent or good, which of course could amount to a vote of confidence in the show the newsrooms had put on. Another poll asked a different question, whether the US coverage was 'fair and reliable.' The answer was a resounding yes; around two-thirds of respondents found the performance of the media met expectations. A third query discovered that viewers and readers were overwhelmingly pleased by the innovation of embedded journalists, whose reports they found 'fair and objective.' People were especially confident (at an 80 per cent level) about the accuracy of military reports, placing even more trust in the Pentagon and Central Command than they did in the newsrooms. One complaint, and that from only a quarter of respondents, was that the media had been too critical of the military. Another, this from the hawks amongst the public, was that the media gave too much coverage to the antiwar cause. Whatever their views on the war, most Americans felt they had heard too much from the 'armchair generals.'

The real-time war did exact a psychological toll on viewers because the TV coverage proved so involving. From the beginning, some Americans suffered a kind of burnout, exhausted by the images of bombing and the columns of tanks sweeping through the desert. Many more were saddened by the experience, perhaps because they recognized how the war, any war, was a tragedy. A surprisingly large number of viewers admitted feeling depressed and frightened, especially near the end of March. Why? Because they worried about American soldiers or new terror attacks? The survey had no answers. But it did discover that nearly three of every ten viewers found the war did not 'seem real,' possibly because it came in the form of infotainment. Unfortunately, no one asked the other question: how many viewers found the war exciting or stimulating. Certainly the majority, right to the end, had been absorbed by the war, with many viewers unable to stop watching the news.

There was a certain irony here because the populace was also on record, in these and other surveys, as favouring a type of war coverage that was 'neutral' rather than 'pro-American' – 'no propaganda, please.' The welter of results demonstrated nonetheless the great success of the marketing effort mounted by the newsrooms and the Pentagon: they had produced a commodity, this real-time war, that aptly suited the tastes and the patriotism of much of the American public. The one exception was the small group of antiwar stalwarts, around one-fifth of respondents, who had an inkling that the American media was still promoting war: too much war, too little news on civilian casualties, and not enough on costs – though even their dissent was mild. Most people simply were not aware of how one-sided and biased the coverage had been. Instead, they believed the news media had served the country well. (see figure 6.2.)

The collapse of the Iraqi regime on 9 April was taken by most Americans as proof of the wisdom of Washington and the might of its military. President Bush got a big boost in popularity (from 55 to 74 per cent), though not as massive as

Figure 6.2 The misguided public (© 2003 Tribune Media Services, Inc. Reprinted with permission.)

Ann Telnaes captured one of the ironies of the American situation. The technology of American television had made it possible for Americans to be anywhere in the world at the moment of a major happening. Yet the market orientation of American networks ensured that the flood of information they supplied could just as well insulate the public from the world outside. Television could so easily create an ersatz reality that seemed both complete and captivating because it satisfied the presumptions and met the needs of the viewing public. Glenna found that the war experience reminded her of a scene from François Truffaut's *Fahrenheit 451* (1966), 'where the woman who is almost zombie-like sat in front of the TV all day and watched reports of the news of the war that was going on in the frontiers, and it was always wonderful, and it was all, all artificial, and her whole world was artificial, meanwhile they were burning the books and trying to keep everyone from finding out what was really going on.'

his father had enjoyed after the first Gulf War. People were inclined to see the conflict just as the Pentagon and White House wanted, namely, as a victory in the overall war against terrorism, even believing that the downfall of Saddam Hussein indicated the US was winning that war. The smoking gun no longer mattered as much as before the war: a majority did not think the justice of the war depended upon Hussein possessing weapons of mass destruction. Indeed, a considerable number of Americans actually thought they had been found: William Dorman cited a post-invasion poll that found one-third of the public claiming the US army had discovered these weapons, and slightly over a fifth claiming chemical or biological weapons were used against the coalition. The public recognized well enough that the reputation of the United States in the world at large and in particular in the Islamic world had suffered. One stray poll, however, came up with an intriguing finding: 61 per cent believed a real benefit of the Iraq War was the fact that other governments around the world were now more afraid of the United States. Apparently the war as ad had worked well.

III

The marketing of war worked an opposite effect in the Middle East: by all accounts it just reconfirmed the fury the Arab street directed against America. Washington had hoped to press home the message to the Arabic and Islamic world that the Iraq War was about liberation, not oil, even sending out top officials to deliver that message. After all, Saddam Hussein did have a dark reputation as a tyrant, especially in Kuwait, invaded by Iraq a decade ago, much less so in Palestine, where he had sent money to the families of suicide bombers in the war against the Israeli occupation. But the war immediately proved a public-relations disaster for Washington, at least outside of Kuwait. The conflict swiftly became a clash between us and them, Muslim against Christian, the West versus the Middle East. Although the Arab channels might show American successes or present Washington's case, they imposed a framework on events that identified the United States as the Arab enemy. Dream TV, an Egyptian service, early on played and later repeated a three-hour discussion by Arabic military experts on why Iraq would defeat the invasion. The language of war was so very different: coalition troops were called 'aggressors,' dead Iraqi soldiers were 'martyrs.' US warplanes were said to target civilian, not military, sites. Arab viewers were treated to repeated, horrific scenes of the mangled bodies of civilian casualties. Consider this report regarding the behaviour of Al-Jazeera. 'On Friday night, for example, US Defense Secretary Donald Rumsfeld's briefing was broadcast on half the screen, while the other half ... showed video of bloodied bodies of civilian victims being evacuated from the latest bombing raid on a market,' reported NBC (31 March). 'A few days earlier, Secretary of State Colin Powell's exclusive interview with Al-Jazeera was later dissected by two pro-Iraqi analysts, the editor of an extremist newspaper and an Iraqi analyst from Baghdad.' (See figure 6.3.)

The yo-yo effect applied in the Middle East as well; indeed, the highs and lows were likely much more intense, except here it was the reverse of the pattern that prevailed in the United States. (Much of the evidence of this, ironically, came from interviews published in the North American media, notably the *Washington Post*, which provided a series of excellent reports on the views of ordinary people around the world.) What many viewers wanted was a revenge flick, something akin to say *Independence Day*, a movie in which an Arab power struck back for all the wrongs of the past. What they saw instead was another kind of melodrama – which many people believed, apparently, was a continuation of the tragedy of an Islam invaded and dominated by the West. The Iraqi regime scored a major propaganda victory early in the war when the video of dead American soldiers and the POWs, no matter how few, buoyed up hopes that the invasion might fail. 'I saw this and I thought, "Good, President Bush knows his fancy missiles don't work,"' said Osami, a father of three children,

Figure 6.3 Democracy is coming (Chappette, in *Neue Zürcher Zeitung* / www.globecartoon.com)

Chappette, who was born in Pakistan, captured the terrible ironies of the American case for liberation. How could you free a people by bombing their regime into submission? Rami Khouri of the *Beirut Star* tried to make this clear to a Western audience when he was interviewed on the CBC radio show 'As It Happens' on 9 April. Liberation was not a gift for Washington to bestow. 'The Iraqi people would have done it themselves, just as the people in Eastern Europe did, and the Philippines, and Iran, and Indonesia, and every place else in the world.' The problems the Arabs have suffered 'at the hands of Western military invasions and Western political neo-colonial powers are much worse than what we have suffered at the hands of our own tyrants.' Khouri thought the main reason for the war was 'to change the whole political culture in the Arab world' to suppress terrorism.

living in Cairo (*Washington Post*, 24 March). 'We will win this war because God knows we are right.' There were less hostile responses to the images of dead or captured Americans. 'Poor guys, poor guys. But what did they expect?' said Maha Mahmour, a mother of three children, watching in Amman, Jordan. 'The mother part of me is sad. But the Arab part of me is happy.' Slowly the optimism waned, but not the rage. One of the angry protesters in Cairo, reported the CBC (28 March), asked Americans, 'Do you want to own all the world? You want to live in the world alone? ... Will you eat all the food?' And always there were the images of the dirty war. 'America has killed thousands of Iraqi children,' said Hassan, another Egyptian, living in a small town near Cairo (*Washington Post*, 28 March). 'They want to destroy Islam as a religion.' A few days later Leila, a well-off woman living in Riyadh, Saudi Arabia, delivered a message of hate to the Americans via the *Washington Post* (30 March): 'If America wants to step over everybody, then we will fight. I will kill Americans in the street.' She herself threatened to become a suicide bomber, widely honoured as martyrs to the causes of Palestinian freedom and Islamic assertion.

The charges against America might differ, but not the message of aggression: this was a new Christian Crusade, America was bent on establishing dominion over the Middle East, Washington wanted Iraq's oil reserves. Running through such outrage was not only a sense of Arabic and Islamic identity – we are all Iraqis now, a notion that sparked efforts to organize Arab volunteers to go and fight against the coalition – but also a fear of who would be next, what other country would become the target of American bombers and tanks.

Arabs were always looking for evidence that Iraq would put up sufficient resistance to force the Americans to stop the aggression. So the swift collapse of the regime in the second week in April, then the scenes of jubilation in Baghdad, the tearing down of the symbols of the regime, the looting of government buildings, the welcoming of American troops – these signs all broadcast by Al-Jazeera and the other channels – bewildered many Arabs. None of this was taken as proof the Americans had waged a war of liberation, except again in Kuwait, where people also celebrated the downfall of the dictator. Instead, so Al-Jazeera reported (10 April), the American conquest of Baghdad evoked shock, sadness, and shame. Had Saddam Hussein struck a deal with the Americans? Was he yet another traitor to the Arab cause? 'I am very sad. All of Egypt is sad. My wife was weeping this morning,' said Adel Farouq, identified as a taxi driver. Whatever his sins, Saddam Hussein was widely admired as an Arab strongman with an Arab army who had resisted Anglo-American pressure for a decade. Now he too was gone. 'It's a day of shame,' claimed a Palestinian engineer. 'On this day Arabs have become slaves. The only man who dared to say "no" to the Americans' face has vanished today. What is left is a bunch of bowing and scraping Arab leaders.' The West had once again reasserted its dominion. 'Once more the Arabs have been humiliated and deceived like the crushing defeat we faced during the 1967 war with Israel,' noted a businessman in Amman. Similar reports from Western sources conveyed how a sense of loss and humiliation had swept through the Arab street. Yet it was a commentator on Al-Jazeera who summed up the mood, his gloom provoked by the brief shot of a marine putting the American flag over the head of a statue of Saddam Hussein: 'Everything that happens from now on will have an American smell.'

IV

In June Pew Research released another in its ongoing series of reports on global attitudes, called 'Views of a Changing World,' based on a survey of 16,000 people in twenty-one states during the previous month. The report took stock of public opinion after the severe shock administered to the international system when America and its 'coalition of the willing' invaded Iraq. The image of the United States had got a lot better across the globe, except in the Islamic world outside of Kuwait. The clean war and the swift victory had impressed. The numbers of people now willing to say they held a favourable view of the United States was well over 50 per cent in Israel (at 79 per cent!), the United Kingdom, Kuwait, Canada, Nigeria, Australia, and Italy. Although improved over March, the approval figures dropped down below 50 per cent in another group of six nations: South Korea, Germany, France, Spain, Russia, and Brazil. In the Islamic world, though, the figures were really abysmal: Morocco and Lebanon 27 per cent, Indonesia and Turkey 15 per cent, Pakistan 13 per cent, and Jordan and the Palestinian Authority 1 per cent. Everywhere large numbers of people, usually majorities, saw the United Nations as a victim of the war, and no longer so important in the realm of international affairs. Indeed, a different poll, by Ipsos-Reid in May, found that substantial majorities in the European Union, Canada, and Russia believed that nobody, neither the UN nor any other country, could 'stop the US doing whatever it wants in the world today.' (People were more modest in the United States itself, where only 50 per cent agreed with the statement.) No wonder that Pew found an increased worry about American military power, not only in Muslim lands but in Russia as well. Particularly striking were the large numbers of people in some Islamic countries who put their faith in Osama bin Laden 'to do the right thing,' presumably because he had proven willing to stand up to Washington. The confidence levels were especially high in Palestine, Pakistan, Morocco, Jordan, and Indonesia.

These statistics demonstrated the way the war had promoted American hegemony. Sizeable numbers of people in Europe, according to Ipsos-Reid, still believed the United States should not have played Rambo and invaded Iraq. But these same people, or rather many of them, had also come to accept the inevitability of American dominance. Not so in the Islamic world. The war on terror, never very popular there, had been replaced by a war against American imperialism, in which Osama bin Laden was widely esteemed as the champion of the Arab and the Muslim cause. In short, events had repositioned the Iraq War, which now, or rather in May 2003, appeared to be the opening salvo in a future 'war of civilizations' between the West and Islam.

This prospect spooked my citizens' panel. People on every side of the issue of war were made uneasy about the messianic tone running through the rhetoric of politics. No one could miss the religious flavour of the cries for jihad against the West in the proclamations of bin Laden and radical Muslims: both constantly spoke in the name of Allah. Saddam Hussein had tried to exploit this mood when he called for a holy war against the infidel invaders. The troubling fact was that George W. Bush and his associates also appeared caught up in their own brand of religious passion for world-saving. 'Like *Independence Day*, there's this moral sense of justice,' said Stephanie, 'and the Americans are going to kick everybody's ass with these super high-tech weapons and they save the day.' The President sometimes took on the guise of 'an Old Testament prophet' (Bruce W), especially when he kept referring to God in his public speeches. Always in the background lurked a sense of 'Christian righteousness' (Reza) or 'a religious fundamentalism' (Bob) that set his regime apart even from the government of his father, or indeed any of his predecessors. The Americans imagined themselves as 'the saviours of the world, the protectors of countries' (Melissa).

Were such worries exaggerated? President Bush's speech on 1 May aboard the USS *Abraham Lincoln* conveyed a slightly secularized version of the gospel of salvation. 'Men and women in every culture need liberty like they need food and water and air,' he argued. 'Everywhere that freedom arrives, humanity rejoices. And everywhere that freedom stirs, let tyrants fear.' Hence this conclusion: 'The advance of freedom is the surest strategy to undermine the appeal of terror in the world.' Bush did not directly espouse the wisdom of exporting freedom and democracy to the more benighted realms of the world by force of arms. He did suggest that course, however. Likely he was aware that the American people accepted an updated version of what used to be called 'the white man's

Figure 6.4   After Iraq ... (© Chappette, in *Le Temps* (Geneva) / www.globecartoon.com)

Chappette expressed the widespread unease outside the United States that the conquest of Iraq marked the emergence of something new to the world, a formal American empire. In the post-invasion summer a few hawks began to speculate about, not an actual empire, another Rome, but certainly a dominion. Or as Robert Kaplan put it, 'a reluctant imperium,' when he outlined in *The Atlantic Monthly* his 'ten rules for managing the world' in order to fashion a new liberal, international order, and thereby realize America's historic mission. In fact, the once unlamented British Empire had suddenly come back into fashion: Max Boot, for example, speculated in the *Financial Times* (2 July) about the need for an institution comparable to the old Colonial Office to look after Iraq and whatever other country might need to be 'rebuilt' in the near future. Perhaps we would look back to Iraq and 9/11, mused Thomas de Zengotita in *Harper's* (July), as the beginnings of 'Empire properly so called, intoxicated with images of its own might – unabashed, raw.'

burden': according to a CBS poll of 26–27 April, the public accepted the proposition the United States had a responsibility to intervene, to use force, in 'trouble spots' around the world. He told his captive audience of warriors, 'Wherever you go, you carry a message of hope, a message that is ancient, and ever new. In the words of the prophet Isaiah: "To the captives, 'Come out!' and to those in darkness, 'Be free!'"' Perhaps it was all no more than an allowable expression of exuberance. Even so, this had the makings of a revamped marketing strategy to sell a grand vision, and a moral one at that, of a New World Order. (See figure 6.4.)

SEVEN

The Phallic Dimension

Time and again I have been conscious of a wholesale concentration on the technical, tactical aspects of warfare ... small boys' fascination with toys,' said Kate Adie, a veteran ex-correspondent, once attached to the BBC (the *Telegraph*, 19 April). 'It means that those things which conventionally interest the male audience are concentrated on, and women disappear from a landscape in which tanks are rolling and missiles shooting.' The hope was to concoct jeopardy and peril, to boost the action, to show the big guns, the very kinds of material men traditionally liked to see at home and in the movies – weapons systems were a 'guy thing,' in Irene's words (see figure 7.1).

She was not the only person to discern a gender bias to war coverage. In a marvellous discussion of 'The Romance of Empire,' written for *Harper's* (July 2003), Thomas de Zengotita talked about the intrinsic 'glamour of gear,' which he found in action entertainment as well as the war experience. 'Ah, the gearing-up scene. Suspense heaven, foreplay supreme, leather fetish for the multiplex.' Gear fused the individual with the mission. 'It always did, historically, in the coordinations of legions and fleets, but now we can take part not just derivatively – hearing the news, cheering the parade – but vicariously, through our gear, the TV, the computer.' Indeed some critics worried that viewers had been subjected to a porno-

Figure 7.1 Real-time war (Angel Boligan, Cartoonists & Writers Syndicate / cartoonweb.com)

graphic spectacle, in which violence was treated like sexuality to enhance the appeal of the war to TV audiences. '... This is what it's come down to: an obscene, pornographic view of a reality that's been distorted,' claimed Savino. 'I feel guilty about it too.'

At least since Sigmund Freud, and especially his *Civilization and Its Discontents*, the intimate association, often a rivalry, sometimes an alliance, of Eros and Thanatos has inspired all kinds of learned disquisitions. Aggression and sex not only involve intense emotions but draw upon the same unbridled drive for pleasure, especially in the case of the masculine libido. War can replace sex. One of the trivial results of the Iraq War was how it changed, briefly, the pattern of searches on the Internet: reports came out that the hunt for sex sites, consistently the favourites on the web, had been upstaged by the hunger for war news. But sex and war can also go together. The fascination with all things Nazi in the world of pornography is one sign of the way perversion explores the darker side of lust and violence. Not that the Iraq War was necessarily another exploration of that unhappy union, any more than any other war in the past century. Rather, the way the invasion was represented, especially on TV, and how it was sold amounted to a case of machismo rejuvenated. That may explain why polls found stronger support for the war among North American males than females (a spread of up to 15 percentage points).

I

The sexualizing of war and peace issues was hardly a major topic of discussion in the respectable realms of the media. It existed only on the margins of the news. But exist it did. The pro-war forces supported their charge that the Iraqi regime was fundamentally evil by citing instances where rape was used to terrorize the population. That formed part of the British dossier against Iraq, released in December 2002 and used to justify a war of liberation at a time when the peace

movement was rapidly gaining strength in the United Kingdom. At a more popular level, tales of the sadism and the
appetites of Uday, one of Saddam Hussein's sons, made the
rounds in the media. On Fox News (8 April), one of Bill
O'Reilly's guests claimed Uday had an obsession with raping
virgins, arranging with high school principals to send a supply of girls, 'as young sometimes as 12 or 13,' from which he
would pick a couple for his pleasure. O'Reilly's parting words
were that 'the protesters, the peace people, the Pope really
need to hear this.'

Some elements of the antiwar movement used sex in a
different way to attract media attention. One early protest,
'Dickheads for War!', targeted the dangerous phallus mobi-
lized by Washington. The plan was to dress the protesters up
'in corporate drag, a suit and tie, with a plastic dildo on their
head,' Ben Shepard wrote later. 'Like the US military does
with its missiles, prominently painted on the side would be
the words such as "USA" or "Fuck You Saddam."' The protesters' costumes and their antics earned them a few seconds
and a couple of lines in the news.

A later, more sedate effort, the Lysistrata Project worked the
opposition between sex and war in its marketing of peace.
Lysistrata was an ancient comedy written by Aristophanes in
which the heroine encouraged a group of fellow Greek women
to go on a sex strike to compel their war-mad husbands to
bring an end to hostilities. Two New York performers decided
to schedule a reading of the play in March as part of the effort
to stop Washington's drive toward war, and the idea of a
'theatre of peace' caught on around the globe. 'Nobody can
resist an ancient Greek dick joke,' said Kathryn Blume, one of
the organizers. Two of the performances in New York, full of
fun and energy, featured balloon phalluses, presumably to
mock the war power.

The poster designed to promote the Amsterdam Lysistrata
show asked, 'War or Sex – what's it going to be, boys?' That
question highlighted the feminist character of the project, the
assumption that war was a man's game, which did not al-

ways sit well with observers. Still, the notion that war was just a case of men playing out their power fantasies with big toys, substitutes for the penis, was a persistent motif (see figure 7.2). In any case, the Lysistrata Project won the notice of the AP news service, CNN, and other outlets. This sort of carnivalesque marketing was a fine way to win attention, although the trouble was that the novelty of the packaging usually overwhelmed the message itself.

The outbreak of hostilities brought the expected burst of slightly pornographic humour. That kind of imagery has always found favour as a way of dishonouring leaders: indeed, pornography before 1800 was often a form of political satire before it was a means of provoking sexual arousal. Oscar recalled receiving an e-mail that featured Saddam Hussein, George W. Bush, and Osama bin Laden engaged in sexual acrobatics, a case of one man screwing another. The word 'embedded' offered an opportunity to cartoonists that was impossible to resist. Milt Priggee put the dazed American media in the sack with a muscular military type. Jack Ohman had a compliant Al-Jazeera sharing Saddam Hussein's bed. One journalist turned jokes like these into a hypothesis. Writing in *The Village Voice*, Richard Goldstein contended that one purpose of the war, this 'horny' war, was to boost the American libido: 'a quick victory is the ultimate Viagra.' Bringing down Hussein's statue was a way of overcoming the ill effects of 9/11, when that libido had suffered so because of the fall of the twin towers. Later Goldstein turned a pornographic eye to the pilot's outfit the President wore when he landed on the deck of the USS *Abraham Lincoln* to deliver his victory speech on 1 May. The military dress accentuated his package, a display of a manly attribute meant to prove the President had the balls to do the job: 'Clearly Bush's handlers want to leave the impression that he's not just courageous and competent but hung.' Such flaunting assuaged the anxiety of the American male after so many decades of sexual uncertainty. 'A lot of people root for Bush to make it as a man, and they're happy to see his big basket (even if it does suggest a male version of the

Figure 7.2   Macho games (By permission of Mike Luckovich and Creators Syndicate)

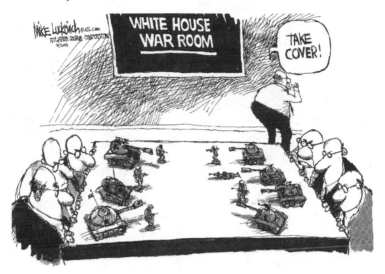

Luckovich captured the idea of boys-with-toys, a favourite way of mocking the pro-war types. Witness this outburst from a columnist at barfi Culture, a website devoted to the Asian community in the United Kingdom: 'Iraq is, and was in the previous war, a chance for the Pentagon boys-with-advanced-toys to test out their Mother-Of-All Bombs and other such macho grandiose names to keep their "boys" salivating over the strength of its own army.' In fact, this line of satire worked off a slightly dated conception of gender roles, given the involvement of women at the Pentagon and the White House selling war – not to mention the involvement of women in the American armed forces. Still, though women were now nearly as responsible as men for war, the masculinist cast of the military endeavour, especially actual combat, remained. Luckovich's paunchy old men, however, represented the aged types whose war games sent young people off to die, a different kind of motif in antiwar commentary.

push-up bra).' All of which turned Bush's victory dress into a species of stealth marketing: apparently our subconscious picked up the message.

Norman Mailer's take on the war was more convincing, although less witty, because he dropped the pornography. He too believed the key purpose of fighting Iraq was to display machismo: America attacked because Washington knew it could win easily. That swift victory was designed to overcome all the slights and blows suffered by the embattled egos of the country's white males, who could no longer claim dominance even in the realm of sport. They could identify with a military so chock full of marvellous machines and staffed, at the top, by white officers. (Well, except for the black face of Brigadier Vincent Brooks, the photogenic spokesman of Operation Iraqi Freedom in Central Command in Doha.) But why limit the yearning for brute force to just the white male? Surely so spectacular a display of machismo as the conquest of Iraq had a much wider appeal, to black and white and Hispanic, to men and women?

A Gallup poll (28 March) did find one ethnic group decidedly unhappy with the invasion: the African-Americans (the war was only supported by 29 per cent of such respondents), apparently because they interpreted the event in the light of their own resentments about a perceived repression at home. Overall men (78%) were more pro-war than women (66%), a not-uncommon finding in like crises; Republicans (93%), naturally, much more than Democrats (53%); rural and suburban (75%) more than urban (62%); and haves (around 79%) more than the less fortunate (58%). Seniors, once strongly opposed to war, had rallied to the flag once the invasion began (the over-sixty-fives were 73% pro-war). A survey released by the Pew Hispanic Center (reported in the *Chicago Tribune*, 10 April) found that three-quarters of Hispanics born in the United States also favoured the war, as against slightly over half of Hispanics born elsewhere. Thus, Mailer's thesis had some merit, though it was far too simple and restricted.

Playing tough had been a ploy that American political leaders used time and again to win office or firm up public support. True enough, Bill Clinton had not marketed himself this way during the 1990s. Such an absence of macho was unusual. The most iconic of recent presidents, John F. Kennedy, got that way partly because he stood up to the Soviet Union, and talked tough, especially over the Cuban missile crisis. Ronald Reagan made a lot of his muscular approach to foreign policy in contrast to the softer style of his predecessor, Jimmy Carter. George Bush senior had a 'wimp' problem that his handlers thought he needed to deal with before he could gain the full confidence of the public. Thus, the macho style was a recurring phenomenon in presidential politics.

The disaster of 9/11 certainly encouraged a revival of machismo in American culture. Or perhaps it just confirmed an existing trend: Richard Goldstein, writing this time in *The Nation*, found the roots of Washington's war fever in the broader story of a macho revival, citing a couple of Michael Douglas's movies, gangsta rap, and in particular Eminem and his hit movie *8 Mile* (2002). The celebration of the heroism of New York's firefighters was one of the signs of the return of the 'old' male to public esteem. Likewise the sanctifying of Rudy Giuliani, the mayor of New York, who had performed so well in the aftermath of the disaster, made authoritarianism, the take-command style, very saleable in political life. Even more significant was the arrival of permanent war, the ongoing war on terror, because battle was traditionally a masculine arena (no matter that women now served) where the hard virtues and harder bodies prevailed. The hawks in and around Bush's administration were particularly articulate advocates of the moral wisdom of aggression in world affairs.

George W. Bush had some initial difficulties fitting into the role of macho star. He had once flirted with a softer image, presenting himself in 2000 as a compassionate conservative. He had wobbled briefly in the immediate aftermath of 9/11, seemingly shaken and frightened by al-Qaeda's onslaught on the symbols of American power. Cartoons captured the doubts about his manly attributes. 'Look at the face cartoonists have given Bush,' claimed Goldstein. 'The ears are outsized while the nose is modest. Big ears are not exactly phallic signifiers; if anything, they connote a state of permanent childhood, à la Mickey Mouse.'

Nevertheless, he and his handlers soon responded to the cultural shift. He enjoyed playing at being the nation's father, the Christian preacher and prophet, even more the tough-minded sheriff of the Old West, all patriarchal roles. He had what Hendrik Hertzberg called his 'Clint Eastwood' moments when he talked rough. Hertzberg cited a comment he made in his famous State of the Union address of 2003 about the arrest of suspected terrorists: 'Let's put it this way: they are no longer a problem to the United States and our friends and allies.' Nearly six months later, as CNN reported (3 July), he warned the anti-American guerrillas in Iraq of the rough justice they could expect: 'Bring 'em on.' It was exactly this kind of macho rhetoric, backed up by unilateral actions, which cultivated the impression, especially in Europe, that Bush was no more than a cowboy out of Texas (see figure 7.3). Foreign polls indicated that a large part of the mistrust of American intentions before and after the war focused on Bush himself. Ironically, American polls demonstrated that since 9/11 Bush had consistently enjoyed the longest and highest approval ratings ever recorded. The cowboy was something of an American archetype, honoured on the screen as the rugged individualist, the man willing to go it alone, the man who walked tall and carried a mean gun, the man who adhered to a code of rough justice to bring order to a land of chaos. So when Bush presented himself in the guise of a sheriff, whether his comments were spontaneous or rehearsed, he was marketing himself as a particularly American kind of phallic hero to a domestic audience, and many of these consumers were ready to buy the illusion.

II

The Western media were crucial to the display of machismo because they became the distributors of 'war porn.' The trouble

Figure 7.3 Bush as cowboy (Peter Schrank, Cartoonists & Writers Syndicate / cartoonweb.com)

Schrank presented a strange mix of stereotypes in this critique of Washington's headlong rush into battle. Bush himself might be dressed like a cowboy, but he looked like a mad monkey. America became the bull with the lethal horns rendered even more phallic by being turned into warheads. The world at large was the helpless little man, hardly able to slow the momentum of the American beast. 'The Germans initially didn't take him seriously,' Susann Park, a university student majoring in American studies, said of Bush to a reporter for the *Washington Post* (2 April). 'Phrases like "Either you're with us or against us," they're so much like something from Western movies. It appals you, because it seems so narrow-minded.' In fact Europeans had never much cared for American machismo, in politics at least because they had also lapped up the versions that Hollywood marketed in film. One of the more famous cartoons of Ronald Reagan, popular in Europe back in the 1980s, had him dressed as a happy cowboy riding a missile down to earth.

was that what some observers saw as obscene others deemed news. Now, the phrase 'war porn' can have a variety of different meanings, other than simply the depiction of sexual matter. There was little of this evident during the war, although Dave recalled a scene where some jubilant Iraqi males were shown thrusting their pelvises against a portrait of Saddam Hussein. Sometimes war porn refers to the so-called pornography of violence, where the sheer scale and repetition of destruction, or the weapons that cause such destruction, becomes intrinsically obscene. Sometimes it means the display of humiliated or wounded or dead bodies in ways that highlight their submission or their penetration: that definition fits the broader sense of pornography that scholar Carolyn Dean has attached to any material seeking 'to describe the violation of the dignified human body in a variety of contexts,' not just sexual but 'aesthetic and political' as well. But war porn always implies a particular way of seeing, an effort to position the consumer so that he or she can derive a shot of pleasure that is erotic, or akin to the erotic, from whatever is on the page or the screen. (See figure 7.4.)

The first type of war porn that television retailed were the loving depictions of American weaponry, the impressive Abrams tanks, the sleek fighters, the phallic missiles, the really big bombs. Linda Williams, a professor of film who had written on pornography, explained to the British journalist Emma Brockes just how this worked:

> CNN have this special thing they do whenever they introduce a new weapon. It reminds me of the way athletes are introduced in coverage of the Olympics: a little inset comes out with their bio and stats. This weapon they had just now was something called the AC130H-Spectre – some dreadful machine – it came flying out and turned this way and that so that you could see it from all angles ... This is the kind of spectacular vision you get in porn – where the point is to see the sex act from every angle. It's narcissistic; boys getting together admiring their toys. It is about us proudly displaying our weapons and there is something sexual about that.

Figure 7.4 The big media (© 2003 Tribune Media Services, Inc. Reprinted with permission.)

Telnaes's cartoon might take on a number of different meanings. It spoke of the enormous size of the media presence. It suggested the huge amounts of material this establishment had produced to inform and entertain the American public. The stance of the man and his accoutrements signified the centrality of television in this world of the media. But above all it captured the phallic overtones of a media that had worked to impose a version of reality on the events in Iraq. A CBC correspondent, speaking on the radio program 'Dispatches' (13 August), reflected on the tastes of her male colleagues. 'Many men really get off on this war-zone thing, I've noticed as a female reporter. They know all the kinds of guns, they know their names, they know the munitions, they know the name of that vehicle ... Me, I like the stories, I like the people.'

The whole display was jazzed up with simulations, fancy graphics, and tech talk, classifying and categorizing, sizing up the body (e.g., what armour it has, look at those wings) and celebrating the potency of the weapon (how large the gun is, what a bomb burst it will make) in ways similar to how the human body is treated in adult movies and literature. No one on the citizens' panel, be it said, drew the connection between these displays and pornography, though Geoff found it all reminiscent of the video games of his youth.

The second type of war porn came from the bombings of Baghdad, which were reproduced live on television screens around the world. Judy Rebick told the Canadian Press news service (27 March) that she was having considerable difficulties watching the spectacle of war manufactured by American television. Rebick was a noted activist and author who had recently taken a chair in social justice and democracy at Toronto's Ryerson University. 'The thing that I find most troubling is this kind of excitement about the bombing, you know, almost sexual excitement,' she said. 'I find it deeply disturbing, really morally repugnant, this thrill over the technology with no comprehension that people are dying.' The bombings obeyed a weird aesthetic of lethal beauty: the clouds of smoke, the boom-booms, these were like the explosions in so many action movies, where the spectator was supposed to get a small rush from the pictures of devastation. It was not just the imagery but the play-by-play, the commentary attached to the live war, that caused upset. '"Slam, bam, bye-bye Saddam," a guest colonel blurted on CNN as the first missiles fell on Baghdad,' Goldstein recalled: there was an outburst full of testosterone. American television celebrated in words and images the penetration and the mutilation of the supine body, allowing viewers to 'vicariously participate in the rape of Baghdad, enjoying the feeling of power that comes with being a citizen of the most militarily powerful country in history,' according to Titus North on his web news site.

The third type of war porn were the pictures of humiliated and mutilated bodies, especially when these pictures were constantly repeated. That was when television became the voyeur's delight. American television stayed away from a lot of this kind of imagery, though it did show some dead soldiers as well as Iraqi prisoners of war. One of the most gripping pieces of television Orsolina recalled was the videotape of the American POWs. 'First of all to see the fear on their faces ... You could really see that they didn't understand what was happening ... It's not like they were prepared for an interview ... I remember the face of the female, from Texas, just the look of shock, eyes were open and just looking right at the interviewer ... The next person had a broken nose, all bruised and damaged ... he was on a bed ... Somebody lifted up his head so that he could speak ... You could tell he was in pain.' Not only was she captivated, she was deeply moved by the plight of that woman and the other soldiers: war porn can have a moral effect.

The US networks backed off airing the whole of the Iraqi video of dead and captured Americans under pressure from the Pentagon – a demand that seemed especially hypocritical when a few months later the Pentagon released to the media photos of the ruined faces of Saddam Hussein's two sons. A viewer needed to tune in to the Arabic channels to get the full force of the dirty war. Indeed, the sanitizing of war on Western TV led one outsider, writing in the *Namibian* (14 April) to call for more war porn to bring home the blood and the gore of battle, because that might well undo the public support for further wars. In fact, the print media and the Internet offered a lot more pictures of devastated bodies than television: the burned, armless body of Ali Ismael Abbas, a twelve-year-old boy whose parents died in the same missile attack that mutilated him, became a symbol of the horrors of war.

The most important spectacle of humiliation, however, was broadcast live when the networks displayed the toppling of the twelve-metre-high statue of Saddam Hussein in Baghdad's Firdos Square on 9 April. All day television had been carrying scenes of the sweep of American tanks into Baghdad and the welcome its citizens gave the soldiers who really did, for that moment, look like liberators. TV had also shown the Iraqis caught up in a mood of carnival, destroying symbols of the regime and looting its office buildings. Then in the late afternoon a crowd apparently gathered at the foot of the most recent of Hussein's large statues, erected about a year earlier in honour of his sixty-fifth birthday. The Iraqis hoped to bring the statue down, even attaching a noose to carry out the feat. To no avail: the statue would not budge. Then the Americans came to help, again. Troops attached chains to a military crane. Television waited patiently. A marine corporal briefly put an American flag over the head of Hussein, then removed this when a commander realized the optics were very bad: this might suggest occupation, not liberation. The vehicle hauled down the statue, leaving only the hollow boots attached to the concrete, and the crowd cheered madly. So too did TV. 'That is at once a pathetic and symbolic representation of Saddam Hussein,' intoned the MSNBC announcer, in a deeply male voice. 'It says it all about what is going on. He has been toppled from his pedestal, head down, no dignity, no power, no standing ...' The head of the statue was dragged through the streets by the crowd, who pelted it with shoes and garbage. Thus ended the ritual castration of the Iraqi regime.

'The visual footage of that one statue being pulled down, that was really stunning, triumphant,' recalled Mike, otherwise no great fan of TV's war, 'a moment of triumph captured on film, and these films will be shown as long as the histories of these wars are recounted.' The event was immediately compared to those other moments celebrated in the legends of democracy like the fall of the Berlin Wall or the standoff in Tiananmen Square. Even the CBC's Don Murray imposed the approved narrative of liberation on the news of the day – and his report was a very good job, a nice mix of images and words and sounds – which excluded any other frame of understanding. Still, downing the statue was more than just that, or maybe it was less real, because, unlike those other events, this was another marketing triumph, again a co-production of the new imperial authority and of that nation's networks. The event looked staged, especially when the camera took a panorama shot: the square contained some Iraqis, a lot of journalists, and the American military, whose tanks had sealed off the square. The toppling of Saddam Hussein was one of those made-for-TV moments: a grand, symbolic act that completed the drama of the real-time war. It had that magic quality of any stunning image, the ability to simplify something, to sum up a situation, to say, in this case, liberation and triumph. John Doyle, a *Globe and Mail* TV columnist (10 April), called this 'the money shot,' a direct reference to that moment in a porn film where the male ejaculates, usually on the female's body. One great phallic symbol had been torn down for all the world to see, and by the Americans. It was the cartoonists who remarked that something equally potent might replace the statue (see figure 7.5).

III

The staged triumph of 1 May found Bush playing a slightly different kind of role. He flew in to the USS *Abraham Lincoln* at the controls of a jet that made a striking tail-hook landing. He arrived wearing a pilot's outfit, full of gear, looking every bit the skilled warrior ready for battle. He strode across the deck of the aircraft carrier, exchanged some words with the sailors, and announced the end of major hostilities in Iraq. The performance may have lacked class but it certainly had swagger. 'I thought from the point of view of getting a message across about triumph and power it was something, it was the most powerful thing I'd ever seen,' remembered Mike.

The performance recalled other masculine moments in the history of political theatre. It might bring to mind vague memories, ersatz memories of course, created out of pop culture, memories of victorious generals and emperors parading through the streets of ancient Rome, except that Bush brought none of the defeated Iraqi leaders along to mark the enemy's shame and his glory. It did evoke in the mind of one of my

Figure 7.5 The new master (Graeme MacKay, *The Hamilton Spectator*)

Cartoonists had a lot of fun pointing out just what the toppling of the Hussein really meant. Cam Cardow of the *Ottawa Citizen* also replaced a dour Saddam Hussein ('Baghdad Last Week') with a happy Ronald McDonald ('Baghdad Next Week'). Rob Rogers of the Pittsburgh *Post-Gazette* had a crazed-looking Ronald holding up a tray with a drink, a Big Mac, and fries, all to celebrate the opening of a new restaurant. Godfrey Mwampembwa (Gado) of *The Daily Nation* in Nairobi, Kenya, put the Golden Arches atop the pedestal between the hollow boots of Hussein, whose statue lay below. Both Rogers and Gado added a few awed Iraqis looking on at the new monument. It all signified the succession of power in Iraq, the arrival of the American way in what another wag now called 'Bushdad.' And it gave new meaning to a comment made by a commentator on Al-Jazeera (10 April): 'Everything that happens from now on will have an American smell.'

university colleagues the imagery of the Third Reich, because of the obsession that regime had with organizing mass spectacles in which Hitler received the adulation of the faithful. Indeed, the totalitarian art of the early twentieth century, fascist as well as communist, had a taste for this kind of motif where the leader and his followers were linked as one in a single-minded devotion to the mission, whatever that might be. But there were many less sinister moments, as in all those sports movies where the coach addressed his team, usually to urge everyone to strive for victory. I thought of the scene in *Independence Day* when President Thomas J. Whitmore, himself an ex–fighter pilot, lauds his compatriots as they set off to do battle for the United States and 'mankind.' Bob decided it was 'a parody of Star Wars, the second Star Wars where the emperor arrives on the Battle Star and the troops are all arrayed to greet [him].' The point is not which, if any, of these models helped to script the event. Rather, what counts is that, again, the spectacle was arranged so as to resonate, to conjure up in the minds of viewers those ersatz memories of moments when men and women rallied or celebrated behind their leader, their coach, their commander, memories that are part of a mythology of our times constantly refreshed by pop culture.

Critics of Bush – Mailer for one – were quick to point to the hypocrisy of a President dressed in battle costume who had effectively evaded service in Vietnam so many years ago by playing at being a pilot in the air force of the National Guard. 'So phoney,' 'absolutely inexcusable,' said Richard. But Bush was not so much referring to his own past as a warrior. Rather, he was showing solidarity with the returning victors, the real men and women who had done a superb job in Iraq. These warriors, he said, had continued the glorious tradition of the American military: 'the daring of Normandy, the fierce courage of Iwo Jima, the decency and idealism that turned enemies into allies.' The optics were good: the President had lined up with the very kind of ordinary pros, the firemen, the policemen, the soldiers and sailors and pilots, who had been so much celebrated since 9/11 – people not so much of thought but of action, people who were team players, people who served the greater good of their land. Once again, the performance was designed in particular for the television audience back home. The moment marked the final scenes of Iraq the movie, when the phallic hero can declare an end to the drama – until the next time.

In his May address Bush called the affair 'the battle of Iraq,' like the earlier 'battle of Afghanistan,' where America had successfully engaged the enemy in the ongoing struggle to achieve security at home and peace in the world. He denied the war on terror would prove 'endless.' Yet he left the clear impression there would be other engagements. Bush was very much the war president, not only because his place in history now rested on the waging of a war against terrorism, but because his administration used the threat of terror to organized domestic politics. Already the chattering classes had begun to speculate about who was next: was it Syria, another Baathist regime akin to the one destroyed in Iraq, and a danger to Israel; or the Islamic republic of Iran, still militant and supposedly bent on acquiring the infamous weapons of mass destruction; or maybe North Korea, which was rapidly developing a nuclear capability that would menace its neighbours and perhaps, eventually, the continental United States? David Remnick, writing in the *New Yorker*, warned there were some high-placed hawks in the administration – he mentioned James Woolsey and Richard Perle – who really did dream of endless war. Once the beast of war was unleashed, could it ever be restrained again? Hence a travel joke making the rounds, as Oscar recalled: 'Visit the United States before the United States visits you.'

EIGHT

The Propaganda State

'There is one thing that stories also have that this doesn't to me which is [an] end, a wrap up, a denouement, a solution,' said Bruce R. 'I find it a very unsatisfying story because ... I don't think it is a story, it may be a chapter ... There isn't really closure, I don't think.' Other members of the citizens' panel made similar comments: the beginning of 'a very, very long war' (Sam), part of an 'endless war' (Stephanie), perhaps the coming of 'another Rome' (Bruce W). Bruce R was right. The Iraq War was only a chapter in a series of other stories.

One of the most important of these stories was the trajectory of democracy in America. The state of politics in the United States has always been a matter of heated discussion, and often the cause of much gloom, because of America's role as the premier advocate of democracy in the world at large. At one point, beginning in the 1970s, attention had focused on the question of legitimacy: did governments enjoy public support, since polls consistently indicated that a large number of Americans distrusted Washington? (That was much less of a problem now because of the vigour of war patriotism.) Margaret Atwood's classic dystopia *The Handmaid's Tale* (1985) embodied one fear of the 1980s, that the religious right might stifle American democracy. More recently, during the 1990s, attention had shifted to complaints about the falling level of citizen involvement in politics, given that roughly half of the electorate never bothered to cast a vote for president, and even more failed to participate in municipal contests. America, it was feared, had become a republic of haves where money ruled, where the rich and the affluent had effectively captured Congress and government. 9/11 provoked a different anxiety about the onset of a surveillance state where video cameras and computer databases worked together to monitor the behaviour of the populace. Washington seemed intent on limiting the legal rights of citizens and residents to privacy, if not yet dissent.

Since the war on terror took hold, the power of spectacle has become as serious a menace to democracy as the police power. Or maybe, as Chris feared, spectacle and surveillance constituted a single structure of domination: Washington had to stoke the momentum of war, 'or else people are going to turn off, from apathy they're going to become frustrated and start asking questions about why so many of their civil liberties are being curtailed.' The Iraq crisis and the Iraq War gave notice of the return of the propaganda state. A propaganda state refers to a regime in which the governors, whether official or unofficial, employ a constant stream of messages to propel the population toward some desired condition of right thinking and right acting. The propaganda state is the dark shadow of democracy, its counter, its contradiction. Both polities are at bottom discursive phenomena, meaning they are grounded in the manipulation of symbols, words and images, except that propaganda relies more on spectacle and assertion than on argument. The propaganda state thrives when other voices are silenced.

That political condition may look similar to the notorious 'hegemony' model of the mass media fashioned by Edward Herman and Noam Chomsky in works like *Manufacturing Consent* and *Necessary Illusions*, both published in the late 1980s. Their theory has not faired well in academic circles in North America, although in practice similar kinds of arguments, notably 'the indexing hypothesis' announced initially by Lance Bennett, have found much favour to explain how the media handle foreign-policy issues. In any case, Chomsky and Herman took aim at the reputation of the news media as 'cantankerous,' always in search of truth, adversaries of authority and agents of democracy. Instead, they claimed, the US media had typically acted as a propaganda arm of the prevailing economic and political elites. That was chiefly because of the corporate ownership of the media, their dependence on advertising revenues, their reliance on official experts and information, the impact of official criticism or 'flak' used to discipline dissent, and the force of anti-communism as a national religion (now, perhaps, anti-terrorism fulfils that role). These operated as a series of 'filters' through which the news was purified to ensure it suited the official agenda. Herman and Chomsky backed up their claims by exploring the wide differences between the ways the media reported the global activities of the American state and of America's enemies. What was crucial, likewise to Bennett, was an elite consensus which established the parameters of debate: when authority – the government, the bureaucracy, Congress – agreed on some agenda, then the media toed the line, so to speak, delivering a brand of news that embodied the wisdom of that authority. In a recent updating of their theory, Herman and Chomsky have emphasized the increased import of the public-relations industry, read marketing, 'as mechanisms of elite influence' to fashion both flak and expertise. Even so, their theory presumes that the captive condition of journalism is systemic rather than intentional: reporters are, as it were, unknowing servants of their masters. Here is one crucial difference – intention is a leading characteristic of the propaganda state.

Allow me a short journey through the history of the twentieth century. The term 'propaganda state' was first applied to the Bolshevik regime in the early years of the revolution, when the Communist party set out to remake Russia. That regime prohibited dissent and employed posters, advertising, school books, plays, paintings, newspapers, cinema – all of the apparatus of persuasion – to fashion the new socialist man and woman. During the 1930s Nazi Germany took the lead as

a propaganda state: Joseph Goebbels, that genius of persuasion, commanded the press, radio, art, and cinema to program minds and stigmatize enemies. In both cases what died
was debate, what prevailed was monologue. The public sphere
was transformed into a public stage where the regime effectively put on a show to compel obedience and celebrate una-
nimity. Perhaps the most notorious examples were the Nazi
party's mass rallies, a spectacle immortalized by Leni
Riefenstahl's film *Triumph of the Will* (1935).

During the Second World War Goebbels employed not
just the mass media but even what was called 'whisper' (or
person-to-person) propaganda to ensure a uniform set of messages that expressed the Nazi vision of war. Goebbels had
looked to radio as the main instrument of persuasion in the
1930s. Now the most impressive propaganda was visual because it promised to encourage a sense of vicarious participation in the great national effort. He took a keen interest in the
fashioning of newsreels designed to persuade audiences
abroad and at home, where the showing of this brand of news
was made compulsory at every film presentation. War cameramen produced huge quantities of raw film, in the beginning of victories, used by teams of editors and officials to craft
a series of newsreels, complete with voice-overs and stirring
music, touting the inevitable triumph of the new Reich. These
productions proved immensely popular with German audiences, David Welch has suggested, since they presented the
war 'in such an immediate way,' and were thus a distant
precursor of the real-time war. They were supplemented by
feature-length documentaries, for example *Feuertaufe* (1940),
which celebrated the Luftwaffe's blasting of Poland and War-
saw. Propaganda infected entertainment as well: *Der grosse
König* (1942), one of the most successful and expensive efforts,
mythologized the indomitable will of Frederick the Great, a
much-embattled ruler of Prussia. Even when events turned
against the German army, the Ministry for Propaganda nonetheless found material, indeed manufactured material, using
for example a camera that captured a double negative, thus

multiplying the enemy killed, to maintain the illusion of military might. Such tricks did not work very well by 1944, of course: war propaganda had lost much of its credibility – audiences took to waiting outside theatres to avoid seeing the newsreels (until the theatres were told to close their doors). Still, in popular memory, Goebbels remained the grand master in the sombre history of propaganda.

No matter how necessary to a totalitarian regime, any mechanism suited to the propaganda state might seem inimical in a democracy, where some sort of dialogue between the governors and citizens was of fundamental importance. But there was one type of emergency when the political situation changed, when democracy gave way to discipline: what was called 'total war,' a phrase, by the way, made famous by Goebbels. Britain and later the United States discovered the necessity of propaganda during the First World War. They learned well: Lenin, for example, modelled his ideas of 'agitprop' on the practices of Britain's propagandists in the Great War. Again, the Allies fashioned an elaborate structure of propaganda and censorship during the Second World War, which encompassed at one point the news of the CBC and the movies of Hollywood. Although these structures were mostly dismantled after the victory, propaganda in one form or another remained commonplace. During the early years of the Cold War in America the language and the views of anti-communism filled the American media, affecting not just the news but Hollywood as well, censoring scenes, actors, and shows that might be labelled 'pink' or 'red.' Thereafter, an ensemble of authorities, private as well as public, have employed advocacy advertising and public relations to advance their causes in the phoney 'wars' against drugs or crime or cigarettes or AIDs. All these campaigns have threatened harm to the practice of democracy – the United States, and indeed most of the affluent zone, has been thoroughly penetrated by this and other kinds of propaganda – but the waves of promotional noise were never sufficient to deliver anything like a fatal blow.

The arrival of a real conflict, the war on terror, very much a shooting war – that created the necessary preconditions to fashion America's own brand of the propaganda state. What was new about this version of the state, or as Oscar put it, 'the American equivalent to Goebbels'? How did the experience differ from past ventures in other democracies during the twentieth century? The war on terror was in some ways akin to the earlier world wars, if not Vietnam. Since 9/11 Washington had established a context of permanent warfare, building something similar to the embattled mentality fashioned by totalitarian regimes, where the populace was attuned to the need for action. The administration maintained the appropriate mood by publicizing a series of alarms, security procedures, and arrests of terrorists, thereby producing the necessary climate of anxiety. 'What surprised me most of all about living amongst the Americans was how paranoid of everything they have become, and I think it's because of the media that surrounds them,' mused Geoff, who had resided in the United States in the fall of 2002. 'So there were lots of people I met who thought if we didn't get Saddam Hussein first there were going to be mushroom clouds in New York.' In short, Washington came close to creating that sense of total war which was the one excuse for the propaganda state.

Under the circumstances it was hardly surprising that the boundaries of the permissible, what could be said, had contracted. The public yearned for closure. So too did the politicians, and the invasion of Iraq looked like a way to advance the war on terror. The decision of the Democrats in Congress to remain silent severely restricted the potential for media debate of the war policy. There existed the very kind of elite consensus that drove dissent to the margins of journalism. The news media covered the antiwar protests early in 2003, although there clearly were limits on the ability of peace activists to get their message out across the United States. Once the bombing started, the big media rallied to the cause of war, as did so much of the public, leaving even less room for dissent. Television news shows might, sometimes, criticize the execution of the invasion. They did not challenge its merits or objectives.

Neither the Pentagon nor the White House imposed censorship in the domestic arena; the newsrooms did. Very few of the voices called upon to comment during the war were drawn from the ranks of the antiwar movement; many more were from the circles of military and security experts. FAIR, a media watchdog, found that during the conflict fully two-thirds of the guests were pro-war on six major TV news programs, only 10 per cent were antiwar, and few of these were American. Indeed, it could be dangerous to a person's livelihood, though not to his or her freedom, to actually speak out in a way that was critical of the new American mood. FAIR reported that MSNBC cancelled Phil Donahue's talk show because he had earned a reputation as preferring anti-war guests. According to an item in the *Globe and Mail* (12 April), a Canadian company working with CBS, Alliance Atlantis Communications, had actually fired its executive producer for a new miniseries on Hitler's rise because he dared to draw a comparison between the attitudes prevailing in Germany in 1933 and America in 2003. In practice, debate was largely shut down, which had also happened in the early stages of wars in America and other democracies during the twentieth century.

However, the product offered was very different from times past. The excuses for war were so contrived that it reminded Jennifer of *Wag the Dog* (1997), a black comedy where a political consultant and a movie producer combine forces to fabricate a war in order to protect a president in trouble. The attack on Iraq constituted a small war, a smart, relatively clean, and swift campaign against a feeble enemy, and a war conducted by a professional military, mostly according to a plan designed by the Pentagon. 'What kind of a war is this,' wondered Irene, when TV kept reporting what was going to happen, complete with maps detailing military operations. This, the scripted war, was not at all like the long, drawn-out, dirty contests of the Second World War or even Vietnam, fought mostly by conscripts, where the enemy was all too formidable. Thus, the Bush administration did not face the same difficulty of mounting a propaganda offensive over a period of years in the face of defeats abroad and sacrifice at home. What need for the propaganda of old when, as Mike put it, the war was 'so easy, and so successful'? Instead, Washington sought to promote a stunning victory that justified war as commodity. 'The proof of American toughness is partly what this is all about,' Mike pointed out. 'It's giving a message to people who oppose the United States – you're going to be destroyed.'

Moreover, the Bush administration acted during what I have called marketing's moment. Neither Churchill nor Roosevelt, not even Kennedy or Johnson, thought in terms of marketing; Bush and his associates did, most especially his top political strategist Karl Rove. 'The President is surrounded by a huge infrastructure, very talented people,' concluded Chris; 'there's all kinds of PR and marketing people, experts who come up with really clever phrases that are going to win over people.' Marketing provided a language and a technology for managing the desires and the fears of the public in ways that did not appear to harm democratic practice. Although there was nothing so ominous as Goebbels's Ministry for Propaganda, the new Office of Global Communications plus a wide array of institutions and personnel throughout the political and military bureaucracies were devoted to managing the news. 'The capacity of the administration to so successfully push deceptions and misrepresentations through a docile press to an emotionally volatile public may stand as the most ruthless press control operation in history,' observed Lance Bennett.

The war coverage was 'better in terms of keeping you informed' than it was during the first Gulf War, claimed Michael, but you were 'almost always manipulated.' Nearly constant polling gave Washington the ability to track public attitudes, the ups and the downs of support, of morale, and so to shape the propaganda to suit the need, a kind of knowledge only recently made possible by technology. The existence of an all-day, all-night news stream penetrating virtually all homes provided a method of getting the messages out to nearly everyone at any time through television, the most involving, the most believable of media. No doubt Goebbels would have envied such an instrument of persuasion, especially given the willingness of the networks to endorse Washington's war. The result was a shift from the past obsession with secrecy and censorship to a new obsession with promotion and publicity that took on the appearance of dialogue. 'Once you get beyond the lie, the actions of the people in Washington are pretty transparent: you know, they actually did say what they [would] do, they have largely said why, and they apparently believe it,' claimed Bob.

Propaganda during the Second World War had spoken mostly in the language of bombast and fear in order to awe or scare its audience. That was as true of Allied as it was of Nazi efforts. The style had not disappeared. Saddam Hussein's Iraq had been one state where the old ways of haranguing the citizenry still prevailed. Indeed, the thrust of America's 'PsyOps' in Iraq looked much like an application of the scare copy of past times. But now, in America, the Bush administration and its media allies offered not just hard sermonizing but a softened propaganda, less coercive and more seductive, a real-time war aimed at satisfying the audience's desires for thrills, excitement, pathos, triumph, and pride. War was 'not real anymore,' lamented Savino. 'It's become like a set-up, contrived, glorified video game.' Hollywood, Madison Avenue, and television had built a common repertoire of characters, motifs, and styles that could be readily exploited to sell war. Neither the war news nor Iraq the movie convinced most of my citizens' panel, all of whom were distanced from the event by the fact of being Canadian. 'It was so constructed to gain the best result from or approval of the American people,' argued Melissa. Which it did: polls and surveys demonstrate how the war coverage did please enough Americans. The propaganda state came to America in the guise of popular culture.

Pop culture could cut both ways, however. It was always a contested realm, where a series of different myths and archetypes persisted, which could be deployed by the critics as well as the champions of war. The success of the ensemble of authorities who produced the war experience recalled a bad dream that had already caused much popular comment. In 1999 Warner Brothers released what became a big hit of the year, *The Matrix*, a movie that won a raft of awards and earned around $450 million worldwide at the box office. It told the story of a renegade hacker called Neo who led a small gang of rebels against the rule of intelligent machines some two hundred years in the future. The movie featured stunning visual effects, especially slow motion and levitation, as well as lots of explosions and much gunfire, enough to make it a gripping scifi thriller, full of action and excitement, no doubt the main source of its appeal to American and foreign audiences (it did better at the box office outside than inside the USA). But what intrigued many fans, and sparked all kinds of discussion on the web, was the dystopian vision of the writers, the Wachowski brothers. The matrix was a counterfeit world of 1999 created in the minds of domesticated humans, whose life force was harvested to supply energy to maintain the dominion of intelligent machines over the physical world. So the movie probed the whole question of reality, what reality was and how we knew that reality, presuming in fact that the real world was no more than a fake used to control an oblivious humanity, a notion that had been around in one form or another since the anxieties over brainwashing back in the 1950s. Why it seemed so apt at the end of the twentieth century was because it addressed the fears endemic in a world where media and marketing were so pervasive. *The Matrix* can be taken as the paranoid fantasy of the propaganda state, a regime where a constant flow of illusion enables an elite to rule over the citizenry.

Once the government of Saddam Hussein collapsed, the spectre of the propaganda state also receded, as had happened throughout the twentieth century whenever a war emergency ended. The monologues died away. The big TV networks returned to the normal task of programing sitcoms and dramas and sports, etc., so they could sell the eyeballs of viewers to advertisers. The news media talked about much else than Iraq, about problems in Israel and Palestine for instance, but emphasizing, once again, the priority of the domestic scene, especially because the public was worried about jobs.

Yet the fact remained that Washington had sold the commodity of war against the grain of democracy. The precedent, and the apparatus, remained. The weapons of mass destruction were bogus, at least this time round. The weapons of mass persuasion were not. They were used, and with deadly effect, in the United States. Democracy did not die, as had happened in communist and fascist lands. Nor was democracy put on hold, as to some extent occurred in North America in the Second World War. Rather democracy was overwhelmed by a torrent of lies, half-truths, infotainment, and marketing. Who can doubt that these tools will be deployed once again when the next chapter in the story of permanent warfare gets written?

Postscript: Summer/Fall 2003

The cover headline of the October 6th *Time* read 'MISSION NOT ACCOMPLISHED.' It was superimposed on a picture of a smiling George Bush, dressed in his pilot's outfit, surrounded by the sailors of the USS *Abraham Lincoln*, taken during his triumphant address on 1 May. The reference was to a banner on the deck of the aircraft carrier that had proclaimed 'MISSION ACCOMPLISHED.' Inside the magazine was a series of stories, full of references to officials and experts and politicians, that detailed how badly things had gone wrong in post-invasion Iraq: the persistence of guerrilla assaults in and around Baghdad, the failure to find the weapons of mass destruction, the way American soldiers were increasingly viewed by Iraqis as occupiers rather than liberators, the continuing sad state of Iraqi oil and electricity supplies. Perhaps the fall of Baghdad had not marked a victory: rather, the war had unexpectedly entered a new phase, whether against the remaining diehards loyal to Saddam Hussein, a new group of Iraqi nationalists, or jihadists recruited from outside the country. (By early November *Time* had taken to calling the insurgents 'resistance fighters.') The scale of the problem was made all the more obvious by the administration's recent request for a whopping $87 billion to manage and reconstruct Iraq (and Afghanistan), causing a serious case of sticker shock in the minds of many Americans, not the least some Republican congressmen.

What and who was to blame? *Time* had a lot of answers. There was the intelligence failure, the fact that Washington did not receive, or perhaps did not listen to, evidence of the degraded state of services and industry in pre-war Iraq. Also important was the ongoing feud between the State Department and the Pentagon over control of policy, a feud that predated the war campaign launched in September 2002, which had undermined the effort to establish peace and security in Iraq. The stories took note of the naiveté of too many government officials, notably Paul Wolfowitz, who had expected American rule would be welcomed by the populace of Iraq. They had listened too readily to the siren songs of men like Ahmed Chalabi, an exiled Iraqi leader, who were out of touch with Iraqi realities. Donald Rumsfeld was too pig-headed to see reason about the need for more troops. Paul Bremer, the interim governor of Iraq, had made 'the disastrous decision' to disband the Iraqi army, thus putting a lot of unemployed soldiers on the streets. The names went on and on; it seemed no one really knew what he or she was doing.

What *Time* did not do was to speculate about the wisdom of leaving Iraq and turning the country over to its citizens, realizing liberation (if not the American style of democracy) as soon as possible. It certainly was not prepared to label the invasion a mistake, even if it noted how Europe remained unwilling to assist the United States, despite Bush's pleas. Nor did the magazine raise the general issue of whether the radical foreign policy of the administration, its commitment to pre-emptive action in the war on terror, had proved a dangerous failure. Some questions were still out of bounds in early October for a mainstream news source, just as Chomsky and Herman had predicted. Still, *Time* had certainly painted a picture of inefficiency, incompetence, and confusion.

The stories showed just how swiftly the hegemony of Washington had unravelled since Bush's moment of triumph. The victory in Iraq had spawned a new set of political problems and opened a new front in the war on terror. That elite consensus over the war in Washington had evaporated. The Democratic opposition had revitalized; indeed, Howard Dean and

Wesley Clark, both presidential hopefuls, were attempting to exploit antiwar sentiment and a new mood of public disenchantment. The press, in turn, had become increasingly critical of Bush and Washington, since the disputes in high places justified a closer scrutiny of the administration's misdoings. Besides, as Michael Schudson has pointed out, the American news media were particularly event-driven, focusing much more on concrete actions than on ideas. The ongoing wave of bombings, rocket attacks, and deaths – of American soldiers and Iraqi civilians and UN and foreign-aid personnel – this news proved irresistible and belied administration claims that things were getting better in Iraq. Public-opinion polls indicated the turn of fortune: Bush's own ratings dropped dramatically, at one point reaching 50 per cent early in the fall, the lowest since 9/11. Likewise, the polls indicated much of the public had little faith in the administration's Iraq policy. A Gallup survey of 6–8 October found that fully 58 per cent thought things were going badly for the United States.

All of which was both a cause and an effect of the remarkable collapse of Washington's marketing exercise. One of the *Time* essays, coyly entitled 'Operation Oprah,' noted how the administration 'may not be communicating well, or Americans may just not be buying what the White House is selling.' No wonder. It did not help the President that evidence had come to light he had exaggerated the menace posed by Saddam Hussein's Iraq, and its purported nuclear capabilities, in his State of the Union address in January. As early as June, again according to the polls, the public was increasingly sceptical about the veracity of Washington's war marketing, although most thought Bush had exaggerated or stretched the truth rather than lied. Excepting Republicans (and habitual viewers of Fox News, who may well have been the same sort of folk), most Americans disagreed with Bush's claim that the news media were making the situation in Iraq seem worse than it really was, according to a Pew Research survey (21 October).

The trouble was that Washington no longer had a product, a public good, that was easily saleable. The price alone, that

$87 billion, was too high, especially when the Bush administration (as *Time* pointed out) was so unwilling to spend anything approaching the same sums of money on jails, police and firefighters, electricity, and the like in America. No less worrisome was the cost in lives: by the beginning of November, the number of soldiers killed during the occupation topped the number slain in the invasion itself, with no end in sight. Furthermore, neither the other powers in the world nor Arab and Muslim countries seemed especially willing to lift much of the burden, in men and money, off the shoulders of the United States. There were a lot of 'free riders' happy to let Washington finish what it had started.

Even more serious, however, was the difficulty of positioning the reconstruction of Iraq so that it met the perceived needs of the American public. A Pew Research survey around the third anniversary of 9/11 found that Americans were still full of fear, three in four counting the world a more dangerous place than it was a decade earlier. The elimination of the regime of Saddam Hussein (except that he, like Osama bin Laden, was still on the loose, and that was a continuing source of concern) had satisfied one long-standing wish for security. Rebuilding Iraq, in itself, did not have the same cachet. There was one way out: preach the American mission of democracy. Nation-building in Iraq might then appear as the centrepiece of a strategy of democratic reform throughout the world. 'The establishment of a free Iraq at the heart of the Middle East will be a watershed event in the global democratic revolution,' President Bush claimed (*New York Times*, 9 November) when he signed the aid bill for Iraq. He said much the same in a speech he delivered to the National Endowment for Democracy early in November, where he linked the success of a freed Iraq and the rise of Arab democracy to the future elimination of the political conditions that generated terrorism. However, the zeal to build democracy across the globe had so far only captured the fancy of neo-conservatives – and frightened their left-wing critics with the spectre of a new wave of American imperialism. Barring some dramatic escalation in the jihadist assault on the West, there was little evidence such a marketing exercise would win the support of the elites or the public in general.

Washington had hoped, if not promised, that its 'war of liberation' would deliver a grateful country, similar in spirit to a newly freed France in the aftermath of the Second World War. Instead, after a summer and fall of increasing resistance, the invasion had produced yet another quagmire, all too reminiscent of Vietnam, an unstable Iraq where American soldiers were bogged down in constant combat. A headline in the *New York Times* (9 November) put it best: Americans might be 'Watching Iraq,' but they were 'Seeing Vietnam.' It was hard to escape the burden of History, especially the history of imperialism. Not even the capture of Saddam Hussein changed that fact.

APPENDIX

Consumer Voices / Citizens' Panel

Listed below are the dates and the subjects of my interviews. In each case participants were guaranteed a degree of anonymity, and they were allowed to select a pseudonym if they so wished. I have identified the participants by their professions, the dates of the interview, and whether the interview was joint (that is, involving a discussion among more than one subject). The nature and the process of the interviews was informed not so much by the techniques of the social survey, employed by the sociologist, as by the approach of the cultural analyst, where the purpose is to discover what meanings people construct from their use of symbolic products and how they consume or create narratives and spectacles. I used a script to elicit opinions: the volunteers were asked about their use of the media, their understanding of the war as both story and spectacle, as well as their views about the war as an event and about the performance of the leading participants.

1. University community

Bob: professor (21 May)
Bruce R: graduate student (12 May)
Chris: graduate student (9 May)
Geoff: graduate student (13 May), joint
Mike: professor (15 May)

Reza: graduate student (16 May)
Richard: retired professor (20 May)
Stephanie: graduate student (13 May), joint

2. General community

Bruce W: retired teacher (8 May), joint
Dave: teacher (13 May), joint
Dennis: teacher (15 May), joint
Glenna: artist (8 May), joint
Irene: entrepreneur (21 May)
Jennifer: teacher (15 May), joint
Melissa: teacher (15 May), joint
Michael: lawyer (20 May)
Orsolina: teacher (15 May), joint
Oscar: retired engineer (10 May)
Sam: editor (7 May)
Savino: teacher (15 May), joint

Sources

The references below list both the principal secondary sources I used in preparing the book, other than the newspaper reports that are dated in the text, as well as a few works that may be useful for readers who wish to pursue particular matters of interest. The sources are cited by chapter, and they are only noted the first time they appear, though they may heen used in later chapters of the book.

1. Marketing's Moment

Balnaves, Maik, James Donald, and Stephanie Hemelryk Donald. *The Penguin Atlas of Media and Information*. Toronto: Penguin Canada 2001.

Bennett, Tony, and Janet Woollacott. *Bond and Beyond: The Political Career of a Popular Hero*. Houndmills and London: Macmillan Education 1987.

Chapman, James. *Licence to Thrill: A Cultural History of the James Bond Films*. London and New York: I.B. Taurus 1999.

Gitlin, Todd. *Media Unlimited: How the Torrent of Images and Sounds Overwhelms Our Lives*. New York: Henry Holt 2002.

Herman, Edward S., and Noam Chomsky. *Manufacturing Consent: The Political Economy of the Mass Media*. 2nd edition. New York: Pantheon Books 2002; first published 1988.

Lasch, Christopher. 'Journalism, Publicity and the Lost Art of Argument.' *Gannett Center Journal* 4, no. 2 (Spring 1990), 1–11. The whole issue was devoted to publicity in the United States.

Pratkanis, Anthony, and Elliot Aronson. *Age of Propaganda: The Everyday Use and Abuse of Persuasion*. New York: W.H. Freeman 1991.

Robinson, Daniel. *The Measure of Democracy: Polling, Market Research, and Public Life 1930–1945*. Toronto: University of Toronto Press, 1999. Robinson charts the origins of a 'marketing polity' in Canada, focusing particularly on polling.

Rutherford, Paul. *Endless Propaganda: The Advertising of Public Goods*. Toronto: University of Toronto Press 2000.

– *The New Icons?: The Art of Television Advertising*. Toronto: University of Toronto Press 1994.

2. The War Debate

Ackerman, Spencer, and John Judis. 'Deception and Democracy: The Selling of the Iraq War.' *The New Republic*, 30 June 2003, 14–18, 23–5.

AEI Studies in Public Opinion. *America after 9/11*, an American Enterprise Institute compilation (updated 4 July 2003).

Canadian Broadcasting Corporation (CBC), National Radio News and Current Affairs. 'Protest.' Web One (online feature), 2003.

EKOS Research Associates. 'EKOS/CBC/SRC/Toronto Star/La Presse Poll, February 21, 2003.'

Ellul, Jacques. *Propaganda: The Formation of Men's Attitudes*. New York: Vintage Books 1973.

MoveOn.org. *National TV Highlight Reel*, a RealVideo record, available on the MoveOn.org website (July 2003).

Pew Research Center for the People and the Press. 'America's Image Further Erodes, Europeans Want Weaker Ties: A Nine Country Survey.' 18 March 2003.

– *Views of a Changing World June 2003*. Washington 2003.

Rampton, Sheldon, and John Stauber. *Weapons of Mass Deception: The Uses of Propaganda in Bush's War on Iraq*. New York: Penguin 2003. This book contains a fine discussion of Charlotte Beers's campaign, among much else.

'Text of George W. Bush's News Conference,' 17 July 2003. Available, with the RealVideo record, on CBC's website, June 2003.

Toffler, Betsy-Ann, and Jane Imber. *Dictionary of Marketing Terms.* 2nd edition. New York: Barron's Educational Series 1994.

3. Managing War

Arlen, Michael. *Living-Room War.* New York: Penguin 1982; first published 1969.

Beelman, Maud. 'The Dangers of Disinformation in the War on Terrorism.' *Niemann Reports* 55, no. 4 (Winter 2001), 16–18.

Boot, Max. 'The New American Way of War.' *Foreign Affairs* 82, no. 4 (July/August 2003), 41–58.

CBC News Online. 'Reality Check: Psychological Operations – Cheaper than Blood.' 26 March 2003.

CBS News. 'Words as Weapons.' 18 March 2003.

Hallin, Daniel. *The 'Uncensored War': The Media and Vietnam.* New York: Oxford University Press 1986. The standard, highly regarded work on Vietnam war coverage, as well as one source of the 'indexing' hypothesis referred to briefly in chapter 8.

Marlin, Randal. *Propaganda and the Ethics of Persuasion,* 194–9. Peterborough, ON: Broadview Press 2002. On the incubator babies story.

Parker, J., and Jerold Hale. 'Psychological Operations in the Gulf War: Analyzing Key Themes in Battlefield Leaflets.' In Thomas McCain and Leonard Shyles, eds, *The 1,000 Hour War: Communication in the Gulf,* 89–109. Westport, CT: Greenwood Press 1994.

Smith, Terence. 'Real-Time War: Defining News in the Middle East.' *Columbia Review of Journalism,* May/June 2003, online edition.

Taylor, Philip M. 'Conflict and Conflicting Cultures: The Military and the Media.' Paper presented at a conference on media oversight, Budapest, 6–9 February 2003; online at www.dcaf.ch, the website of the Geneva Centre for the Democratic Control of Armed Forces.

Ullman, Harlan K., and James P. Wade. *Shock and Awe: Achieving Rapid Dominance.* Washington: National Defense University Press, 1996. Available on the website of the Command and Control Research Program (CCRP) within the Office of the Assistant Secretary of Defense (May 2003).

Woodward, Gary C. 'The Rules of the Game: The Military and the Press in the Persian Gulf War.' In Robert Denton, Jr, ed., *The Media and the Persian Gulf War*, 1–26. Westport, CT: Praeger 1993.

4. Real-Time War

Bourdieu, Pierre. *On Television*. Trans. Priscilla Parkhurst Ferguson. New York: New Press 1998.

Engstrom, Nicholas. 'The Soundtrack for War.' *Columbia Journalism Review*, May/June 2003, online edition.

Guardian Newspapers. *The War We Could Not Stop: The Real Story of the Battle for Iraq*. Ed. Randeep Ramesh. London: Faber & Faber 2003.

Kuttab, Daoud. 'The Arab TV Wars.' *New York Times Magazine*, 6 April 2003.

Lawson, Annie. 'US Broadcasters' War Stance under Scrutiny.' *The Guardian*, 14 April 2003. [On Rupert Murdoch.]

Livingston, Steven, and Sean Aday. 'TVNewscan,' A Project of the George Washington University. Presented 3 October 2003 (online at smpa.gwu.edu/index.gw). The project compared news at ABC, NBC, CBS, CNN, and Fox.

Pew Research Center for the People and the Press. 'War Coverage Praised, but Public Hungry for Other News.' 9 April 2003.

– 'How Global Publics View: Their Lives, Their Countries, the World, America.' 4 December 2002.

Poniewozik, James. 'Whose Flag Is Bigger?' *Time*, 14 April 2003.

Postman, Neil. *Amusing Ourselves to Death: Public Discourse in the Age of Show Business*. New York: Viking Penguin 1985.

Rutenberg, Jim, and Bill Carter. 'Spectacular Success or Incomplete Picture? Views of TV's War Coverage Are Split.' *New York Times*, 20 April 2003.

5. Consuming War

Gerbner, George. 'Persian Gulf War, the Movie.' In Hamid Mowlana, George Gerbner, and Herbert Schiller, eds, *Triumph of the*

Image: The Media's War in the Persian Gulf – A Global Perspective, 243–65. Boulder, CO: Westview Press 1992.

Habermas, Jürgen. *The Structural Transformation of the Public Sphere: An Inquiry into a Category of Bourgeois Society*. Trans. Thomas Burger with Frederick Lawrence. Cambridge, MA: MIT Press 1991.

Hallin, Daniel, and Todd Gitlin. 'The Gulf War as Popular Culture and Television Drama.' In W. Lance Bennett and David Paletz, eds, *Taken By Storm: The Media, Public Opinion, and U.S. Foreign Policy in the Gulf War*, 149–63. Chicago: University of Chicago Press 1994.

Newspaper Audience Databank. *2002 NADbank Study*. Canada (online at www.nadbank.com).

6. Perceptions of War

CBC. 'Your Space: Letters on the War.' Online at the CBC website, Spring 2003.

Canadian Television Network (CTV) website. 'Text of U.S. President George Bush's Speech.' Posted 2 May 2003.

De Zengotita, Thomas. 'The Romance of Empire.' *Harper's*, July 2003, 31–9.

Dorman, William. 'Stop Me before I Shill Again: American Journalism and the Iraq War.' Roundtable, International Communication Association and American Political Science Association, vol. 13, no. 3 (Fall 2003) (online at www.ou.edu/policom/1303_2003_fall/dorman.htm).

Gallup. 'American Public Opinion about Iraq.' 6 May 2003.

Gallup News Service. 'Speech Watchers Believe Iraq Victory Aids U.S. in War on Terrorism.' 2 May 2003.

Ipsos-Reid. 'On the Eve of G-8 Summit in France ...' 29 May 2003.

– 'Canada and the Iraq War: Two Solitudes Emerge.' 6 April 2003.

Kaplan, Robert D. 'Supremacy by Stealth.' *Atlantic Monthly*, July/August 2003, 65–83.

Pew Research Center for the People and the Press. 'To the Victor Go the Polls.' 30 April 2003.

- '60% the War's Going Very Well – 69% We Haven't Won Yet.'
  10 April 2003.
- 'War Coverage Praised, but Public Hungry for Other News.'
  9 April 2003.
- 'TV Combat Fatigue on the Rise.' 28 March 2003.

7. The Phallic Dimension

Brockes, Emma. 'What Is It about Men and Guns?' *The Guardian*,
  26 March 2003.
Coleman, Sarah. 'The Lysistrata Project: Theater of Peace.' *World
  Press Review*, 27 February 2003 (online at www.worldpress.org).
Dean, Carolyn. 'History, Pornography and the Social Body.' In
  Jennifer Mundy, ed., *Surrealism: Desire Unbound*, 227–43. London:
  Tate Publishing 2001.
Freud, Sigmund. *Civilization, Society and Religion: Group Psychology,
  Civilization and Its Discontents and Other Works*. Vol. 12 of the
  Penguin Freud Library, ed. Albert Dickson, 243–340. Harmonds-
  worth: Penguin 1991.
Gallup Poll, 28 March 2003. At www.seniorjournal.com (in October
  2003).
Goldstein, Richard. 'Bush's Basket: Why the President Had to Show
  His Balls.' *The Village Voice*, 21–27 May 2003.
- 'War Horny: Victory Is the Ultimate Viagra.' *The Village Voice*, 16–
  22 April 2003.
- 'Neo-Macho Man.' *The Nation*, 24 March 2003.
Hertzberg, Hendrik. 'Blixkrieg.' *The New Yorker*, 10 February 2003.
Mailer, Norman. 'The White Man Unburdened.' *New York Review of
  Books*, 17 July 2003, 4 and 6 (an earlier version appeared in the
  London Times, 29 April 2003).
North, Titus. 'The Transformation of the Free Press into War Por-
  nographers.' Wombat News Center (online at www.pitt.edu/
  ~ctnst3/news/warporn.html).
Pollitt, Katha. 'Phallic Balloons against the War.' *The Nation*,
  24 March 2003.
Remnick, David. 'War Without End.' *The New Yorker*, posted on the
  web 14 April 2003.

Shepard, Ben. 'Absurd Responses vs. Earnest Politics; Global Justice vs. Anti-War Movements; Guerrilla Theater and Aesthetic Solutions.' *Journal of Aesthetics & Protest* 1, no. 2 (January 2003) (online at www.journalofaestheticsandprotest.org).

8. The Propaganda State

Bennett, Lance. 'Operation Perfect Storm: The Press and the Iraq War.' Roundtable, International Communication Association and American Political Science Association, vol. 13, no. 3 (Fall 2003) (online at www.ou.edu/policom/1303_2003_fall/bennett.htm).
– 'Toward a Theory of Press–State Relations in the United States.' *Journal of Communication* 40, no. 2 (Spring 1990), 103–25.
Chomsky, Noam. *Necessary Illusions: Thought Control in Democratic Societies*. Montreal and New York: CBC Enterprises 1989.
Entman, Robert. 'Cascading Activation: Contesting the White House's Frame after 9/11.' *Political Communication* 20 (2003), 415–32. An updating of the indexing hypothesis.
FAIR (Fairness & Accuracy in Reporting). 'Amplifying Officials, Squelching Dissent.' *Extra*, May/June 2003 (online at www.fair org/extra/0305/warstudy).
– 'Media Advisory: Some Critical Media Voices Face Censorship.' 3 April 2003 (online at www fair.org/press-releases/iraq-censorship).
Kenez, Peter. *The Birth of the Propaganda State: Soviet Methods of Mass Mobilization, 1917–1929*. Cambridge: Cambridge University Press 1985.
Stark, Nans-Günther. 'The Eye of the Dictator.' Video-recording. London: Charisma Films 1994.
Welch, David. *The Third Reich: Politics and Propaganda*. London and New York: Routledge 1995.

Postscript: Summer/Fall 2003

CBSNews.com. 'Americans More Skeptical on WMD.' 14 June 2003.
Gallup. 'Questions and Answers about Iraq.' 14 October 2003.

Pew Research Center for the People and the Press. 'Rising Job
Worries, Bush Economic Plan Doesn't Help.' 21 October 2003.
– '75% Say It's a More Dangerous World.' 4 September 2003.
Schudson, Michael. 'If You Start with Autonomous Journalists, Will
You End Up with a Free Press? Or Why We Need an Unlovable
Press.' Reilly Center for Media and Public Affairs, Louisiana State
University, March 2003 (online at www.lsu.edu/reillycenter/
batonrouge228.pdf).

Index

Abbhas, Ali Ismael (hurt child), 177
ABC (American Broadcasting Corporation), 45, 83, 91, 102, 130; news, 33, 74, 76, 104
Abdo, Hassan (Egyptian tailor), 144
Abu Dhabi TV, 78, 83, 87
Action/adventure, 7, 18–19, 20, 69, 71, 86, 94, 132, 135–7, 141, 176
Adie, Kate (journalist), 164
Advertising, 10, 12–13, 17, 19, 29, 30–1, 32, 38, 58, 59, 60, 65, 78, 90, 100, 102–3, 111, 119, 155, 185, 193; advocacy, 14–15, 36, 43, 45, 112, 187; attack ads, 59; clutter, 11; Creative Revolution, 12; green, 14; issue campaigns, 14, 15; political, 14. See also Marketing; Propaganda
Advertising Age, 31, 102, 103

Advertising Council, 14, 30
Afghanistan, 19, 26, 72, 73, 83, 93, 182, 194
Africa, 11, 73
Air Canada, 58
Al-Arabiya, 83, 84, 97, 116
Albuquerque Journal, 112
Al-Jazeera, 4, 30, 31, 78, 83–4, 87, 96, 99, 100, 101, 104, 107, 116, 156, 158–9, 168, 180
Al-Karram, Tamara (Jordanian journalist), 90
Alliance Atlantis Communications, 189
Al-Manar, 28, 83
Al-Qaeda, 24–5, 26, 33, 36, 73, 120, 123, 171
American Enterprise Institute, 33
American Idol (TV), 107
Americans (public), 11, 25, 30, 31, 71, 86, 105, 119, 142, 161, 175, 188, 191, 192; media

habits, 9, 10, 110; views, 22,
33–4, 35, 38, 46, 100, 102–3,
150–5, 183, 196
Amman, 30, 47, 158, 159
Anglo sphere, 123, 149
Anti-Americanism, 29, 31, 43,
48, 83, 113, 122, 130, 145, 146,
148, 172
Antiwar (peace) cause, 6, 24,
32, 37, 38–49, 41, 53, 119,
124–5, 130, 133, 141, 142, 147,
148, 149, 151, 152, 153, 167,
169, 188–9, 196; Vietnam, 49,
71
Apocalypse Now, 18
Arabs, 6, 26, 83–4, 85, 87, 100,
107, 116, 124, 129, 133, 139,
177, 197; opinion, 27–31, 104,
123, 144, 155–9, 160
Aras (Iranian student), 144
Argentina, 71
Aristophanes, 167
Arlen, Michael (author), 70
Armageddon, threat of, 39, 45
Armchair generals, 67, 68, 85,
127, 128, 152
Arnett, Peter (journalist), 97,
107
Arnot, Bob (journalist), 94
'As It Happens' (radio), 157
Asia, 18, 169
Associated Press, 43
Atlanta Journal-Constitution, 169
Atlantic Monthly, 162
Atrocity story, 61, 96
Atwood, Margaret (novelist),
183

Audiences and viewers, 3, 4, 5,
7, 12, 19, 20, 21, 23, 24, 30, 31,
34, 35, 37, 52, 65, 80, 81, 86,
87, 96, 100, 111–12, 132, 149,
157, 166, 172, 176, 181, 182,
191, 193; cynicism of, 119;
disbelief of, 32, 112, 120;
tastes and habits, 9, 83, 102–
5, 107, 138, 139, 144, 152–3,
154, 156, 164, 186–7, 192, 196
Australasia, 10
Australia, 160
Automobile industry, 102
Axis of evil, 27, 92

Baathist Party, 57, 182
Baez, Joan (protest singer), 49
Baghdad, 50, 60, 64, 66, 78, 83,
93, 94, 97, 101, 129, 137, 156,
194; bombed, 4, 46, 53–4, 86,
87–91, 100, 102, 103, 108, 117,
119, 136, 151, 176; captured,
52, 74, 76, 77, 85, 114, 126,
139, 140, 152, 158–9, 177–9,
180
Barfi Culture (website), 169
Basra, 21, 95, 96
Baudrillard, Jean (theorist), 86
BBC (British Broadcasting
Corporation), 4, 69, 78, 83,
104, 108, 116, 125, 129, 164
Beelman, Maude (journalist),
61
Beers, Charlotte (ad executive),
29, 30, 31
Behrendt, Fritz Alfred (cartoonist), 44

Beirut Star, 157
Bell, Martin (journalist), 78
Ben Casey (TV), 34
Benetton, 15
Bennett, Lance (media scholar),
   184, 185, 190
Berlin, 39, 144, 178
Big Brother (TV), 107
Bin Laden, Osama, 25–6, 28, 29,
   30, 33, 124, 139, 160–1, 168,
   197
Black Hawk Down, 70
Blade Runner, 132, 136
Blair, Tony, 22, 32, 47, 60, 96
Blitzkrieg, 54, 93, 97, 118, 150
Bloom, David (journalist), 93–4,
   135
Blume, Kathryn (protester), 167
Bob (participant), 48, 114, 118,
   119, 123–4, 131, 133, 135, 136,
   138, 140, 161, 181, 191
Bob Coen Insider's Report, 12
Boenigk, Ingeborg (German
   teacher), 144
Boer War, 124
Boligan, Angel (cartoonist), 165
Books, 9, 154, 185
Boot, Max (author), 52, 55, 56,
   162
Bosch, Hieronymous, 89
Bourdieu, Pierre (theorist), 81–
   2, 108
Bowles, Cynthia (journalist), 76
Bowling for Columbine, 132
Brand America, 30, 31, 59
Branigin, Walter (journalist), 96
Brazil, 12, 160

Bremer, Paul, 195
Brockes, Emma (journalist), 174
Brookings Institution, 76
Brooks, General Vincent, 65,
   67–8, 170
Brosnan, Pierce (actor), 19, 21
Brown, Aaron (journalist), 100,
   125
Bruce R (participant), 84, 117,
   119, 120, 126, 135, 136, 137,
   138, 141, 183
Bruce W (participant), 32, 35,
   113, 118, 119, 127, 133, 139,
   141, 161, 183
Buck Rogers (sci-fi character),
   131
Burridge, Air Marshall Brian,
   106, 108
Bush, George H.W., 171
Bush, George W., 5, 11, 16, 17,
   24, 26, 27, 29, 31, 32, 39, 41,
   43, 46, 47, 49, 60, 61, 92, 96,
   105, 153, 156, 195; addresses,
   34–6, 38, 62, 161, 163, 179,
   181–2, 194, 196, 197; administration, 22, 25–7, 32–3, 41, 62,
   64, 65, 97, 118, 146, 171, 182,
   188, 190–1; image, 21, 40, 52,
   122, 123, 140, 148, 161, 168,
   170, 171–2, 173. *See also*
   Washington: regime, White
   House

Cairo, 144, 158
Calais (Maine), 151
Calderon, Francisco José
   (cartoonist), 109

Canada, 14, 48, 90, 115, 123, 124, 128, 142, 145, 146–50, 160; media, 10, 103, 104–5, 114, 115

Canadians, 6, 40, 47, 48, 85, 117, 142; opinion, 27, 38, 39, 48, 91, 150, 160

Cardow, Cam (cartoonist), 180

Carnival, the spirit of, 5, 22, 168, 178

Carter, Jimmy, 171

Cartoons, 5, 113, 139, 173

Casciari, James (cartoonist), 80

Casualties issue, 33, 51, 53, 56, 62, 76, 91, 94, 100, 104, 129, 130, 131, 133, 137, 150, 151, 153, 156, 196

Cavuto, Neil (journalist), 97

CBC (Canadian Broadcasting Corporation), 4, 40, 47, 49, 61, 74, 77, 83, 85, 87, 90, 91, 103, 104–5, 108, 113, 115–16, 117, 125, 126, 128, 129, 139, 146, 148, 150, 157, 158, 175, 178, 187

CBS (Columbia Broadcasting System), 28–9, 53, 71, 76, 91, 98, 102, 104, 163, 189

Celebrities, 11, 41, 49

Celluci, Paul, 147

Censorship, 13, 70–2, 187, 189, 191

Central Command, 4, 55, 57, 65, 67, 152, 170

Cerre, Mike (journalist), 76

Chalabi, Ahmed, 195

Chan, Jackie (actor), 69

Chaplin, Charlie (actor), 132

Chappette, Patrick (cartoonist), 157, 162

Chater, David (journalist), 91

Cheney, Dick, 26, 40, 85

Chicago Tribune, 170

Children, motif of, 13, 18, 47, 101, 104, 110, 129, 133, 138, 158

China, 20, 125

Chomsky, Noam (theorist), 15, 184, 185, 195

Chrétien, Jean, 47, 122, 124, 147, 148

Chris (participant), 39, 117, 119, 120, 126, 129, 139, 184, 190

Churchill, Winston, 38, 61, 190

CIA (Central Intelligence Agency), 28

Citizens, people as, 7, 11, 16, 17, 24, 46, 49, 61, 70, 107, 111–12, 141–3, 146, 147, 149, 177, 183–4, 187. See also Consumers, people as

Citizens' panel. See Consumer voices / citizens' panel

Clark, General Wesley, 128, 196

Clarke, Victoria, 61, 66, 72, 76

Class issue, 170, 184

Clean war, motif of, 21, 51, 56, 90, 100, 129, 137, 150, 152, 160

Clement, Gary (cartoonist), 128

Clinton, Bill, 41, 171

CNN (Cable News Network), 10, 11, 41, 45, 60, 71, 80, 83, 85, 86, 91, 93, 98, 100, 103,

104, 105, 108, 109, 113, 116–
17, 125, 128, 129, 130, 142,
168, 172, 174, 176
CNN effect, 60, 117
Coalition of the Willing, 36, 39,
64, 101, 119, 122, 159
Coca-Cola, 11, 48
Cold War, 53, 187
Comcast, 41
Comedy, 75, 139, 167, 189
Comical Ali (Mohammed
Saeed Al-Sahaf), 63, 139, 140
Comics, 15
Commando Solo II, 57, 60
Committee on Public Educa
tion, 13
Commodity, 16, 19, 39, 80, 131;
war as, 4, 7, 18, 49, 53, 106,
113, 118, 119, 123, 153, 190,
193
Communications, 6, 9, 62, 65,
79, 81, 111
Communism, 13, 18, 181, 185,
193
Congress, 24, 32, 41, 128, 184,
185, 188
Consumers, people as, 4, 5, 6, 7,
8, 11, 12, 16, 17–18, 19, 32, 35,
48, 61, 62, 63, 108, 111, 112,
172, 174. See also Citizens,
people as
Consumer voices / citizens'
panel, 5–6, 18, 35, 47, 112–43,
147, 161, 176, 183, 191
Cooper, Gary (actor), 38
Cowboy image, 172, 173
Creel, George (official), 13

Cronkite, Walter (journalist), 71
CTV (Canadian Television
Network), 104–5, 115, 116,
125
Cuban missile crisis, 171
Cubist style, 86, 87, 91
Culture jamming, 15

Dahler, Dan (journalist), 76
Daily Mirror (UK), 97
Daily Nation (Nairobi), 180
Daisy ad, 42–3, 45
Dave (participant), 26, 44, 118,
127, 139, 174
De Villepin, Dominique, 22
De Zengotita, Thomas (writer),
19
Dean, Carolyn (historian), 174
Dean, Howard, 195
Death Star, 58
Decapitation strike, 21, 54, 64
Defense Policy Board, 26
Democracy, 4, 108, 149, 178,
193, 195; as cause, 27, 30, 38,
44, 123, 161, 197; philosophy
of, 111–12, 141–2, 187; prac-
tice of, 8, 17–18, 23, 82, 120,
123–4, 143–4, 183–5, 188–9,
190, 193
Democratic party, 41, 42, 128,
170, 188
Dennis (participant), 116, 125,
127
Denormalization, 17
Denver Post, 37
Der grosse König, 186
Diana, Princess, 82

Dickheads for War, 167
Die Another Day, 20
DiManno, Rosie (journalist),
   114
Dion, Celine (singer), 30
Direct mail, 11, 15
Dirty war, motif of, 21, 51, 100,
   101, 107, 133, 158, 177
Discourse, 7, 14, 81, 141
Dishonouring, practice of, 17,
   25, 40, 59, 168
Disney Studios, 3, 91
'Dispatches' (radio), 146, 175
Dissent, expression of, 27, 39,
   153, 184, 185, 188
Dixie Chicks (singers), 41
Doha, 65, 83, 170
Donahue, Phil (talk-show
   host), 189
Donvan, John (journalist), 74
Dorman, William (media
   scholar), 155
Douglas, Michael (actor), 65,
   171
Doyle, John (journalist), 179
Dream TV (Egypt), 156
Drehle, David Von (journalist),
   53
Dr Gillespie (TV character), 34
Dr Kildare (TV), 34
Dr Strangelove (movie charac-
   ter), 26, 32, 53, 132
Dr Zorba (TV character), 34
Dyer, Gwynne (pundit), 128

Economist, 113, 125, 130
Editor and Publisher, 76

Egypt, 115, 156, 158
8 Mile, 171
EKOS Poll, 39
Elites, 14, 15, 48, 108, 112, 113,
   143, 185, 188, 192, 195, 198
Ellul, Jacques (theorist), 24
E-mail, 55, 62, 65, 91, 107, 140,
   146, 148, 168
Eminem (singer/actor), 171
Empire, issue of, 40, 101, 122,
   123–4, 125, 160–1, 162, 164,
   197–8
Empire Strikes Back, The, 58
Engstrom, Nicholas (writer),
   98
Enola Gay, 90
Entertainment, 7, 10, 12, 18, 21,
   81, 102, 103, 105, 106, 111,
   115, 131–41, 164, 186
Europe, 10, 38–9, 47, 134, 141,
   157, 160, 172, 173, 195
Eves, Ernie, 148

Fahrenheit 451, 154
FAIR, 189
Falklands/Malvinas War, 71
Falwell, Reverend Jerry, 25
Farce, 140–1
Farouq, Adel (Egyptian taxi
   driver), 159
Fear Factor (TV), 107
Fear-mongering, 36, 37, 43, 58,
   191
Fedayeen, 64, 151
Federal Communications
   Commission, 41
Feminism, 25, 167

Fenton Communications, 42
Feuertaufe, 186
Film, 10, 178, 179, 186
Financial Times (London), 113, 125, 162
Firdos Square (Baghdad), 177
First World War, 13, 187
Fleischer, Ari, 65, 140
Fonda, Jane (actor), 49
Fox and Friends (TV), 97
Fox News, 23, 45, 46, 76, 95, 97–9, 102, 103, 105–6, 116, 146, 167, 196
France, 13, 22–3, 27, 39, 70, 73, 81, 86, 122, 160, 198
Franklin, Nancy (journalist), 91, 94
Franks, General Tommy, 50, 76
Free riders, 16, 26, 197
Freud, Sigmund, 166
Friendly fire, 62, 78, 130, 131
Friends-of-America rallies, 148–9
Frum, David (journalist), 27

Gallup Poll, 28, 33, 152, 170, 196
Garfield, Bob (journalist), 31
Gays, 25
Gender issue, 19, 164, 166, 167, 169, 170, 175
General Motors, 102
Geoff (participant), 113, 117, 119, 126, 127, 130, 135, 136, 138, 176, 188
Germany, 13, 27, 39, 90, 122, 160, 185, 189

Gitlin, Todd (media scholar), 9, 10, 111
Glenna (participant), 3, 6, 32, 35, 47, 113, 119, 131, 132, 133, 135, 139, 154
Global TV, 115, 116
Globe and Mail (Toronto), 76, 77, 85, 102, 114, 123, 179, 189
Goebbels, Joseph, 140, 186–7, 188, 190, 191
GoldenEye, 19, 20
Goldstein, Richard (writer), 86, 88, 168, 171, 172, 176
Goldwater, Barry, 42
Gore, Al, 16
Great Dictator, The, 132
Greenberg, Steve (cartoonist), 40, 101
Greenpeace, 42
Grenada, 71
Guardian (UK), 56, 64, 77, 78, 83, 105, 115, 125, 129
Guiliani, Rudy, 171
Gulf War I, 22, 33, 35, 50, 52, 54, 56, 57, 61, 65, 71–2, 80, 82, 84, 93, 131, 155, 190

Habermas, Jürgen (theorist), 141–2
Halifax, 46
Hamilton Spectator, 75, 180
Harper, Stephen, 147
Hassan (Egyptian viewer), 158
Hawks (American), 22–3, 26–7, 35, 49, 83, 122, 123, 127, 152, 162, 171, 182
Hayden, Tom (protester), 49

Hedges, Chris (journalist), 75
Hegemony, 160, 195; as model, 15, 184
Herman, Edward (media scholar), 15, 184, 185, 195
Hertzberg, Hendrik (journalist), 46, 172
High Noon, 38
Hill & Knowlton, 61
Hiroshima, 53, 54
History Channel, 94, 95
Hitler, Adolf, 35, 148, 181, 189
Hobbes, Thomas, 125
Hollywood, 18, 19, 41, 65, 69, 94, 106, 131, 135, 136, 173, 187, 191
Horsey, David (cartoonist), 98
Hotmail, 62
Hughes, Karen, 61
Human Interest, 20, 82, 137–8
Humanitarian issue, 68, 91, 100, 130, 138
Humour, 20, 34, 140, 168
Hussein, Saddam, 3, 34, 43, 57, 92, 93, 97, 124, 138, 139, 161, 167, 168, 174, 176, 177–9, 180, 191, 192, 194, 197, 198; as hero, 155, 159; statue of, 126, 159, 168, 177–9, 180; as threat, 33, 35, 36, 37, 66, 121, 122, 125, 136, 148, 188, 196; as villain, 21, 31, 32, 44, 58–9, 67, 96, 120, 121, 126, 133, 148, 155, 159
Hussein, Uday, 167

IBM, 9, 11
Independence Day, 26, 132, 156, 161, 181

Indiana Jones (movie character), 18, 85
Indianapolis Star-News, 23
Indian Mutiny, 124
Indonesia, 30, 104, 157, 160
Information, 4, 54–5, 60–1, 69, 72, 74, 77, 78, 82, 95, 110, 115, 117, 131, 139, 141, 154, 185; briefings, 52, 64–5, 67, 96, 120, 126; deception, 54; disinformation, 54, 55, 73; misinformation, 54, 55, 68, 70
Infotainment, 4, 82, 106, 108, 131, 142, 153, 193
Internet, 4, 9, 11, 25, 28, 39, 41, 55, 62, 79, 80, 108, 109, 114, 115, 139, 142, 166, 177
Ipsos-Reid poll, 149–50, 160
Iran, 27, 92, 125, 157, 182
Iran-Iraq War, 96
Iraq, 19, 23, 27, 31–8, 40, 42, 53, 57, 60, 83–4, 120, 123, 125, 134, 150, 162, 166, 172, 184, 191, 194–8
Iraqi regime/government, 4, 32, 41, 62, 63, 73, 90, 101, 153, 156, 166, 178, 179
Iraqis, 50, 57, 68, 69, 118, 120, 127, 150, 151, 174, 178, 179, 194, 195, 196; military, 51–2, 55, 56, 57–60, 61, 66–7, 85, 95, 121, 123, 128, 136, 137, 139, 156; as victims, 44, 56, 58–9, 64, 74, 96, 100, 101, 107, 122, 129, 130, 133–5, 138, 157, 158, 180
Iraq War, 3–4, 6, 21, 22–3, 27, 46–7, 50–2, 53–4, 55–60,

60–70, 72–8, 79–81, 82–110,
101, 112–43, 144–63, 164–6,
168–82, 183, 184, 188, 189,
195, 197, 198
Irene (participant), 48, 113, 116,
119, 124, 125, 126, 131, 132,
133, 137, 138, 140, 164, 189
Islam, 6, 17, 26, 27–31, 45, 47,
60, 83, 101, 104, 118, 121, 124,
155–6, 158–9, 160–1, 182, 197
Israel, 21, 28–9, 31, 83, 113, 122,
155, 159, 160, 182, 193
Italy, 12, 27, 39, 73, 160
ITN (Independent Television
News), 77
ITT, 58
Iwo Jima, 181

Jakarta, 104
James Bond saga, 19–21, 80, 90
Japan, 10, 12, 53, 54, 90, 145
Jennifer (participant), 117, 127,
130, 139, 189
Jews, 6, 13, 28, 29
Jihad, 29, 124, 161
Jihadists, 17, 25, 26–7, 45, 124,
194, 197
Jodoin, Debbie (pro-war activ-
ist), 148–9
Johnson, Lyndon, 71, 190
Jordan, 10, 28, 30, 47, 158, 160
Journalism, 7, 16, 64, 70–2, 77–
8, 81–100, 101, 105–6, 108,
125–32, 135, 185, 188; embed-
ded, 64, 70, 72–7, 85, 86, 91,
93–5, 96–7, 107–8, 115, 126–7,
130, 131, 135, 152, 168; objec-
tivity in, 16, 73, 76, 105, 125,

130, 152; sensationalism in,
20, 95, 130, 138
J. Walter Thompson, 29

Kaplan, Robert (author), 162
Karbala (Iraq), 96, 129
Keefe, Mike (cartoonist), 37
Kelly, Greg (journalist), 76
Kennedy, John F., 171, 190
Khouri, Rami (journalist), 157
Kirkuk, 93
Klein, Ralph, 148
Koppel, Ted (journalist), 99
Kosovo, 83
Kristol, William (writer), 26–7
Kurds, 35
Kuwait, 10, 61, 72, 93, 135, 155,
159, 160

Lakey, James (journalist), 97
Language of war, 62–4, 100,
119, 156
Lapham, Lewis (editor), 125
La Presse (Montreal), 114
Lasch, Christopher (theorist),
15
Latin America, 122, 145
Lawrence of Arabia, 132
Leaflets, 4, 57, 58
Lebanon, 28, 160
Le Devoir (Montreal), 114
Left/liberal (political views), 6,
14, 25, 41–3, 64, 108, 113, 122,
141, 162, 197
Legitimacy issue, 3, 23, 112, 183
Leila (Saudi Arabian viewer),
158
Lenin, Vladimir, 187

Liberal party, 149
Liberation issue, 19, 36, 38, 44,
  51, 60, 62, 66, 96, 100, 101, 120,
  123, 138, 149, 150, 155, 157,
  159, 166, 177–9, 194, 195, 198
Lobbying, 15, 32
London, 39, 65, 144
London Times, 19
Looting, 133, 134, 158, 178
Lopez, Jennifer (singer), 11
Los Angeles Times, 42
Luckovich, Mike (cartoonist),
  169
Lynch, Private Jessica, 68, 69,
  70, 135, 138, 151
Lysistrata Project, 167, 168

Machismo, 20–1, 164–72, 173,
  174, 175, 178, 179, 181–2
Macintosh PC, 9
MacKay, Graeme (cartoonist),
  75, 180
MacKenzie, Major-General
  Lewis (pundit), 128
MacMillan, Kent (Canadian
  viewer), 91
Madison Avenue, 12, 191
Madonna (singer), 48
Madrid, 24
Magazines, 4, 9, 11, 12, 26, 79,
  102, 114, 142, 194
Mahmour, Maha (Jordanian
  mother), 158
Mailer, Norman (novelist), 170,
  181
Mansbridge, Peter (journalist),
  87, 89, 90

Margulies, Jimmy (cartoonist),
  51
Marines, 64, 94
Marketing, 4, 5, 6, 7, 8–18, 19,
  24, 25–6, 30–1, 32, 53, 55,
  57–60, 61–2, 62–3, 67, 70, 72,
  82, 97–9, 105–6, 108, 110, 113,
  118–21, 142, 148–9, 155, 163,
  167–8, 170, 171–2, 178–9, 185,
  190, 192, 193, 196, 198. *See
  also* Advertising, Propaganda
Marketing polity, a, 17
Marketplace, 8, 11, 12, 17, 48, 80
MasterCard, 102
Matrix, The, 192
McCaffrey, General Barry
  (pundit), 128
McCann-Erickson, 12, 30
McCarthy, Sheryl (journalist),
  99
McDonald's, 180
McInerney, Jay (novelist), 20
McLuhan, Marshall (theorist),
  81
Media, 4, 10–11, 20, 22, 24–5,
  55, 60–1, 78, 79–81, 82, 83–5,
  96–7, 106, 108, 109, 110, 111–
  12, 139, 156, 165, 166, 167,
  172, 177, 186, 187, 192, 193;
  Canada, 103, 104–5, 146, 147;
  Middle East, 10, 28, 29–30,
  31, 60, 83–4, 133, 156;
  Toronto panel, 113–17, 126,
  129, 130–1, 135–6, 141, 142;
  US, 9–10, 14, 15–16, 17, 23,
  32, 41, 43, 45, 49, 52, 53, 59,
  64, 66, 67, 68–9, 71–2, 77, 95,

100, 102–6, 152–3, 168, 175, 184–5, 188–9, 191, 196
Media relations, 18
Melissa (participant), 37, 116, 130, 161, 191
Melodrama, 20, 156
Metallica (rock group), 98
Mexico, 10
Michael (participant), 35, 47, 117, 118, 130, 131, 133, 140, 171, 190
Mickey Mouse, 172
Middle East, 10, 21, 28–9, 35, 36, 43, 104, 107, 120, 121, 145, 155–9 197
Mike (participant), 65, 114, 117, 118, 119, 121, 126, 132, 133, 135, 137, 138, 140, 142, 178, 179, 190
Mission, American sense of, 25, 32, 38, 161–3, 197
Mission Impossible (TV), 69
Mogadishu, 99
Monty Python (TV), 140
Moore, Michael (writer), 41, 61
Morality, language of, 13, 14, 17, 21, 23, 34–5, 39, 44, 49, 52, 112, 122, 125, 132, 140, 148, 161, 163, 171, 177
Morocco, 160
MoveOn.org, 41, 42, 43, 45
Movies, 7, 9, 10, 18–19, 20, 24, 26, 36, 50, 69–70, 71, 80, 87, 90, 91, 93, 111, 144, 156, 164, 171, 173, 176, 181–2, 186–7, 189, 191, 192; Iraq the movie, 131–41, 182, 191

MSNBC, 98, 103, 178, 189
Murdoch, Rupert (media owner), 10, 20, 105
Murray, Don (journalist), 77, 178
Musée de la publicité, 13
Museo de Jamon, 24
Mwampembwa, Godfrey (cartoonist), 180
Mystery, 138–9

NAACP, 42
Nagasaki, 53, 54
Nahwa Al-Hurrich (TV service), 60
Namibian, 177
Narrative, 4, 34, 68, 95, 135, 178
Nation, The, 75, 171
National Air and Space Museum, 90
National Council of Churches, 42
National Endowment for Democracy, 197
National Guard, 181
Nationalism, 57, 113, 148, 194. See also Patriotism
National Organization for Women, 42
National Post (Toronto), 7, 114, 123, 125, 128
Nazis, 14, 18, 166, 181, 185–6, 191
NBC (National Broadcasting Corporation), 45, 64, 69, 83, 93, 94, 97, 102, 103, 104, 107, 128, 156

Neo-conservatism, 26–7, 39,
114, 122, 197
New Coke, 9
News, 8, 79, 111, 164, 167, 176,
178, 186, 187, 189; discourse,
10, 11, 17, 20, 28, 30, 45, 52,
53, 81–2, 95, 100, 101, 106–10,
113–18, 125–7, 128, 129–31,
138, 144, 166, 174; impact,
151–2, 153, 154, 155, 156, 158;
management, 60–9, 70–7,
119–20, 190, 191; media, 15,
24, 32, 83–5, 99, 102–6, 112,
168, 195
Newsday, 99
NewsNet (CTV), 103
Newspapers, 3, 4, 6, 9, 11, 15,
28, 69, 79, 85, 95, 96, 104, 106,
108, 114–15, 119, 123, 133,
142, 156, 185
Newsreels, 186, 187
Newsrooms, 4, 96, 108, 130,
132, 152, 153, 189
Newsweek, 83
Newsworld (CBC), 103, 115,
116
New World Order, 163
New York, 12, 24, 28, 125, 167,
171, 188
New York Daily News, 86
New York Times, 42, 51, 52, 63,
64, 65, 86, 92, 114, 115, 145,
197, 198
New Yorker, 46, 50, 91, 182
Nicholson, Peter (cartoonist),
56
Nigeria, 160

9/11, 24–6, 28–9, 32–3, 45, 100,
102, 105, 142, 150, 168, 171,
172, 181, 184, 188, 196, 197
96.3 FM (Toronto radio station),
113–14
Normandy, 70, 181
North, Oliver (journalist), 146
North, Titus (news analyst),
176
North Korea, 20, 27, 92, 125,
182
Nostradamus, 25
Nunberg, Geoffrey (pundit),
63, 64
NZZ am Sonntag (Zurich), 157

O'Farrell, Vince (cartoonist), 63
Office of Global Communica-
tions, 62, 65, 67, 190
Ogilvy and Mather, 29
Ohman, Jack (cartoonist), 168
Oil, 14, 20, 39, 40, 43, 57, 93,
119, 122, 124, 131, 155, 158,
194
Operation Enduring Freedom,
27, 28
Operation Iraqi Freedom, 50,
119, 170
O'Reilly Factor, The (TV), 102
O'Reilly, Bill (journalist), 21,
102, 167
Orlando Sentinel, 145
Orsolina (participant), 25, 177
Osami (Egyptian father), 156
Oscar (participant), 31, 35, 114,
127, 140, 168, 182, 188
Ottawa, 47, 85, 114, 148, 180

Ottawa Citizen, 180
Oxford English Dictionary, 62

Pacifism, 18, 48
Pakistan, 28, 45, 115, 118, 157,
    160
Palestine, 29, 78, 155, 158, 159,
    160, 193
Palestine Hotel, 77, 78
Panama, 71
Paramount Studios, 10
Paris, 13, 47
Pariser, Eli (spokesperson), 43
Park, Susann (student), 173
Patriotism, 25, 41, 43, 46, 97–9,
    101, 105, 108, 142, 153, 183.
    See also Nationalism
Pax Americana, 122
PBS (Public Broadcasting
    System), 66, 73, 87, 108, 109
Penn, Sean (actor), 41
Pentagon, 4, 26, 51–2, 53, 55,
    60–2, 64, 65, 66, 67, 68, 72–7,
    78–9, 91, 95, 99, 100, 108, 118,
    119, 128, 129, 130, 152, 153,
    155, 169, 177, 189, 195. *See
    also* Bush: administration,
    White House, Washington:
    regime
Pepsi-Cola, 11, 102
Perle, Richard, 26, 182
Permanent warfare, idea of, 26,
    188, 193
Peterson, Roy (cartoonist), 134
Pew Research Center, 27–8, 38,
    46, 81, 103, 110, 151, 159–60,
    170, 196, 197

Pittsburgh Post-Gazette, 180
Plante, Bruce (cartoonist), 92
Poland, 39, 186
Pollack, Kenneth (author), 121
Polls, 6, 7, 17, 27–8, 33, 38–9, 46,
    69, 100, 111, 145, 147, 149–50,
    151–3, 155, 160, 163, 166, 170,
    172, 183, 190–1, 196
Popcorn, Faith (pundit), 103
Popular culture, 3, 4, 7, 12,
    18–19, 21, 30, 34, 41, 69, 108,
    131, 179, 181, 191, 192
Pornography, 20, 48, 106, 107,
    164, 166, 168, 170, 172, 174,
    176–9
Poseidon Adventure, The, 24
Posters, 13, 15, 185
Postman, Neil (media scholar),
    81, 82, 86, 108, 109
Powell, Colin, 22, 29, 123, 156
Pre-emptive war, strategy of,
    27, 195
Preventive war, 122
Priggee, Milt (cartoonist), 168
Prisoner of war issue, 138, 146,
    150, 156, 177
Procter & Gamble, 32, 100
Production of fear, 26, 188
Project for a New American
    Century, 27
Promotion, 8, 16, 17, 19, 62, 80,
    119, 187, 191
Propaganda, 73, 74, 83, 97,
    101, 104, 106, 142, 156, 192;
    antiwar, 41–3, 45; apparatus
    of, 15–16, 32, 61, 65, 189–91;
    'Big Lie,' the, 28–9, 37, 120;

222   Index

history of, 12–14, 71, 185–7;
Iraqi and Arab, 63, 76, 83, 97,
99, 137, 139, 146, 177, 191;
and the media, 15, 99–100,
153, 184–5, 188–9; and the
panel, 113, 118–22, 125, 126,
127, 130, 131, 140; theory of,
13, 16–18, 24, 184; US government, 27–31, 33–8, 49, 55,
57–60, 62–4, 65–70, 76–7, 90,
150, 191. *See also* Advertising;
Marketing
Pro-war cause, 23, 32, 36, 40,
44, 46, 105, 122–3, 124–5, 133,
146, 148, 166, 169, 170, 189
Proxy regimes, 28, 124
PSAs (public service announcements), 14, 15
Psychological operations, 4, 54,
55, 57, 59, 60, 61, 191
Public affairs, 5, 7, 15, 17, 21,
26, 42, 45, 74, 129, 138, 141,
149, 161, 171, 173, 182, 183
Public goods, 16–17, 18, 21, 38,
99, 112, 196
Publicity, 8, 11, 12, 29, 30, 45,
53, 72, 76, 121, 142, 191
Public opinion, 7, 17, 33, 102,
112, 141–3, 149, 152, 159
Public relations, 8, 15–16, 23,
42, 61–2, 67, 112, 155, 185,
187, 190
Public sphere, 11, 13, 49, 112,
115, 141–2, 186
Pundits, 83, 87, 90, 99, 116, 125,
127–9, 130, 156, 185, 189, 194
Pyle, Ernie (journalist), 73, 136

Qatar, 10, 30, 65, 83
Quagmire, spectre of, 67, 69,
97, 198

Race issue, 14, 29, 170
Radio, 4, 9, 11, 28, 30, 57, 59, 61,
79, 85, 104, 108, 110, 113, 115,
117, 126, 135, 146, 148, 150,
157, 175, 186
Radio Sawa, 30, 104
Rambo (movie character), 18,
68, 69, 160
Rather, Dan (CBS anchor), 98
Reagan, Ronald, 171, 173
Reality TV, 7, 86, 87, 106–7, 132
Real-time war, 79, 81, 82, 84–92,
93–100, 101, 102, 103, 107–8,
111, 117, 126, 129, 131–2,
135–6, 142, 144, 149, 152–3,
179, 186, 191
Rebick, Judy (social critic), 176
Reid, Chip (journalist), 64
Religion, 17, 26, 30, 158, 161,
183, 185
Remnick, David (journalist),
182
Republican Guard, 66, 93, 139,
152
Republican party, 25, 26, 27, 42,
170, 194, 196
Reuters News Service, 79, 144
Reza (participant), 47, 48, 52,
100, 115, 116, 117, 118, 119,
120, 123, 124, 129, 130, 133,
135, 137, 138, 140, 161
Rice, Condoleezza, 29, 32
Richard (participant), 26, 35,

48, 113, 116, 118, 122–3, 127,
130, 136, 137, 139, 140, 171,
181, 182
Riefenstahl, Leni (film-maker),
186
Right (political views), 6, 22,
27, 105, 108, 183
Rivera, Geraldo (journalist), 93
Riyadh, 158
Robbins, Carla (journalist), 96
Robertson, Nic (journalist), 86
Robinson, Daniel (marketing
scholar), 17
Rodgers, Walter (journalist), 85
Rogers, Rob (cartoonist), 180
Rosie the Riveter, 13
Rumsfeld, Donald, 26, 32, 39,
45, 50–2, 61, 65, 66, 67, 73, 76,
85, 91, 96, 99, 122, 134, 140,
156, 195
Russia, 18, 74, 185

Sadism, 20, 167
Safwan (Iraq), 74
Salamon, Julie (journalist), 86
Salutin, Rick (journalist), 85
Sam (participant), 114, 117, 119,
127, 129, 133, 183
Sanger, David (journalist), 92
Sarandon, Susan (actor), 41
Saudi Arabia, 10, 158
Saving Private Ryan, 69, 70, 132
Savino (participant), 11, 117,
121, 132, 139, 166, 191
Schrank, Peter (cartoonist), 173
Schudson, Michael (media
scholar), 196

Schwarzenegger, Arnold
(actor), 38, 94
Schwarzkopf, General
Norman, 50
Science fiction, 20, 136
Scripps Howard News Service,
45, 80
Seagal, Steven (actor), 19
Seattle, 39
Seattle Post-Intelligencer, 98
Second World War, 13, 53, 70,
73, 90, 109, 145, 186–7, 189,
191, 193, 198
Security, motif of, 16, 26, 31, 36,
37, 147, 182, 188, 195, 197
Security Council (UN), 23, 36
Seeger, Pete (singer), 49
Sex, issue of, 20, 48, 69, 166–8,
174, 176
'Shared Values' campaign, 30–1
Sheen, Martin (actor), 41
Shepard, Ben (writer), 167
'Shock and Awe' (war phrase),
4, 52–5, 62, 64, 86, 87, 91, 92,
119, 137, 147, 151
Simpson, O.J., 82
680 News (Toronto radio
station), 113
Sky News (UK), 91, 103
Smart weapons, 54, 55, 56, 65,
89–90, 100, 136
Smith, Terence (journalist),
66
Smokey the Bear, 14
Soccer, 25
Social risks, 16–17, 18, 36
Somalia, 61, 72, 99, 150

Sony, 32
South Africa, 123
South Korea, 160
Soviet Union, 52, 171
Spain, 39, 160
Spectacle, 4, 11, 80, 87, 108, 132,
  166, 170, 174, 176–9, 181, 184,
  186
Sports, 19, 111, 132, 181, 193
Stalin, Joseph, 59
Stalingrad, memory of, 66, 121,
  139
Stallone, Sylvester (actor), 69
Star Trek, 132
Star Wars saga, 18, 19, 58, 132,
  136, 181
State Department (US), 29, 65,
  195
Statistics Canada, 115
Statue of Liberty, 13
Stein, Janice (pundit), 127, 128
Stephanie (participant), 117,
  119, 126, 129, 139, 161, 183
Studio 2 (TV), 116
Suhendro (Indonesian), 104
Suicide bombers, 26, 45, 155
Summers, Dana (cartoonist),
  145
Sunday Chronicle, 42
Supreme Court (US), 25
Survivor (TV), 86, 107
Syria, 92, 182

Taliban, 26, 33, 73, 125
Talk shows, 28
Taylor, Philip (propaganda
  scholar), 61

TBS (Turner Broadcasting
  System), 19
Technology, 25, 190–1; machinery of television, 79, 84, 96,
  136–7, 154; machinery of
  war, 54–5, 58, 89–90, 91, 136,
  174, 176; motif of, 21, 51, 53,
  56, 135, 164, 170, 175, 192
Teenagers, 11
Tehran, 144
Telegraph (UK), 106, 164
Telephone, 11, 55, 87, 137
Television, 3, 4, 8, 15, 28, 30, 32,
  42, 55, 57, 67, 71, 85, 119, 152,
  164, 182, 191; cable TV, 10,
  41, 45, 65, 81, 82, 95, 96, 97,
  102–6, 108, 115, 116; content
  of, 34, 45, 47, 60, 65, 68–9, 85–
  95, 97–100, 101, 106–7, 128,
  132, 133, 135, 146, 174, 176–9;
  critique of, 11, 61, 81–2, 96–7,
  107–10, 126, 127, 129–31, 154,
  165, 166, 188–9; institution
  of, 12, 45, 49, 70, 83–4, 102–6,
  175, 193; satellite TV, 10, 55,
  83, 95, 108, 116; usage of, 9,
  10, 19, 79, 80, 115–18, 142,
  144, 145, 153
Television commercials, 8, 11,
  12, 30, 32, 102
Telnaes, Ann (cartoonist), 154,
  175
Terminator series, 18, 38, 132
Terrorism, 16, 24–6, 27, 29, 31,
  33, 36, 37, 39, 139, 153, 157,
  161, 172, 185, 197
Tet Offensive, 70, 71

Theatricality, 54
Thompson, Robert (pundit), 87, 91
Three Kings, 93, 132
Tiananmen Square, 178
Time, 10, 17, 37, 97, 104, 194–5, 196, 197
Time Warner, 10
Titanic, 10
Tokyo, 144
Tomorrow Never Dies, 20, 21
Toronto, 3, 5, 47, 49, 113, 114, 115, 127, 144, 147, 176
Toronto Star, 69, 85, 91
Toronto Sun, 113
Totalitarianism, 181, 187, 188
Towering Inferno, The, 24
Tragedy, 133–5, 140, 153, 156
Trever, John (cartoonist), 112
Tribune Media Services, 154, 175
Triumph of the Will, 186
Truth issue, 34, 61, 63, 65, 73, 121, 125, 129, 142, 185, 196
Turkey, 28, 104, 160
Turner, Ted (media owner), 105
TVNewscan, 95, 99
TVOntario, 115, 116, 125, 128
TV-7 (Indonesia), 104
Twentieth-Century Fox, 10

Ugly American, The, 26
Ullman, Harlan (author), 52–5
Umm Qasr (Iraq), 95
unilaterals (independent journalists), 73–4, 77, 107, 115

United Arab Emirates, 10, 83
United Kingdom, 16, 19, 20, 21, 22, 23, 27, 37, 39, 47, 48, 49, 64, 71, 101, 103, 106, 109, 115, 123, 124, 147, 148, 160, 162, 166, 167, 169, 187
United Nations, 3, 22–3, 32, 33, 35–6, 39, 41, 46, 47, 122, 123, 142–3, 147, 160, 196
USS Abraham Lincoln, 76, 161, 168, 179, 194

Valour and the Horror, The (TV), 90
Variety, 69
Varvel, Gary (cartoonist), 23
Ventura County Star, 40, 101
Viagra, 168
Vichy France, 13
Video games, 9, 86, 88, 132, 136, 176
Video news releases, 15
Vietnam, Vietnam War, 18, 33, 49, 59, 67, 70–1, 122, 150, 151, 181, 188, 189, 190
Village Voice, 86, 168
Violence, issue of, 18–19, 20, 124, 146, 148, 158, 166, 171, 174

Wag the Dog, 132, 189
Wallace, General William, 66
War on drugs, 14, 15, 41, 187
War script, 51, 66–8, 75, 90, 97, 99, 127, 128, 130
War on terror, 26, 27, 29, 32, 33, 36, 41, 147, 155, 160, 171, 182, 184, 188, 195

Washington, 26, 41, 42, 195;
regime, 3, 23, 25, 27, 28, 31,
32–3, 37, 39, 40, 41, 43, 46, 49,
51–2, 64–8, 79, 90, 92, 99,
118–19, 120, 121, 124, 125,
127, 131, 140, 148, 150, 153,
155–6, 157, 158, 160, 167,
170, 171, 173, 183, 184, 188,
190, 191, 193, 196–7, 198. *See
also* Bush: administration,
Pentagon, White House
Washington Post, 19, 53, 67, 96,
102, 104, 114, 144, 145, 156,
158, 173
Washington Times, 97
Wayne, John (actor), 52
Weapons of mass destruction,
16, 27, 32, 36, 37, 57, 59, 89,
120, 121, 122, 125, 139, 141,
155, 182, 193, 194
Weekly Standard, 27, 72
Welch, David (propaganda
scholar), 186
Wells, Paul (journalist), 125

Westmoreland, General Will-
iam, 71
White House, 27, 32, 61, 62, 65,
67, 71, 72, 79, 118, 119, 147,
155, 169, 189, 196. *See also*
Bush: administration, Penta-
gon, Washington: regime
Williams, Linda (pornography
scholar), 174
Willis, Bruce, 11, 136
Windows 95, 8
Wolfe, Tom (cultural critic), 20
Wolfowitz, Paul, 26, 32, 35, 195
Woodstock, 48
Woodward, Gary (media
scholar), 71
Woolsey, James, 182
Workman, Paul (journalist), 74
World Is Not Enough, The, 20
World Trade Center, 24, 28
World Wide Web, 80, 114, 115,
166, 176, 192

Zerbisias, Antonia (journalist),
85